JOB–SONG OF SOLOMON

Morning Conversations

on the Wisdom of the Ages

Days 437–679 of your
devotional journey through
the Old Testament with

JON R. ROEBUCK

© 2022

Published in the United States by Nurturing Faith, Macon, GA.
Nurturing Faith is a book imprint of Good Faith Media (goodfaithmedia.org).
Library of Congress Cataloging-in-Publication Data is available.

ISBN: 978-1-63528-191-0

All rights reserved. Printed in the United States of America.

Scripture quotations taken from the (NASB®) New American Standard Bible®,
Copyright © 1960, 1971, 1977, 1995, 2020 by The Lockman Foundation.
Used by permission. All rights reserved. www.lockman.org

Scripture quotations marked (NLT) are taken from the Holy Bible, New Living Translation,
copyright ©1996, 2004, 2015 by Tyndale House Foundation. Used by permission of Tyndale
House Publishers, Carol Stream, Illinois 60188. All rights reserved.

Scripture quotations marked (NIV) are taken from the Holy Bible, New International Version®,
NIV®. Copyright © 1973, 1978, 1984, 2011 by Biblica, Inc.™ Used by permission
of Zondervan. All rights reserved worldwide. www.zondervan.com The "NIV" and
"New International Version" are trademarks registered in the United States Patent and
Trademark Office by Biblica, Inc.™

Scriptures marked KJV are taken from the KING JAMES VERSION (KJV):
KING JAMES VERSION, public domain.

Dedication

This volume is dedicated to my lifelong friend, Chaplain Colonel Stan Campbell, whose love of both music and the mystery of the faith, has inspired me, challenged me, and taught me for the past 40 years. I am a better man because of his example and presence in my life.

Contents

Preface 1

Job 3
       Days 437 through 478

Psalms 45
       Days 479 through 628

Proverbs 195
       Days 629 through 659

Ecclesiastes 226
       Days 660 through 671

Song of Solomon 238
       Days 672 through 679

Preface

Welcome to Volume 3 of a 5-Volume collection of devotional thoughts drawn from each chapter of the Bible. *Morning Conversations on The Wisdom of the Ages* takes the reader through all five books of wisdom literature. Once again, I invite you to join with me in a fresh devotional read through the pages of the Old Testament text. My goal in writing is not to exhaustively interpret, translate, or provide full commentary on every chapter of the Old Testament, but to help you engage with the text and perhaps draw some meaningful application for each day. I have discovered a number of fascinating ways the truth of God's Word leaps off the page and into my heart. It is my hope that some of my reflections will help you with your discovery of scripture and the role of faith in your life. I use the word "Conversations" with great intentionality. I think Bible study should happen that way. God is revealed to us through stories of our faith, and then we reflect and offer back to God the thoughts of our hearts. It is a conversation… a back-and-forth dialogue. Conversations invite us to ponder, reflect, inquire, learn, and grow.

As you read through these volumes, my hope is that you will take the time, not to simply read what I have written, but to reflect with me on what the ancients have written. Let me challenge you each morning to take a moment to read the suggested focus chapter from a trusted translation before you dive into the words I have written. Read and reflect. As you make your way through this book, and the other volumes in the set, you will discover a lot of my life story written into these pages. But more importantly, I hope you will discover a lot about God's story… the one carefully crafted and preserved for you. For in hearing God's story, you will hear the echoing refrain of God's desire to know you, to love you, and to redeem you. Welcome to the conversation.

Morning Conversations Volumes 1-5

Morning Conversations on the Creation of a People and Place is the first volume of a set that follows the natural order of the Old Testament canon, and spans the Biblical narrative from the opening chapter of Genesis to the end of the book of Ruth.

Morning Conversations on the Rise and Fall of Kings and Kingdoms continues the orderly progression, spanning the books of 1 Samuel through Esther.

Morning Conversations on the Wisdom of the Ages covers all five books of wisdom literature from Job to the Song of Solomon.

Morning Conversations on the Prophetic Word wraps up the Old Testament with a look at the books of prophecy, covering both the Major and Minor prophets, Isaiah through Malachi.

Additionally, *Morning Conversations on the New Testament* is the final volume of this collection which offers perspective from each chapter of the New Testament.

Day 437 — Job 1: You Think YOU Are Having a Bad Day

> "In all of this, Job did not sin by blaming God." Job 1:22 (NLT)

Observation
Job lived in the land of Uz. He was described as blameless, a man of "complete integrity." He feared God and stayed away from evil. His life was very blessed. He had seven sons and three daughters, as well as large numbers of sheep, camels, oxen, donkeys, and servants. His children customarily gathered to feast at the home of one of his sons. Focused on righteousness, Job would make a sacrifice the morning after such a celebration on behalf of his children, just in case they had sinned. This opening chapter describes a scene in heaven where the heavenly court gathers to meet with God. Satan joins the group and he and God discuss Job's righteousness. Satan argues that it is only because of Job's blessings that he loves God to the extent that he does. The lie goes like this, "Take away the blessings and he will curse you to your face." God allows Job to be tested. In a single day, all that Job loves is lost. His servants are killed, his livestock are all destroyed or stolen, and worst of all, all his children die when a windstorm blows down the house in which they were gathered. And yet… Job refuses to curse God. The account records that on this terrible day he did two things. First, he grieved over his loss, and then he worshipped his God.

Application
We all have good days and bad days. How we respond to both are indicative of our faith. When we experience a day that brings untold blessings, answered prayers, safety, and security, surely as people of faith, we take moments to acknowledge the gracious God who has given us all things. Failure to praise God is an abuse of God's grace. But what about the bad days? Hopefully, none of us will experience a day like the one that Job experienced. Hopefully, our valleys will not be as deep, nor our grief so devastatingly poignant. But difficult days will be a part of our life experience. None of us are immune. Dark days might include loss, but could also include the pain of brokenness, the anxiety of job loss, the fear of financial instability, or the onslaught of a medical problem. How we respond can be a test of our faith, and maybe even a testimony to the resiliency of our relationship with God. Look at Job's example. He took the time to grieve. He acknowledged his loss, he felt the sting of the moment, he surely offered a gut-wrenching cry as he tore his clothes as a sign of mourning. But then he worshipped. He acknowledged that even in such darkness, that God was with him and worthy to be praised. I pray that you will know more joy than sorrow this day. Most of all, I hope you will know God.

Prayer
Father, may we feel your presence in both the good and difficult days of life. Amen.

Day 438 — Job 2: The Ministry of Presence

> "When they saw Job from a distance, they scarcely recognized him. Wailing loudly, they tore their robes and threw dust into the air over their heads to show their grief. Then they sat on the ground with him for seven days and nights. No one said a word to Job, for they saw that his suffering was too great for words." Job 2:12-13 (NIV)

Observation

Again, there is a gathering of the heavenly court and, once again, Satan argues with God over Job's faithfulness. Satan insists that Job remains faithful in adversity simply because he still has his health. "Take away his health and he will surely curse you to your face!" Once again, God allows Job to be tested. He is struck with a terrible disease that causes terrible boils from head to toe. In his misery, Job's wife adds to his pain by suggesting that he curse God and die. Even with the opposition and suffering, Job refuses to displease or dishonor God. Three friends who have heard of his tragedy arrive to comfort and console him. They hardly recognize him because of his terrible affliction. They wail and weep and grieve over the state of their friend. Unable to offer words, they simply sit with him in silence for seven days. (As they work through their thoughts about Job's affliction, they too will join the chorus offering both explanation and blame. But at least initially, they have modeled an important element of care... presence.)

Application

There are moments of ministry that require our physical presence. Sometimes it is not sufficient to just call, or text, or email, or post on Facebook. Sometimes the situation demands that we travel to the place of need and join with those who are hurting. I call this the "ministry of presence." Sometimes those in need require a flesh and blood presence of Christ that can only come through our actions. We interrupt our schedules, we reprioritize our day, and we make the effort to be present. At times, our presence is all that is needed. In those moments, what do we need to say? What would bring comfort? What would be the exact word from the Lord to share? Maybe we don't need to say anything. Maybe we just need to be present and sit quietly as our friend mourns, weeps, and heals. In fact, people seldom remember what is said in such a moment but they will remember that we were physically present when they needed us. Let me encourage you to be the kind of supporter, friend, and Christian that will place the importance of a friend's moment of need above the inconvenience that such ministry will cost. Be real. Be present.

Prayer

Father, allow us to be your representatives to those who are hurting. Amen.

Day 439 — Job 3: Calling on an Expert

> "Let those who are experts at cursing—whose cursing could rouse Leviathan—curse that day." Job 3:8 (NIV)

Observation
After an entire week of sorrowful suffering, grief, and silence, Job finally speaks. From the depths of his anguish he begins to curse the very day of his birth, wondering why he would be born only to endure such suffering. He wishes that he had never been born. He speaks from the depths of his pain, which is both physical and mental. He goes to great lengths to curse the day he was born. He wishes the day could be erased, that it would be blotted off the calendar. He curses the day for not shutting his mother's womb, and for allowing his birth. He cries out, "Why be born to see all this trouble… why is life given to those with no future?" It is a very emotional, powerful, and understandable rant in the face of his hardship. As I read this narrative, I was struck with the words of our focus verse. Job blurts out, "Let those who are experts at cursing… curse that day."

Application
When I read the focus verse, I am reminded of a line from one of my favorite Christmas movies, *A Christmas Story*, where Ralphie, speaking retrospectively about his father and his father's propensity for cussing says, "He worked in profanity the way other artists might work in oils and clay. It was his true medium: a master." Ralphie's father offered a plethora of colorful words during the course of the movie. He *was* an expert. In the Biblical narrative, Job is so distraught, so angry, so grief-stricken that he calls upon experts in cursing to curse the day that he was born. To get the job done well, he wanted an expert to take on the challenge.

Don't we do the same? Whenever we face a challenge in our lives, we want experts to help meet our needs. We want a well-qualified doctor to perform our surgery. We want an expert in finance to counsel us about our retirement income. We want a licensed plumber to fix the leak, or a well-trained electrician to wire our homes. We will gladly pay a mechanic a large fee if we know he or she can fix our car. In terms of our sin problem, we have an expert on the case. Knowing that we will never be good enough, or righteous enough, or pure enough to overcome our sinful desires and habits, we have an expert who pleads our case before God. And more than simply representing us, Jesus pays the price of our sins. He forgives us completely and calls us his beloved. Who else would we call on for such a solution, other than the one who suffered on the cross, died for sins, and rose to give us life?

Prayer
Father, thank you for the expert who deals with our sins. Amen.

Day 440 — Job 4: Guilt or Innocence

> "'Can a mortal be innocent before God? Can anyone be pure before the Creator?'" Job 4:17 (NIV)

Observation
After a week of silence followed by Job's speech, Eliphaz responds to Job's grief and loss. He is most likely the oldest of Job's three friends because the protocol of the day would suggest that the oldest would speak first in such a situation. He attempts to address the turmoil in Job's life and attempts to counter some of Job's thinking. He reminds Job that Job has been a source of great encouragement and strength to others during times of difficulty and hardship. Now that his own life has taken such a strange turn, why can Job not hear his own counsel? Eliphaz asks, "Where is your confidence, where is your hope?" In his eyes, Job has been able to give counsel, but not receive it. He then suggests that Job must be suffering because of sin. And because of the severity of his suffering, there must be a great sin, though maybe even unknown, in Job's life. Eliphaz claims that this truth has been given to him through a "disturbing vision" at night. The truth has been "whispered" into his ear. He asks, "Can a mortal be innocent before God? Can anyone be pure before the Creator?" (Though Eliphaz's comments certainly reflect the popular thought of the day that suffering was a result of sin, such an indictment does not apply to Job in this situation. He was innocent and blameless at the time of his difficulty.)

Application
This concept of suffering because of sin is widely broadcast even in our day. To be honest, some of the hardship and pain in our lives is indeed the direct result of our sinfulness. We abuse our bodies, we destroy relationships, and we live well outside the boundaries of godly living. In such cases, we should expect that our "sins" will catch up to us. However, at other times, it is foolish to insist that suffering is a result of some sin committed. We live in a flawed world. Our bodies are not perfect. Sometimes the only cause of our pain is from the natural result of living life here on earth, regardless of our faithfulness to God and God's demands. Simply put... all illness and suffering are not a direct result of some disobedient behavior. So, Job's friend might have gotten his theology a little wrong. But there is an element of truth in his words. When he asks the rhetorical questions spoken in our focus verse, he makes a valid point. The truth is, "for all have sinned and fall short of the glory of God" (Romans 3:23 NASB). Our sinfulness, however, doesn't lead directly to illness, it leads to separation from God. But the good news is that ,through the atoning sacrifice of Jesus, our sins are erased and we stand both innocent and pure before God. Now that's quite a vision!

Prayer
Father, thank you for taking away the sins that should demand punishment. Amen.

Day 441   Job 5: Good Word, Wrong Application

> "But consider the joy of those corrected by God! Do not despise the discipline of the Almighty when you sin. For though he wounds, he also bandages. He strikes, but his hands also heal." Job 5:17-18 (NIV)

Observation
This chapter continues the speech that Eliphaz offers to Job in response to Job's misery and grief. He reminds Job that such calamities and tragedies are the result of sinful actions. Bad things happen to those who sin... or at least that is Eliphaz's theological approach. He calls for Job to confess his sins and surely God will fix his predicament. Verse 7 is an interesting perspective on life. Eliphaz says, "People are born for trouble as readily as sparks fly up from a fire" (NLT). Many have used that verse to point to the difficult state of the human condition. But Eliphaz's interpretation is that people bring trouble on themselves, which he believes is the case for Job. He warns Job not to despise the discipline of God, but to embrace it as a way forward. Eliphaz insists that if Job would admit his guilt, that surely God would bring promised relief. Taken on their own merit, these two verses spoken by Eliphaz are good and true. Indeed, we would be wise to embrace God's discipline when we have committed sinful mistakes. Through God's discipline, we are healed, forgiven, and transformed. However, in the context of this story, these words have no merit, simply because they do not apply to Job's situation.

Application
Sometimes good advice can be offered at the wrong time. Sometimes, even scripture, when taken out of context, provides further injury instead of healing grace. I often think of the "well-meant" phrases that people toss out at the time of a death. "Well, he is in a better place," or, "I guess God just needed her in heaven more than we do." Or how about this one... "I guess it was just God's will" (as though God wills injury, pain, and sadness on any of us). In our attempts to provide solace, we sometimes make matters worse. In fact, if we are not careful, we can even distort the image of God so that God becomes some type of celestial villain rather than a loving Father. It is vitally important to know the Word of God. We need to read it, memorize it, and internalize it. It is the very bread of life. It is also vitally important to have the wisdom to apply it correctly. God's Word should heal, comfort, correct, and offer grace. We need to make sure that we use God's Word as a tool for redemptive mercy and not as a club to injure people in their difficult moments. As Paul once admonished young Timothy, "Be diligent to present yourself approved to God as a workman who does not need to be ashamed, accurately handling the word of truth" (2 Timothy 2:15 NASB). Be careful with God's Word.

Prayer
Father God, teach us to know your Word and apply it wisely. Amen.

Day 442 — Job 6: The Pain of an Unreliable Friend

> My brothers, you have proved as unreliable as a seasonal brook that overflows its banks in the spring when it is swollen with ice and melting snow. But when the hot weather arrives, the water disappears. The brook vanishes in the heat." Job 6:15-17 (NIV)

Observation

This chapter is dedicated to Job's response to Eliphaz's charges in which Job continues to defend his innocence. Remember that Eliphaz has insisted that Job's sufferings are a result of sinfulness in his life. Job is quick to say that he would not be complaining about his grief and turmoil if it were justifiable punishment. Throughout the chapter, he describes the misery of his plight. He states that his misery and grief outweigh all the sands of the sea. Becoming very disillusioned with life and feeling a sense of hopelessness, Job prays that God would end his life. Perhaps worst of all is the cruel response and rebuke that he has received from his friends. Rather than offering comfort and help, they only add to his pain. He compares his friends to a dry riverbed in summer that provides no water when needed the most.

Application

Ever have an unreliable friend? They never show up when they should. They don't keep their word. They make promises they can't keep, and they even stick you with the bill at dinner! Often, we avoid friends like that at all costs. We prefer stability, honesty, dedication, and reliability. We want to surround ourselves with people upon whom we can lean on in times of trouble, weep with in times of sorrow, and laugh with in times of joy. Friends should lessen our pain, not make things worse.

I've discovered over the course of my life that friendship is a two-way street. If we desire to have strong, confident, reliable friends in our lives, then we must offer the same in return. I have also noticed that friendships are forged on the anvil of time and shared experiences. Friends "are there for each other." Friends are consistent over time. Friends keep confidences. Friends forgive. Friends make investments in the lives of those they love. It is both my hope and prayer that you have at least one or two "true" friends in your life. If you do, count yourself blessed.

So, here's my challenge for you this day. Think of a way to express your gratitude to your best friend or friends. Send an unexpected gift. Write a note and mail it. Call them and offer them a few minutes of uninterrupted time. Plan an event and invite them to go along with you. We will never regret the moments we spend with our friends. Just make sure that you have created plenty of those moments.

Prayer

Father God, I thank you today for my life-long, soul-nurturing friends. Amen.

Day 443　　　　　　　　　　　　Job 7: The God Who Watches

> "For you examine us every morning and test us every moment."
> Job 7:18 (NIV)

Observation
Job is slowly losing hope. His words once again turn to the physical agony of his disease. He graphically describes the sores that cover his body using the words, "maggots, scabs, and oozing pus." Sounds fun, right? He cries out to God, bemoaning the brevity of his life. He believes that he will never feel happiness again. Though he never curses God, he does question God in terms of his affliction. He longs to know how he has disobeyed God and missed the mark of God's intention. (He uses three different Hebrew words for wrongdoing. He uses the word "sin," that means to miss the mark. He uses the word "transgression," which means rebellion. He uses the word "iniquity," which means infraction or perversity.) He is at a loss to explain why such things have happened in his life. His words are the musing of a man with a weary mind, a pain-wracked body, and a defeated spirit.

Application
Like any other campus across America, here at Belmont University, the safety and well-being of our students is the number one priority. Belmont is blessed to have a very well-trained and well-equipped security team. One of the security measures in place is video cameras that give constant, 24-hour watch care over the students. There are more than 200 strategically placed cameras that watch every vital portion of the campus. In fact, there is a security officer stationed in front of a wall of monitors, carefully watching all that takes place, every hour of every day.

In his desperate cries to God, Job acknowledges that God "examines us every morning." Job is fully aware that God is always giving careful attention to everyone who inhabits the planet. None of us are outside the scrutiny of God's vigilance. Even the prophet Jonah, while running from God and swallowed by a fish at the bottom of the sea, was watched and heard by God. I hope that you will take comfort in God's attention to your life this morning. God watches every step, sees every detail, hears every conversation, and knows every thought. God's watch care over us is not punitive in nature. God is not trying to catch us in some poor choice or bad moment. Rather, God watches over us to protect us, to guide us, and to offer us the comforting presence of the Spirit. The watch care of God is a good thing. In fact, it's a great thing. God loves us and longs for us to succeed. As you go about this day, take comfort in the fact that your Father is carefully watching over your life.

Prayer
Father God, thank you for your constant, vigilant, and protective care over us. Amen.

Day 444 — Job 8: The Wisdom of the "Aged"

> "But those who came before us will teach you. They will teach you the wisdom of old." Job 8:10 (NIV)

Observation

Bildad is the second of Job's friends to speak in the midst of Job's great misery. The tone and the attitude of Bildad's words are much harsher than the words that Eliphaz had offered a few moments earlier. Both friends share the same mentality and theology concerning sin. Both view calamity as the direct result of sin. Bildad throws some shame at Job's children, suggesting that the children must have committed sins and their punishment is well deserved. He goes further to give a simple answer to the complex problem of Job's situation. He tells Job to simply seek God and God will restore his estate. Towards the end of his speech, Bildad gives a final parting shot... suggesting, "God will not reject a person of integrity" (verse 20). Surely the caustic words of Bildad do nothing to relieve the pain and suffering of Job.

Application

All of us "live and learn." Each experience teaches a lesson. Each relationship offers some wisdom. Every season brings knowledge. And so, the older we become, the more wisdom we acquire. That's not to say that any one of us has a perfect perspective on life or knows all the right answers to each of life's questions. It does mean that sometimes we should pay attention to the senior voice within our midst. Those with a few gray hairs typically have something important to say... certainly something worth hearing. The more I study the topic of leadership, especially in regard to the millennial generation, I am fascinated by the insight that most millennials seek some type of multi-generational experience. In fact, in terms of church life, most millennials are drawn not to a homogeneous body of believers where everyone checks off the same age category, but rather crave a church experience where there can be a give-and-take learning experience between old and young. It's not only a good idea, but also a Biblical concept. Elders should be respected for both their wisdom and example. But there is a caveat... there is more to becoming an elder in the faith than simply celebrating a lot of birthdays. Respected, older leaders should be honored and heard, not because of age, but because of the testimony created by many years of faith practice and the wisdom that has been gained when faith-teaching has been translated into faith-practice. My challenge today revolves around the idea of mentorship. If you are young in your faith, look for someone older who can mentor you as you navigate the difficult intersection of faith and culture. And if you are older in your faith, don't rest on your laurels, thinking that you have done enough. Invest these "best years" in the place it matters most.

Prayer

Father God, thank you for those who can share the wisdom of the aged. Amen.

Day 445 — Job 9: The Advocate

> "If only there were a mediator between us, someone who could bring us together." Job 9:33 (NIV)

Observation
This chapter records Job's speech in response to Bildad's attack. Job agrees with Bildad's theology, which insists that evil people are cut off from God. But what continues to mystify Job is God's apparent punishment in light of his personal righteousness. Job muses that even if he had a day in court before God, what could he say, or what response could he offer to make his case before the Almighty? His words reflect a very strong monotheism, rare in the day in which he lived. He affirms that God is the powerful and great creator of the heavens and the earth, and that God alone can defeat all of the forces of evil. He concludes that God sometimes destroys the guiltless as well as the wicked. Such a notion violates his moral code of how God relates to creation. Therefore, his ultimate explanation can only be that sufferings are in the hands of God to dispense, and God will dispense them according to God's pleasure. The reader does find in Job's remarks, the first hint of the need for a Messiah-Mediator who would act as a go between bringing God in contact with sinful humanity.

Application
I have a friend who is suffering through the break-up of her marriage. It's been a long and drawn-out process that has created a lot of anger and angst on both sides. Because of an inability to come to any rational and peaceful resolve, a mediator has been called in as attempt to find closure. Mediation is needed, not only in marital squabbles, but in many other situations as well. Sometimes businesses require mediation among employees. Sometimes court cases need mediation. Even churches sometimes must bring in an outside mediator to resolve differences within the congregation.

Job longs for some type of advocate to plead his case before God. He longs for a mediator to attempt to bridge the divide that he feels with his creator. At times, we feel such tension in our own lives… especially on those days when we know that we have "missed the mark" of God's intention for our lives and have disobeyed God's purposes. We feel the distance. We feel the separation. We feel the brokenness. But unlike the desperate cry of Job, we have a living hope. Listen to these words from 1 John 2:1, "My dear children, I am writing this to you so that you will not sin. But if anyone does sin, we have an advocate who pleads our case before the Father. He is Jesus Christ, the one who is truly righteous" (NLT). What comfort there is in knowing that through Christ, the gap has been bridged, the brokenness has been mended, and the sins have been forgiven and forgotten.

Prayer
Father God, thank you for the hope of redemption and reconciliation we have in Christ. Amen.

Day 446

Job 10: Hope in the Darkness

> "It is a land as dark as midnight, a land of gloom and confusion, where even the light is dark as midnight." Job 10:22 (NIV)

Observation

Job continues to plead with God throughout this chapter. He begs God to explain why he is being oppressed. Job acknowledges that he has never changed his lifestyle or relationship with God through both prosperity and need. He is confused by his state, feeling as though he has been condemned as being guilty of some great sinfulness. He takes a moment in his speech to reflect on God's creative ability when God brought him to life from his mother's womb. He wants to know why God would now desire to destroy what God has created. Job continues to wallow in despair and once again voices his lament at having ever been born. The entire chapter reflects a very gloomy and desperate tone.

Application

Can you think of a time when you experienced an all-encompassing, deep, physical darkness? I have a very vivid memory of a very deep darkness that I experienced a few years ago in Haiti. I was on a mission trip, working in the small village of Thomaseau, about 25 miles outside of Port-au-Prince. A group of Haitian women prepared the meals for our mission team, and late each night, they had to be transported back to their small shacks, located far up into the surrounding hills. Because it was not safe for one of the team sponsors to travel alone, I rode with him each night as he dropped these women off at their homes. They lived in severe poverty, in places where dirt roads turned to footpaths, where there was no running water, and where electricity had never arrived. As we drove down these small roads, the darkness grew deeper with each passing mile. With a thick canopy of trees overhead, and no light of any kind in the deep recesses of these villages, I experienced a darkness like I had never known. It was eerie, disorienting, and a bit intimidating.

Now let's talk about the darkness of mind and soul. Have you ever experienced one of those moments, not unlike that of Job, where the darkness of gloom, confusion, and adversity seemed overwhelming? Ever been to a place where you were without hope, without answers, and without comfort? Unfortunately, each of us may experience such a moment during the course of our lives. How do we survive the darkness? How do we find comfort and light and hope? I think we have to look in the places where light can always be found. Specifically, we must stubbornly cling to our faith where the light of the world promises His nearness. And second, we must cling to those who walk among us who are bearers of that same light.

Prayer

Dear God, may we experience the light of the Gospel in the midst of darkest nights. Amen.

Day 447 — Job 11: Challenging Fake Religion

> "Should I remain silent while you babble on? When you mock God, shouldn't someone make you ashamed?" Job 11:3 (NIV)

Observation
It is now time for Zophar to speak regarding Job's situation. He is the third of Job's friends to speak. It appears that Zophar had not planned to speak until he heard Job's long outpouring. His condemnation of Job is blunt. He reiterates what the others have said, insisting that it is just common sense to know that people are punished because of their sins, and thus Job must have some great, unconfessed sin. He rebukes Job for his false claims of innocence. He tells Job that he is empty-headed and unable to comprehend the wisdom of God. And like the others, Zophar also reminds Job that if he continues in his sin, he will die.

Application
All of us have seen the State Farm Insurance commercial where a couple of people are talking on a sidewalk. They are discussing some claims made on the internet. The woman, who is waiting on her date, who claims to be a French model, says, "They can't put anything on the internet that isn't true." A clumsy, awkward looking guy, who is clearly not a model, walks up and says, "Bonjour."

We have to be careful these days to separate fact from fiction. We must evaluate claims—in the news, in commercials, on the internet. Misinformation and fake stories are pushed our way each day. It can even happen in terms of faith. Not every voice who claims to share truth has truth to share. Some who claim to have a word from the Lord don't even know the Lord. It is easy to become deceived, confused, and misled. For example, in a response to a tragic mass shooting in 2017 at First Baptist Church of Sutherland Springs, Texas, one pastor boldly proclaimed that the killing of these church goers was "an answer to their prayers." His brand of theology proclaimed that anyone who is killed should rejoice because they get to claim their heavenly reward. I'm pretty sure those words rang hollow in the ears of the victims and were not reflective of God's love and nurturing in our lives.

And so, it happens… we allow preachers, proclaimers, and politicians to babble on without challenging the veracity of their words. When truth is abused and when falsehood is pushed along without question, we should insist on truth, on proper interpretation, and on consistent doctrinal clarity. As Zophar suggested, when someone mocks the name of God, or speaks falsely about God's purpose, we should boldly offer a corrective word.

Prayer
Dear God, grant us the courage to insist on the truth. Amen.

Day 448 — Job 12: Seeking Wisdom

> "Just ask the animals, and they will teach you. Ask the birds of the sky, and they will tell you. Speak to the earth, and it will instruct you."
> Job 12:7-8a (NIV)

Observation
In this chapter, Job speaks in response to Zophar's blistering attack. He offers a severe critique of the ideas that all three of his friends have put forth. He mocks their false piety and condescending counsel. In fact, he offers one of the great lines ever written in response to know-it-alls: "You people really know everything, don't you? And when you die, wisdom will die with you!" (Job 12:2 NLT). Job is quick to remind them that his wisdom is not inferior to theirs. In fact, his words offer some counsel and correction in response to their verbal attacks. He teaches them that God does not always act in predictable ways. There are moments when God delights in undoing human initiatives. God, in infinite wisdom and power, sometimes does the unexpected, at least unexpected in the minds of men. God even reverses the role of earthly kings according to God's plans.

Application
Hopefully, all of us are life-long learners. Our goal should be to seek to learn new lessons, gain new knowledge, and grow in our understanding of all things for as long as we live. We are instructed by the lessons of life. We learn from experience. If we are wise, we keep asking questions, we keep pondering ideas, and we keep wondering at the mystery of life and our place in this world. In our quest to learn, we should look for instruction from a lot of varied sources. We read books. We listen to lectures. We invite conversation. We surf the web. We watch important shows and movies. And… according to Job, even nature can teach us, if we are willing to listen and learn.

It doesn't take a rocket scientist or a well-equipped meteorologist to recognize the coming of a rainstorm. When we observe the gathering of dark clouds, see the birds circle high in the air, watch the leaves suddenly become tossed about by the quickening pace of the wind, or smell the scent of rain in the air, we know that soon drops will fall. When we see daffodils push up from the frozen soil, we know spring is coming. When leaves begin to turn in the fall, we know that cold weather will soon follow. There are lessons and signs and signals all around us. God, who is revealed to us in a multiplicity of ways, sometimes is revealed through the created order. You can learn kindness from a dog. You can learn a work ethic from an ant. You can learn parenting from a hen. So, let me invite you to stop, look, and listen today to the world around you. Is there truth to glean? Does God have something to teach you or reveal to you? Be a life-long learner. Seek wisdom where it is found.

Prayer
God, may we have the good sense to observe your ways in the world around us. Amen.

Day 449   Job 13: Hope in the Midst of the Yet Unexplained

> "God might kill me, but I have no other hope. I am going to argue my case with him." Job 13:15 (NIV)

Observation
As this chapter opens, Job continues to plead his case. He gives his friends a harsh critique. He tells them that they have given no new insights. Their wisdom and knowledge are in no way superior to his own. They are equals in terms of intellect. He describes them as worthless physicians who have done nothing to ease his pain. In fact, their words have only added to his sufferings. He tells his friends to be silent so that he can present his case before God. He knows that even to dare stand in the presence of God could cost him his life, and yet he will not be deterred. He longs to know from God just what he has done to bring such pain and suffering upon himself. With his friends silenced, he begins pleading his case with God as the chapter ends.

Application
Verse 15 is a tricky verse, and one that is often misunderstood. Hebrew scholars tend to translate it in two different ways. Some argue that Job is saying, "Behold, he will slay me, I will not wait." Such a translation has a very defiant tone. It shows Job as impatient, rushing into God's presence and demanding an answer, even though such an impertinence could cause his death. The second translation follows more along the lines, "Although he slays me; I will wait for him." This translation seems to reflect more of the heart of Job. Such an interpretation has Job saying, "Although my sufferings are being brought about by God's hand for whatever reason, still I will keep my hope in him."

Let's chase that second thought for a moment. For me, it's a faithful approach to the trials and sufferings of this life, especially in the moments where we have no answers and no explanations for why we suffer. In such moments, we must affirm several things. First, that this is indeed God's world, and God has mastery over it. Second, God's wisdom is infinitely superior to our own. Third, God's timing is always according to God's purpose and love for each of us. Spin all of that together and the fact of the matter is that we cannot ever fully know the plans, purposes, or timing of God. But we stand confident in the assurance that God knows. We stand confident in knowing that God loves us perfectly, consistently, and constantly. And like Job, I don't think it's a sin to question God, or to be dumbfounded at what is going on around us. Many of the troubles of this present life are indeed confusing and troubling. But our hope is in God, always. We must live this day and every day with the conviction that although we may not understand all things, we are loved by the One who does.

Prayer
God, we thank you that our lives are in your hands. Amen.

Day 450 — Job 14: The Basis of Our Hope

> "Can the dead live again? If so, this would give me hope through all my years of struggle, and I would eagerly await the release of death."
> Job 14:14 (NIV)

Observation

As this chapter opens, Job continues his dialogue with God, speaking about his continued suffering and the frailty of life. He confesses that life is short and full of trouble. He acknowledges that all of life is lived out under God's gaze... that all the days are determined long before they are lived. He poses a rhetorical question of God, reasoning that if the lifespan is already settled, then why not allow him to live out his short life in peace without the suffering? The passage continues with a very dark note concerning the finality of death. In verse 13, Job is struck with a sudden thought, "What if there is life after death?" Such news would give him hope in his struggle. But the reality is that his hope continues to crumble each day like a mountain slowly ravaged by the winds and rain.

Application

President Obama once wrote about the "audacity of hope." Such a great concept, right? Hope gives life in the presence of death. Hope gives promise in the midst of despair. Hope gives comfort in the midst of pain. Hope gives promise in the presence of scarcity. We survive on hope. We move forward on hope. We dream with hope. We exist with the promises that hope brings. Hope connects us to a future that cannot be taken from us.

Part of Job's problem was that he lacked hope. He could see no end to his suffering, no end to his pain, no end to his grief. The promise of an afterlife, where there would be no more pain, or suffering, or heartache would have given him the emotional and physical strength needed to move forward. A little hope can go a long way.

In the Old Testament faith-experience, there was some debate concerning the promise of heaven. The Sadducees of Jesus' day didn't teach it or even accept its reality because the Torah never mentions resurrection. The Pharisees, on the other hand, taught the concept of resurrection with great assurance, especially for those who could keep every fine point of the Law. Jesus took things a step further. He not only talked about it, but also provided it. With his conquering death over sin and the grave, Jesus made the promise of resurrection real and valid and attainable for all of us. We now live in the promise and hope of that better day. We push through difficult moments because of our hope. We endure suffering because of our hope. We do not despair ultimately at the coming of death because of hope. Hope does not give us immunity from the pain and suffering of the present time, but it does give us the ability to see beyond this present moment, to that better day and better place.

Prayer

God, we thank you for the promise and hope of resurrection. Amen.

Day 451 — Job 15: When Helping Hurts

> "What has taken away your reason? What has weakened your vision, that you turn against God and say all these evil things?" Job 15:12-13 (NIV)

Observation
Chapter 15 begins a second round of speeches between Job and his friends. Mostly, his friends repeat themselves, with a much angrier tone than before. Gone are softer words of grace and comfort. In his second speech, Eliphaz delivers a blistering attack, offering a flurry of accusations. He accuses Job of being a "windbag" full of hot air. He tells him that his words have been useless and not profitable. He tells Job that he has a lack of reverence for God. He also attacks Job's piety, asking, "What do you know that we don't know?" Eliphaz reminds him that the wicked will always suffer a terrible fate. He expresses well his retributive theology insisting that if a person is a sinner, God will punish. Certainly, Eliphaz's words bring no comfort to Job. And so, a wounded man is wounded even more deeply by the words of his friend.

Application
Years ago, I traveled with a group of fellow church members to a remote area outside of the capital city of Brasilia, Brazil. Our task was to build a small chapel in the community so that an emerging house church could grow and flourish. Throughout the week of construction, we were surrounded on the worksite by an inquisitive and ever-present group of impoverished children. Each day on lunch break, as we held plates full of beans, rice, and chicken, these children stood nearby watching us. We had been told by the missionaries on site not to offer them our food. They explained that the food we were eating was so rich in calories and sustenance that it would make them sick. The typical diet of these children contained very little protein or nourishment. Sure, we could feed them for a day… but what good would that do? The leaders claimed that wanting to help could actually hurt. I must admit I found it impossible to eat while such hunger swirled around me. I decided that at least I could help one little, small boy that week and so I made him sit with me each day and I gave him my lunch. Each day as he absolutely inhaled his meal, tears ran down my cheeks.

It was a difficult situation. Sometimes well-meaning intentions can cause harm. I get that. Most likely, you will not be confronted this day by a starving little boy as you eat your lunch. But you probably will encounter people who are hurting, people who have needs, people who have lost their way. How will you respond? If you offer judgment, condemnation, or condescension, you are only adding to their pain. As I often remind others, when you are faced with the option of judgment or grace… choose grace every time.

Prayer
God, as we have the opportunity to do so this day, let us be the bearers of grace. Amen.

Day 452

Job 16: Make It Stop

> "And now his archers surround me. His arrows pierce me without mercy. The ground is wet with my blood. Again and again he smashes against me, charging at me like a warrior." Job 16:13-14 (NIV)

Observation
It is time for Job to make his response to Eliphaz's second speech. The reader can surely feel the mounting tension between Job and his friends as the relationship deteriorates. Job dismisses Eliphaz's rhetoric because it carries the same theme as his earlier speech. Job calls his friends, "sorry comforters." Using their own words, he tells them that they are the windbags, filled with hot air. Job then declares that if the situation were reversed and his friends were suffering, that he would not speak words of judgment, but words of solace to ease their pain. As the chapter continues, Job expresses what may be the source of his greatest agony… the way he feels abandoned by God. His life is broken and shattered by God's action. (He is unaware that his misery is not God's doing, but Satan's.) Toward the end of the chapter, he once again declares his innocence, insisting that his prayers are pure.

Application
Can we confess that sometimes we are more like Job's friends than we care to admit? Often, when our friends find themselves at a point of pain or suffering or hardship, we immediately get a little judgmental, and sometimes we even blurt out hurtful words. Instead of speaking grace and comfort, we offer criticism and our pious solutions to their problems. For example, if a friend experiences financial difficulty, we may be tempted to say, "I guess you should not have spent all that money on stupid stuff. You should have saved more. You should have gotten a second job." We offer both answers and judgment with our words. Or, let's say a friend is battling health issues because of obesity. We might say, "That's what happens when you don't pay attention to your diet. You know you should have been getting some exercise." Again, maybe the right answer, but certainly the wrong words. Here's the deal… when people are suffering, they don't want answers, they want their suffering to go away. They want help with their pain, not a guilty explanation as to their situation. Our "answers" can sometimes make matters worse and raise the level of anxiety. There may be times for explanations and answers somewhere further down the road to recovery. Obviously, we don't want our friends to languish in repetitive, destructive behaviors. But our first response must be that of alleviating the suffering. We do that best through our efforts at genuine concern and practically expressed love. Help now. Give answers later.

Prayer
God, may we become healers and not "sorry comforters." Amen.

Day 453   Job 17: You Can Take It with You

> "No, my hope will go down with me to the grave. We will rest together in the dust!" Job 17:16 (NIV)

Observation
In this chapter, Job continues to despair over his sufferings and the inability of his friends to provide any comfort. The words record a very low point in this drama. He states that he is crushed in his spirit and that his life is about to be snuffed out. He also states that he is surrounded by mockers who treat him bitterly. He appeals to God alone in his despair, "You must defend my innocence, O God, since no one else will stand up for me" (v. 3). He fires a shot at his friends suggesting that they have closed their minds to understanding. His friends should have been appalled at the suffering of a righteous man, but instead they continue their guilt-laden assault. Still, Job carries a relentless hope, suggesting in the last verse that his hope will go with him to the grave.

Application
"You can't take it with you." We often recite those words in terms of the material possessions that we value so highly here on this earth but know they are of no value in terms of our future life. We cannot take with us the things that we often prize, like our wealth, our keepsakes, or our homes or cars. (I did read once about a woman in West Tennessee who was killed in a car wreck, along with her beloved dog. The dog was prepared for burial and placed in the casket with her!)

However, there is something that we do take with us to the grave. As Job suggests, "our hope will go with us down to the grave." But let's be clear. Our hope is not something to which we stubbornly cling throughout this life, knowing that it gives strength and comfort as we face difficult times, but will dissolve along with our bodies when we die. Not at all. Hope is transcendent. Hope not only prepares us for the life that is to come, but it is also the promise on which we travel from this life to the next. Hope is vital because of where our hope is placed. If we place our hope in temporary things, like wealth, like status, like popularity, or intellect, then yes, it will surely fail. But if our hope is rooted in the eternal, then hope lives on and so do we.

Take a moment to consider where you have placed your hope… your ultimate hope. Strong walls can't protect you. Wise counsel can't shield you. Good connections can't defend you. Healthy habits can't preserve you. We must hope in Christ alone. As Peter once rhetorically asked of Christ, "Lord, to whom shall we go? You have the words of eternal life" (John 6:68). Hope is the one thing that you can take with you. Pack it carefully.

Prayer
God, thank you for the confidence and victory we claim when our hope is in Christ. Amen.

Day 454   Job 18: Gone and Forgotten

> "All memory of their existence will fade from the earth, no one will remember their names." Job 18:17 (NIV)

Observation

Now it is Bildad's time to offer a second speech in rebuttal of all that Job has declared about his condition and the words of his so-called friends. Bildad lashes out at Job's accusations asking, "How long before you stop talking?" He goes on to remind Job that God snuffs out the light of the wicked. He asserts that the punishment of the wicked is well deserved and that Job has been caught in a snare of his own making. Bildad even offers a biting remark about the loss of Job's children. Obviously, the tension and anger between Job and his friends continues to escalate.

In his description of the fate of the wicked, Bildad offers the words of our focus verse, asserting that all memory of the wicked will fade from the earth. No one will even remember their names once they are gone. That's a difficult indictment against Job and is certainly a difficult word for most of us to hear in terms of the legacy we hope to leave.

Application

I've walked through a few cemeteries in my time… mostly as a pastor officiating funerals of former church members. It's always a solemn and sobering experience. There is a cruel brevity written into each headstone. There is a name recorded, along with the length of that life, and maybe a three- or four-word description. But that's about it. Unless you are a family member of the deceased, the names are meaningless and the stories forgotten. Even the names on the stone are washed away by the passage of time. A stroll through such sacred ground is a reminder of the brevity of life and the difficulty of leaving much behind for people to remember.

And yet we long to be remembered… to leave behind a legacy, a story, a testimony. We want to know that it mattered that we lived and that the things we invested our days in doing made a difference. In his teachings, Jesus taught us how to make a lasting influence. He said, "Don't store up treasures here on earth, where moths eat them and rust destroys them, and where thieves break in and steal. Store your treasures in heaven, where moths and rust cannot destroy, and thieves do not break in and steal. Wherever your treasure is, there the desires of your heart will also be" (Matthew 6:19-21 NLT). Jesus' point is simple and hard at the same time. If you want to leave a legacy, then invest in those things that transcend the grave. Invest in the things that are eternal. Most of us spend our days in the pursuit of the trivial. The lasting impression is made by our commitment to faith.

Prayer

God, may each of us leave behind a few markers that testify to our faith. Amen.

Day 455 — Job 19: The Relentless Encroachment of Hope

> "But as for me, I know that my Redeemer lives, and he will stand upon the earth at last. And after my body has decayed, yet in my body I will see God!" Job 19:25-26 (NIV)

Observation

In this chapter, Job replies to Bildad's relentless accusations. His words have been as "torture" to Job. Job exclaims that his words have crushed him and insulted him 10 times! Job tells Bildad that his words are useless. He tells Bildad that even if he had sinned, it was not his business, nor that of the other friends. It was God alone who had brought on his punishment and so the matter was one for Job and God to solve. Job continues to feel abandoned and rejected by all, even his own family and wife. "Haven't you chewed me up enough?" he asks of Bildad. Though he feels very alone and forsaken, the chapter contains a word of relentless hope. He is confident that his "redeemer" lives and that the day will come, even after death, when he will see God. Despite all that has occurred, Job is confident that God would vindicate his claim of innocence.

Application

I have a friend who is a recovering addict. It started with alcohol and then morphed into a drug addiction. Soon his crack addiction became all-consuming. He told me how he continually went to the ATM to draw out cash to pay for his addiction. He was using more than $1000 a week for many months. His life was out of control. The day finally came when he went to the ATM and it rejected his request, stating there were "insufficient funds." At that moment, he realized that he had burned through all of his savings and retirement money... hundreds of thousands of dollars. He was stunned. He had placed all his hope and future in his wealth and when it was all gone, he was completely and utterly lost. (The story ends on a positive note. My friend is doing well again. He just celebrated another year of sobriety, has a job, and can manage his income.)

Our hope in God and God's plans for our lives are the only inexhaustible resources we hold. If we are confident in God's presence, sure of God's grace, and secure in God's protection, then our hope is forever secured in the promise of God's love for us. That hope has a bearing on every facet of our lives. We escape difficult days and survive the worst of moments because our hope is unshaken. We laugh despite our grief, we smile in spite of our pain, we rejoice in the midst of our hardships, because of our hope. Because we are people of faith we echo the words of Job, "I know that my Redeemer lives." When that phrase is written both on our hearts and minds, we become more than conquerors. As you face the challenges of another day, may you do so with the bright hope of the Gospel to lead your way.

Prayer

God, grant to each of us, a relentless, ridiculous, victorious hope. Amen.

Day 456 — Job 20: The Destruction of a Relationship

> "Then Zophar the Naamathite replied: 'I must reply because I am greatly disturbed. I've had to endure your insults, but now my spirit prompts me to reply.'" Job 20:1-3 (NIV)

Observation

As this chapter opens, it is time for Zophar to respond to Job's latest speech. (This is Zophar's second speech in the book.) It is obvious from his language that he is seething with anger against Job. He offers a long diatribe against wicked people. He states that God's judgment is evident in the life of a wicked person by a loss of wealth and a shortened lifespan. It is obvious that Zophar's condemnation of the wicked is directly connected to the story of Job and his plight. With much imagery, Zophar describes God's punishment of the wicked as he tells of God's bronze arrow of judgment piercing the heart of the wicked. The continual back-and-forth dialogue between Job and his friends reveals a very quick deterioration of friendship.

Application

All relationships require effort. Even the best of friends must work at maintaining the vibrancy and life of a close relationship. For example, I have friends whom I have known for decades. There was a time when we were close. We shared experiences, stories, and life-events. But time and distance have eroded away much of the connection. We still exchange Christmas cards, we "friend" each other on Facebook, and maybe we occasionally call when we are passing through town, but that's about it. To maintain a closer relationship would take time and effort that, quite honestly, most of us are not willing to give. There are just too many other demands on our lives to worry about old friends.

Then there are those stories like that of Job and his friends. An offer of help became an occasion for judgment. Anger began to escalate. Damaging words were spoken. Friends became enemies. I hope that Job's story is not your story. I hope that you don't allow brokenness to destroy the important relationships of your life.

Remember what I said earlier? All relationships require effort... even the best ones. I encourage you to work hard at being a friend. Make the effort. Do the difficult work. Call. Visit. Text. Connect. Do not take your friends for granted. Do not neglect the important things that continue to bind you to one another. Give to the relationship. Put in the effort. Express your thankfulness in tangible ways. Be present when needed. Before this day is done, reach out to your best friends and remind them how important they are to your life. It is one of the most important investments that you will make.

Prayer

Father God, thank you for the friends we hold dear. May we treasure each relationship and work hard at maintaining our friendships with them. Amen.

Day 457 — Job 21: The Art of Listening Well

> "Bear with me, and let me speak. After I have spoken, you may resume mocking me." Job 21:3 (NIV)

Observation
Job responds to Zophar's latest charges. Job builds a strong case against the assumptions and arguments that his friends have brought forth... specifically, that God always punishes the wicked for their actions and wickedness must be the reason for Job's calamities. But Job carefully builds a counterpoint indicating that evil people often thrive in life and suffer very little for their sins. Job takes a long look at the notion of why the wicked seemingly prosper. He invites his friends to listen to his response. He reminds them of the success the wicked often enjoy. He speaks of comfortable surroundings, financial success, health, and long lifespans that even the wicked enjoy. (Job's thoughts, however, do not include any discussion on God's final judgment of the wicked.) By showing the prosperity of the wicked, Job points to the holes in his friends' theology of a prosperity and calamity mentality that rewards the righteous and the wicked consistently.

Application
Amid the back-and-forth arguments between Job and his friends, Job begs for a moment of rational, thoughtful, and patient listening on the part of his accusers. "Bear with me," he insists, so that he can make his case. He tells them that after he has spoken, they can return to their mocking ways. Do you see the dynamic in the dialogue that Job is hoping to introduce? "Stop talking long enough so that you can hear what I am saying. Before you form your next response, at least listen to what I am saying."

Let's talk for a moment about the way in which most of us argue with others. All of us, from time to time, get into those unpleasant, heated, verbal interactions with spouses, children, parents, co-workers, friends, or maybe even caregivers. Somewhere along the way, we stop listening to what others are saying because we are so focused on formulating our response. It goes like this... we hear the initial few words, we gauge the tone, and read the body language. We assume we understand what they are trying to convey. But rather than actively listening, we begin to process our response and thus we don't even hear all of what is being said. Job pleads with his friends to listen to what he has to say before they offer their response. He wants them to at least give him the space to make his case. Most of us need to hear and heed that advice. Part of the art of listening requires that we give time for others to offer their thoughts before we begin to spew out our responses. Even a short delay in our response could help us collect better thoughts and tone down our emotions.

Prayer
Father God, may we develop the habit of listening well to others. Amen.

Day 458 — Job 22: Limitless Grace for Our Limitless Sins

> "No, it's because of your wickedness! There's no limit to your sins."
> Job 22:5 (NIV)

Observation
This chapter marks the beginning of the third round of speeches between Job and his friends. These speeches do little to advance the conversation as they tend to repeat the refrains from the earlier speeches. This time, it is Eliphaz who is speaking. He accuses Job of having become wealthy by abusing the helpless and the downtrodden. This is why Job suffers so greatly, Eliphaz charges. He tells of Job's abuse of all those around him… his brothers, the weary, the hungry, the widows and orphans. He accuses Job of committing sins in defiance of God's sovereignty. He reminds Job that because of his sinfulness that the day will come when he will be completely cut off from God. He calls for Job to adopt an attitude of repentance.

Application
Eliphaz accuses Job of such sinfulness that there is "no limit" to his sins. Same could be said for us, right? Is there a limit to the sins we have committed and will continue to commit? Who could even begin to count such a thing?

A few years ago, a trip to the doctor revealed that my blood pressure was starting to trend upward. He prescribed a low dose of medication and gratefully my blood pressure has been well-controlled ever since. But in those first few months, I felt a little panic about it. So, here is what I did. I bought a blood pressure cuff and began to take a reading every morning, carefully recording the date and the numbers. I kept a log for more than 400 days so that I could prove to myself and to my doctor that things were going well. (I took the notebook with me for my annual physical just so he could see the results.)

What if someone kept a running total of your transgressions? What if every sin committed, every evil thought in the mind, every wayward word spoken, or every non-Christlike attitude was recorded? Surely there would be no limit to our sins. That's bad news, but the Good News is found in the limitless grace of Jesus Christ. As Paul reminds us in Romans 8:1, "Therefore there is now no condemnation for those who are in Christ Jesus" (NASB). Remember the old hymn lyric that taught us about "grace greater than all our sins"? We need to bask in the glow of that realization. Yes, our sins are many… but grace is greater. The God who called us into fellowship has made a provision for our sinfulness. The atoning death of Christ on the cross is supremely sufficient. The price of our sins has been paid and grace has been extended. God has promised to cleanse us from all unrighteousness. So, if in your guilt-infused mind you are keeping a count of all your sins, remember that God is not.

Prayer
Father God, thank you for the freedom that grace provides. Amen.

Day 459 — Job 23: When God Is Absent

> "I go east, but he is not there. I go west, but I cannot find him. I do not see him in the north, for he is hidden. I look to the south, but he is concealed."
> Job 23:8-9 (NIV)

Observation
This chapter records Job's third reply to Eliphaz. It is apparent by what Job says that he has abandoned his attempt to persuade his friends of his innocence. Instead, he longs to plead his case in the court of God. Problematic to his quest, however, is the belief that God is nowhere to be found… that God is veiled in secrecy, hidden from Job's seeking. Still, he longs to plead his case before the Almighty even if it is rebellion before God. He wants to explain his thoughts to God and listen carefully to all that God would say in response. Job indicates that he refuses to be silent even though a very deep darkness has surrounded his life.

Application
Notice the very bleak outlook described by Job as he wrestles with his difficult situation. It is the opposite of the words reflected by the psalmist who asks rhetorically, "Where can I go from Your Spirit? Or where can I flee from Your presence? If I ascend to heaven, You are there; If I make my bed in Sheol, behold, You are there. If I take the wings of the dawn, If I dwell in the remotest part of the sea, even there Your hand will lead me, And Your right hand will lay hold of me" (Psalm 139:7-10 NASB). On one hand, the psalmist describes the inescapability of God's presence, while on the other hand, Job describes a feeling of utter abandonment. Let's be honest… in our walk of faith there are certainly those days when we feel the presence of God in every place and at every moment. But there are also those days when God seems very far away and removed from our story. How can we respond to those moments when God seems absent? How can we discover God and know of God's comforting presence when our lives are enveloped in a terrible and deep darkness? I think there are several steps one may take. First, whenever you feel alone spiritually, don't allow yourself to be alone physically. Surround yourself with fellow believers who can speak hope and light into your darkness. Don't look to them to give you all the answers to your problems but do rely upon them to be present with you as you search for hope. Think in terms of community, not isolation. Second, maintain your spiritual disciplines. Read even if the passages seem empty, pray even if the words seem to be ignored, worship even when the practice is laborious and not invigorating. Light has a way of penetrating even the smallest cracks of our dark boxes. Wrestle with your faith until the light begins to seep in once again. God is always present, even when our life story seems to say otherwise.

Prayer
Father God, may we find you present, even in our darkest hours. Amen.

Day 460 — Job 24: The Exploitation of the Poor

> "They press out olive oil without being allowed to taste it, and they tread in the winepress as they suffer from thirst." Job 24:11 (NIV)

Observation

Job turns his attention to the topic of why the evil seem to prosper. He ponders the way in which God seems to tolerate the terrible evil in the world. Job sees the evidence of injustice all around him and wonders why God doesn't act with swift judgment. He sees the evildoers move the property boundaries of the poor. He sees them steal livestock and mistreat the poor. He sees the extreme poverty of others caused by wicked men's selfish exploitation. Job also points to the heinous acts of evil done in the cover of darkness. He points specifically to murder, theft, and adultery, but claims that surely God can see even in the dark shadows. Towards the end of his speech, Job does seem to allow for the final judgement of the wicked but remains perplexed by the lack of immediate judgment and justice on the part of God.

Application

Some of Job's thoughts are as timeless as today's headlines. Notice in our focus verse how Job describes the exploitation of the poor. They "press out olive oil without being allowed to taste it, they tread in the winepress as they suffer from thirst." It is the image of the poor laborer who works long and hard but never reaps the benefit of his labor. It is the image of a slave who is forced to work endless hours in horrible conditions with no hope of ever bettering her station in life. We'd like to think that such exploitation is just a tale from the pages of ancient history. We'd like to think that slavery ended here in the U.S. with Lincoln's Emancipation Proclamation. But we are fools if those thoughts make sense to us. According to every single, reputable source on slavery, trafficking, prostitution, and exploitation, there are now more people enslaved around the world than at any other time in human history. Lives are being abused. Bodies are being sacrificed. Cultures are being destroyed. And the greed of many remains unchecked. If you want a sobering and frightening realization, call the local agency in your community that deals with human trafficking and get them to tell you how bad the problem is both world-wide and in your community. You will not sleep well. Do some research and poke around the topics of extreme poverty and exploitation and see if some of the companies and products you use every day are on the list. Take a trip to the developing world for a week and ask yourself for an explanation of the inequalities of poverty and wealth. Here's my point… we are all a part of the problem and therefore, we must all be a part of the solution. It's time for the godly to rise up and oppose the structures that keep others oppressed.

Prayer

Father God, give us eyes to see and courage to act. Amen.

Day 461 — Job 25: We Should Stand in Awe

> "God is more glorious than the moon; he shines brighter than the stars."
> Job 25:5 (NIV)

Observation
With very few words, Bildad offers his third and final speech to Job. It is a "last gasp" from Job's accusers. The theme is once again God's punishment of those who are wicked. The dialogue between Job and his friends is obviously winding down… there is no new thought or content to add to the situation that has not already been expressed. These words of Bildad do, however, reflect a slightly different slant. Rather than offer a tirade on the fate of the wicked, he takes a moment to talk about the greatness of God. Verse 4 is a rhetorical question in light of God's majesty and power. Bildad asks how any man can be innocent before God. His question still strikes a blow against Job's insistence of innocence.

Application
Earlier this year, here in middle Tennessee, we experienced what is often referred to as a Super Moon. The moon's orbit around the earth is not a perfect circle… it is more of an oval. That means during certain times of the year the moon is closer to the earth than at other times. This distance to the moon can vary by almost 30,000 miles. A Super Moon occurs when the moon is close and the moon is full. The "moon illusion" as it is sometimes called as the moon peeks over the horizon, makes the moon appear 7% bigger and 16% brighter. On this occurrence, the skies were crystal clear and the image of the Super Moon was really special. As I stepped out to see it, I was reminded of the immense expanse of the universe and the glorious display of God's handiwork.

Sometimes we forget to look up and think of the mystery, majesty, and glory of God. We tend to become so focused "down here," that we forget to look "up there." A few weeks ago, I was teaching a group of bi-vocational pastors in the mountains of Honduras. When the power grid went down at night, it became very dark. And then within moments, the celestial light show came to life… stars, planets, constellations… all displayed across the sky. It was glorious. It was awe-inspiring. It was humbling. It was interesting to me that, to have my focus turned skyward, I had to let go of the distractions that prevented me from seeing God's creativity. It happens. We get so caught up in the here and now, with the noise and distractions of daily living, that we sometimes become blinded to the things God is doing and to the ways in which God longs to be revealed to us. So, let me encourage you to take a moment in the next few weeks, to go outside on a clear night and just look up. No, you might not see a special moon or a shooting star, but you will be reminded of the greatness of God who has arranged the heavenly display for our enjoyment.

Prayer
Father God, thank you for revealing yourself to us in the stars of heaven. Amen.

Day 462 — Job 26: The Rhythm of the Rain

> "He wraps the rain in his thick clouds, and the clouds don't burst with the weight." Job 26:8 (NIV)

Observation
This chapter reflects Job's third reply to Bildad. He rebukes Bildad for his unhelpful words. The first few verses of the chapter drip with irony as he addresses Bildad… "Where in the world would the poor soul be without your amazing counsel and wisdom?" He goes on to ask Bildad where he had gotten his words because he is obviously simply repeating the words of others. Job continues to assert that he knows more about the greatness of God than his friends. He speaks of the way in which God has suspended the earth in space and defined the boundaries of the oceans. It is apparent that although Job could not see through the mysteries of his suffering, he still holds fast to the fear of the Lord.

Application
I'm a well-educated man. I've got plenty of diplomas hanging on the wall, but still there are mysteries that I have yet to understand. Rain is one of them. I get the whole water cycle… the sun heats the water on the surface of the earth, the moisture rises, it collects, and the rain falls. But what I don't fully grasp is how the clouds can hold so much moisture and its massive weight. Sometimes the clouds burst open and inches and inches of rain fall to the ground. How can the clouds above our heads remain suspended in the skies while holding such volume? When the hurricanes blow up from the Gulf, how can the clouds carry the moisture so far and in such abundance? While I am sure that there are any number of scientific explanations for such phenomena, I find myself in awe of God's design who allows the whole water cycle to exist, for the clouds to form, and for the rain to fall.

When I was young, I saw the rain as an interrupter of all the things I loved to do outdoors. The rain could cancel a baseball game, make a clean car dirty, or end a day at the lake. Rain forced me to change plans or cancel events. But as I get older, I don't mind the rain so much. I understand how vital the rain is to the earth, to the crops on which we depend, and to the flowers that we enjoy. Rain brings a solitude, a peace, a calm, a refreshment. Sometimes when it rains here in middle Tennessee, I leave our backdoor open and listen to the sound of the rain striking the back deck. There is tranquility. Maybe even a reassurance of sorts, knowing that the plants will thrive, the grass will grow, and the needs of nature will be met. We used to sing about "showers of blessing." The next time it rains, I challenge you to see the handiwork of God as it falls. It is God's blessing and God's reminder that our needs are met and life is given to our thirsty souls.

Prayer
Father God, thank you for the gift of rain and the abundance of your grace. Amen.

Day 463 — Job 27: Integrity in the Face of Hardship

> "As long as I live, while I have breath from God, my lips will speak no evil, and my tongue will speak no lies." Job 27:3-4 (NIV)

Observation
Job continues his speeches by offering an extended final word to his friends. He begins with, "As God lives…" It is an oath used in ancient courts to prove the validity of someone's testimony. Job is insisting that his testimony is true. According to Job, God had denied Job a right to due process by not allowing him to plead his case in God's presence. This turn of events had made Job "bitter." And yet his response to the mysteries of God exposes the attitude deeply embedded in his heart: "No matter the circumstances of one's life, each person should resolutely trust in God." The latter part of his discourse is directed towards his friends. He refers to their actions as "nonsense." They have acted wickedly against Job and he tells them that they will one day bear the consequences of their actions.

Application
One of the most interesting men I have ever known was named Bruce Montgomery. Before his death a few years ago, Bruce had a long career in law enforcement, first as a Federal Marshal and then as the Sheriff of Sevier County, Tennessee. Bruce was powerful, politically connected, opinionated, passionate, kind, and generous. It was his generosity that always caught my attention. He was one of those guys that was always doing something for someone else. If he saw a need, he tried to solve it. If it was a problem money could fix, he knew ways to make it happen. When cancer invaded his life, he amassed huge debts… hundreds of thousands of dollars. But neither the cancer nor the indebtedness did anything to change one bit of his generosity. Through it all, he remained as benevolent and as giving as always. He taught me the lesson of generosity in the face of hardship.

The story of Job is one of unyielding integrity in the face of difficult circumstances. Though his struggles were harsh and the explanations were non-existent, Job never wavered. Though he could not understand the ways of God, he never cursed God, nor rebelled against God. His integrity was tested in the fires of adversity. All of us will experience adversity over the course of our lives. It could be financial adversity, a health concern, a broken relationship, etc. How we respond in such moments is a measure of the depth of our character and faith. In the face of the shifting sands of our lives, we must anchor our hearts on the solid rock of God's presence, God's faithfulness, and God's grace. As you face the day before you, may your faith be strong, your character unchanged, and your attitudes hopeful.

Prayer
Heavenly Father, give us the strength to face whatever life throws our way today. Amen.

Day 464 — Job 28: Wisdom Quest

> "And this is what he says to all humanity: 'The fear of the Lord is true wisdom; to forsake evil is real understanding.'" Job 28:28 (NIV)

Observation

Chapter 28 reflects Job's words on the wisdom of God. It has been called by many the "heart of the entire book." It is a lofty view of God's providence and wisdom. Job describes the wisdom of God in creation and administration of the universe, as well as God's interaction in the affairs of men. Job asserts that only God could understand the path of Job's life and the reasons why the calamities came his way. Were they for discipline or for teaching? In his speech, Job describes the way in which men tunnel beneath the earth attempting to discover precious stones and valuable ore. And yet, man is unable to "unearth" the wisdom of God. The value of God's wisdom, says Job, is far beyond the worth of jeweled stones. Job closes his thoughts with the idea that true wisdom teaches a person to live under the authority of God. Those who are wise will depart from evil and fear the Lord.

Application

When I made the transition from Woodmont Baptist to Belmont University, I took a week or so to pack up my old office, deciding what to keep and what to throw away, so that I could bring to campus the essential things needed to begin my work. For several of years I used a portable hard drive to back up the data from my work computer. I kept a lot of sermons, funerals, and other important documents on that hard drive just in case my computer ever crashed. Not long after I moved to Belmont, I needed to retrieve some files from the back-up drive. "Now, where did I put it?" I had no idea where I had placed the hard drive, but I did have a distinct memory of saying to myself, "I need to put this in a safe place." I looked in boxes, I searched my office at home, I went through drawers and cabinets and desks, but still no hard drive. Then one day, while looking for something entirely different, I opened the drawer of a desk in our living room at home and found the hard drive, where I had placed it months before.

Sometimes it happens that way. We discover some hidden gem while searching for something quite different. And sometimes, we discover the wisdom of God in our daily routine. Job reminds us that true wisdom comes through our fear of the Lord. He's right. When we choose to live our lives fearful of disappointing God and longing to align our purposes with God's, we discover that God's wisdom is waiting to be claimed, like a jewel hidden in the soil, or a hard drive tucked away in a desk.

Prayer

Heavenly Father, may we discover this day, the wisdom you long to impart to us. Amen.

Day 465 — Job 29: Acts of Faith

> "I served as eyes for the blind and feet for the lame. I was a father to the poor and assisted strangers who needed help." Job 29:15-16 (NIV)

Observation

As this chapter opens, Job reflects on the blessings he once claimed. This chapter speaks of his prosperity; the following chapter will speak of his calamity. As he recalls his life story, he reminds his listeners of his righteousness and the undeserved sufferings he is now experiencing. He certainly recalls the best days of his life when his family was healthy, his business prosperous, and his outlook happy. He "walked in the light of God's favor." He felt that God was his friend and walked with him through each day. He knew great status and influence. He was a respected leader in the city. His wisdom was sought out and the poor and needy knew they could come to him for help. He offered justice with his words and opposed the wicked with his actions. It was a good life, filled with joy, peace, and prosperity.

Application

New Testament writer James reminds us that "faith by itself isn't enough. Unless it produces good deeds, it is dead and useless" (James 2:17 NLT). And he's right, of course. Our faith should always find practical expression. Our faith should be evident in the things we do, the words we say, and the attitudes we hold. In the case of Job, his faith was evident in the way in which he treated the marginalized of his community. He served as eyes for the blind, and feet for the lame. He was a father to the poor and assisted strangers who needed help. Here's what I have noticed about people who truly possess an active and vibrant faith… they live out that faith every day that they walk the planet. Faith-produced actions are not something they have to think about or conjure up at the right moment. No. Because they are people of faith, good works follow them around like a wonderful scent. They perform righteous deeds and noble acts, not to prove their faith, but because of their faith.

Living out your faith is a gradual process. The day of your conversion doesn't just automatically reorient and reprioritize your life. It does begin the process. Daily we become transformed into the image of our Lord. We make conscious choices. We commit deliberate acts. But as we become transformed, faith takes over. We go from learning about our faith to living out our faith. We no longer have to think, "Does this reflect well on my faith?" We move to the point that all we do becomes a faith-filled expression of the lordship of Christ. This very day, the world around you needs you to live out your faith. Love the marginalized. Uplift the downtrodden. Give hope to those who suffer. Speak joy to those who are hopeless.

Prayer

Heavenly Father, may we truly live out our faith this very day. Amen.

Day 466 — Job 30: The Ache of Abandonment

> "I cry to you, O God, but you don't answer. I stand before you, but you don't even look." Job 30:20 (NIV)

Observation

As this chapter opens, the tone of Job's speech takes a dramatic shift. He moves away from describing the memories of his blessed past to a description of his present life of severe anguish. Chapter 29 told of all the things that God had given to Job. Chapter 30 describes all of the things now taken from him. Job indicates that he is dishonored by younger men, the sons of detestable people. These persecutors are in Job's words, "not worthy to run with his sheepdogs" (v. 1). They offer continual insults and spit in his face. They come at him from all directions, attacking every facet of Job's life where he is vulnerable. Job feels that God has left him defenseless. He suffers both physical and emotional pain. He writhes in pain each night and is constantly haunted by depression.

Application

Notice the desperation in the words of our focus verse. These are the words of a man who, from the depths of his depression, feels absolutely abandoned by God. He prays but God doesn't respond. He stands in God's presence, but God never even looks in his direction. We read his words and certainly feel moved by his plight. We feel the pain of his story because, at times, it is also our story. Sometimes we feel separated from God. We pray, but our words go unanswered. We cry out in our pain but find no relief. Why do we experience such moments, and how do we ever escape them?

Sometimes, we put ourselves in desperate moments. We choose disobedience to the ways of God. We allow our sinful actions to separate us from God. That's a simple "cause and effect" situation. But what happens when we feel abandoned or ignored by God while in the careful pursuit of our faith? What happens when our faith disciplines bear no fruit and our study of God's Word provides no answer? In other words, what happens when we find ourselves in the wilderness, wondering where or how to reconnect with God? Let's remember something about the wilderness experiences of the faithful God-followers recorded in scripture (Elijah, David, Paul, Jesus... just to name a few). The wilderness provided a time of reflection, renewal, and reprioritization. The wilderness brought a rediscovery of God. Rather than being abandoned, it is in the wilderness where the presence of God was strongly felt, and God's words carefully heard. You will also discover that after every wilderness experience, the next great moment in that person's life unfolded. So, if you are feeling a little left out these days, not to worry, you are being prepared, not forgotten.

Prayer

Father, may experience enough of you today to be reminded that you are near. Amen.

Day 467 — Job 31: The Scrutiny of God

"Doesn't he see everything I do and every step I take?" Job 31:4 (NIV)

Observation
This chapter records Job's last pleading of his case before the Lord and his friends. Throughout his speech, Job will continue to plead his innocence. In fact, he dares to invoke curses on himself if he is guilty of any of the crimes that he mentions in this chapter. He insists that he "would be glad to suffer" if he were guilty. He mentions sexual sin and lust. He proclaims that he has never even taken a lustful glance. He proclaims that there is no falsehood or deceit in his spirit. There is not even a "spot of wrongdoing" on his hands. He claims that he has never been enticed into an illicit relationship. He has been fair with his servants and has cared well for the poor, the widow, and the orphan in his midst. He further mentions that he has never trusted in his gold or wealth and has never sought revenge.

Application
In defending his innocence, Job asserts that God has seen everything that he has done and has watched every step that he has taken. Nothing can escape the scrutiny of God. If he had sinned, God would surely have seen his actions.

We often consider God's scrutiny and are fearful of it. Knowing that God sees, hears, and knows all things, we sometimes shy away from God's presence, knowing that God has seen our sins and knows of our wayward thoughts. God's scrutiny is at times all but unbearable. We cower in fear at the thought that he has such an intimate knowledge of our lives. But let's consider for a moment, the opposite side of God's scrutiny. Aren't we grateful that God's watch care is so exact, so careful, and so mindful of our needs? Recently I was in charge of watching our one-year-old granddaughter. Though she has not yet taken her first steps, she is quite mobile and can cover a lot of ground as she crawls around the house. And so, I had to be vigilant while she was in my charge. I had to watch her every move and anticipate any dangerous action she might take. I kept unsafe objects out of her reach and monitored every item she held in her hand. That's what a loving grandparent or parent does. They watch those under their charge every moment. They protect. They love. They nurture. They defend. Isn't it comforting to know that God is watching every move you make? Not to catch you in some awkward misstep, but to protect you and guide you every step of the way. Aren't we glad that God "sees everything we do and every step that we take?" As you travel through this day, be comforted in the knowledge that God is watching.

Prayer
Father, thank you for your constant vigil over our lives. Amen.

Day 468 — Job 32: The Source of Wisdom

> "But there is a spirit within people, the breath of the Almighty within them, that makes them intelligent." Job 32:8 (NIV)

Observation

A fourth person has been listening to the exchanges between Job and his friends. His name is Elihu and he had been listening in silence up to this point. The longer he listened, the angrier he became. He was angry at Job for his continual assertions of innocence. He was angry with the three friends of Job because they had not silenced Job with their arguments nor given any proof of their accusations. (There are some scholars who speculate that Elihu may have been the author of the Book of Job.) Elihu acknowledges his junior status among the other men. But he reminds them that being old does not guarantee wisdom. True wisdom comes from "the breath of the Almighty." Having a sense of self-importance and wisdom, Elihu stands ready to offer his words as the chapter closes.

Application

You may have heard that "experience is the best teacher." Surely, if we are wise, we can gain a lot of insight from our experiences. From the time we are very young, we learn what brings both pleasure and pain. Each event registers in our mind and we learn that some things are worth repeating while other things are to be avoided. For example, I learned long ago that fire is hot. I don't have to reach my arm into a campfire every winter to be reminded of that truth. We learn a few things along the way, but wisdom is more than just the acquisition of knowledge and facts. Wisdom is the ability to know when and how to apply those facts. It is the sense of timing and intellect that give wisdom her true power.

When writing about wisdom, James reminds us that "if any of you lacks wisdom, let him ask of God, who gives to all generously and without reproach, and it will be given to him" (James 1:5 NASB). In this passage, Elihu reminds us that because the breath of God is within us, we can lay hold of godly wisdom when needed. We have the ability to discern right from wrong. We can apply insight and teaching to situations that need resolve. But there's the problem for most of us. Even though the ability to display wisdom resides within us, we seldom choose to listen to God's voice. We choose self-reliance over godly wisdom. We offer our opinions and not the counsel of the Lord. What if, before you start out on this day, you sought the heart and wisdom of God? What if you prayed, "God make me wise this day, not for selfish gain, but for the furtherance of your Kingdom and for the glory of your Son." There is a spirit within you… the very breath of the Almighty. Pray that it would make you wise this day and every day.

Prayer

Father, as situations come before us this day, may we display your wisdom. Amen.

Day 469 — Job 33: Hearing from God

> "For God speaks again and again, though people do not recognize it. He speaks in dreams, in visions of the night, when deep sleep falls on people as they lie in their beds." Job 33:14-15 (NIV)

Observation
In this chapter, Elihu continues to speak to Job. He urges him to listen, insisting that he will offer words of sincerity and truth. His words are a bit different in topic than those of the previous speeches given by Job's friends. Elihu will talk about the instructional nature of suffering and how God can use it to correct and heal. Elihu puts himself on the same level as Job as they dialogue by reminding Job that both men have been created by God. He has heard all of Job's declarations of innocence and tells Job that he is wrong to say that God is against him. Elihu offers the counsel that God speaks in various ways, through both dreams and suffering. The purpose of God's words is to help individuals turn from their wrongdoing. Elihu also offers Job a word of hope in this speech by asserting that God might send an angel to intercede for him and even restore him to health.

Application
One of the things that happens as a part of my work at Belmont as the director of a leadership institute is to add content to our website. I write an occasional blog as well as posting a few podcasts. It's always a bit strange to me to offer insight, advice, or counsel, without knowing if anyone out in cyberspace will ever hear those words. It's the old, "if a tree falls in a lonely forest, will it produce any noise if no one is there to hear it" question. Back in the days that I wrote and proclaimed sermons for a living, I was always assured of an audience who would hear the words and hopefully apply them.

Elihu correctly proclaims that God speaks again and again. The question is whether people hear God's voice, and further still, do they respond to God's instruction? To connect with us, God uses many ways to speak truth to our lives. It may well be through a dream or illness as Elihu suggests. But God may also speak through the written Word, or through the advice of a godly friend, or through a song, or through nature, or through the prompting of God's Spirit. The problem is never God's silence, but always our ability to listen. In fact, God will speak to you this very day. God always does. But are you listening? Is your spiritual antenna turned in God's direction? Why not begin this day with the faithful belief that God longs to speak to you today? As you awaken to a new day, ask God to speak clearly, specifically, and lovingly to you. Be sensitive to God's voice in whatever way God chooses to communicate. And then take it one more step… respond with obedience.

Prayer
Father, speak this day, for we are anxiously listening. Amen.

Day 470 — Job 34: The Essence of Repentance

> "Why don't people say to God, 'I have sinned, but I will sin no more'?"
> Job 34:31 (NIV)

Observation
As this chapter opens, Elihu continues his speech directed towards Job. He specifically answers Job's accusations that God is unjust. He appeals to others within the sound of his voice to listen to his words and decide if Job was right or wrong to challenge God with being unjust. He criticizes Job for being irreverent and spiritually ignorant. He further accuses Job of walking with wicked men. In the second half of the chapter, Elihu defends God's justice. It is unthinkable that God would do any wickedness or wrong. He reiterates the theology of Job's other friends by saying that the wicked are punished because they have turned away from following God. In the eyes of Elihu, Job needs to confess his sins so that healing can begin.

Application
Confession is the act of admitting to God our sinful disobedience. It is to agree with God that our actions have been evil in God's sight. It is to acknowledge both to God and to ourselves that we have committed wrong and shameful acts. Repentance takes our confession a step further. To repent is to change directions. It is to act on the confession we have made so that we do not continue to act in sinful and shameful ways. It is to alter the course of our thinking, our actions, and our words so that we move away from those sins that separate us from the presence of God

The trap we may fall into is confession without repentance. We confess our sins, believing that "He is faithful and righteous to forgive us our sins and to cleanse us from all unrighteousness" (1 John 1:9 NASB). We trick ourselves into believing that as long as we have confessed our sins, no further action is needed on our part. And so, rather than alter our behavior, we continue to commit the same sinful acts, reasoning with ourselves that God will always forgive us. Such thinking is an abuse of God's grace. It is a dangerous pattern of behavior that invites us to "feel better" about our sins. We lull ourselves into thinking that sins which are so easily erased, must be of no consequence to our hearts and minds. Nothing could be further from the truth. Christ calls us into transformation. Yes, grace allows us to begin again, to move forward without laboring under the weight of guilt and shame, but repentance calls us to live differently, to make better choices, and to align our hearts and actions with those of God. So, be careful to confess your sins. Name them specifically and honestly. But don't stop there. Change the direction of your actions through repentance.

Prayer
Father, forgive us and then grant us the courage to live a better life. Amen.

Day 471 — Job 35: The God Who Hears

> "But it is wrong to say God doesn't listen, to say the Almighty isn't concerned." Job 35:13 (NIV)

Observation
In this chapter, Elihu reminds Job that God is not affected or dependent upon man's sin or innocence. In other words, sin only affects the person who commits the sin. It does not affect Almighty God. Therefore, God judges impartially as Job is being judged, at least in Elihu's mind. Elihu points out that often people tend to cry out for deliverance when they are suffering. The reason such prayers are not always answered is because such prayers are just pleas for relief and not prayers of true humility before God. Elihu points to three things offered to those who trust in God: songs in the night to comfort them, words to teach them, and knowledge to make them wise. He reminds Job that Job's assertions and accusations are just "non-sense."

Application
Back in the summer of 1980, then Southern Baptist Convention president, Dr. Bailey Smith, offered some words that were heard far and wide in faith circles, words that set Christian-Jewish dialogue back for many years. Smith said, "God Almighty does not hear the prayers of a Jew," shocking words then and now. The assertion that God fails to hear the prayers of any person ought to bother all of us. Certainly, we called out to God long before doing so through the name of Jesus. If not for God's listening, how could God hear the prayers of any sinner, prior to coming to faith? And so those words once spoken by Smith weren't carried along on the stream of good theology or compassionate faith. Surely God hears and responds to the prayers of us all… at least that's the assertion that Elihu makes when talking with Job. "It is wrong to say God doesn't listen."

It is both humbling and exciting to think that God hears every prayer that I make. I'm humbled that my thoughts are so important to the creator of the universe that God would take the time to listen to me. I'm excited to think that God cares so very much. Let's be honest, all of us have had periods in our spiritual lives that seemed like a funk… like living in the doldrums… thinking that somehow God was far away and removed from the affairs of our daily lives. Whenever we feel abandoned, ignored, or distanced from God, let's realize that God is unchanging. God's love for us never wanes. God's compassion for us never dims. God's longing to hear from us never changes. And so, the distance we feel is a separation that we have created and not God. So, pray confidently this morning as your start your day, knowing that God is listening even if we don't feel it.

Prayer
Father, thank you for hearing every prayer we offer. Amen.

Day 472 — Job 36: The Mysteries of God

> "Look, God is greater than we can understand. His years cannot be counted." Job 36:26 (NIV)

Observation

In this final speech to Job, Elihu claims to speak with God's authority. In fact, he has a rather high opinion of his wisdom and counsel. He states, "I am a man of great knowledge" (v. 4 NLT). He emphasizes God's strength, mercy, and justice. He tells Job that God exalts the righteous like kings. If the righteous suffer hardship it is restorative in nature. In other words, God will correct the wayward steps of the righteous. He reminds Job that the key to blessing is repentance. Job must repent while there is still time. Don't complain about suffering, repent of wickedness. Elihu, obviously, still believes that Job's hardships are a result of unconfessed and unrepentant sin. The latter part of the chapter switches focus to the majesty of God. Elihu specifically will speak of the ways in which God's sovereignty is demonstrated by the power of a storm. Perhaps his words are a foreshadowing of the storm (whirlwind) that is approaching through which God will speak to Job.

Application

We are all wired a little differently from one another. Some of us understand certain concepts while others elude us. For example, I have always been good with numbers and directions, but introduce me to a group of people and it won't take me long to forget their names. I have friends who are amazing at reading music and playing instruments, but I've never been able to get too far with such endeavors. All of us have strengths and weaknesses. Our understanding about things is not complete or comprehensive. Sure, we can study and amass knowledge, but still there will be things that are beyond our comprehension. One of them is the majesty and complexity of God. Who can fathom God's ways, or understand God's timing, or reason over God's omnipotence?

It's always been interesting to me how God arranges the people, places, and moments of our lives to God's glory and purpose. The older I become, the less I believe in coincidence and the more I believe in the providence of God. I had two of those God moments recently, when I was in the right spot, at the right time, with the right word of counsel to offer, because God had equipped me for that conversation and placed me in just the right spot. Who can understand God's ways? My faith teaches me not to try to figure out all that God is doing, but to simply accept that God is always at work and somedays you and I are included in the plan. Our lives are woven into the narrative. We have to be okay with the mystery of God. We have to live in faith, not knowing all the intricacies of God's ways, but to be comfortable in knowing that this is indeed God's world, and we are the most important part of it in God's eyes.

Prayer

Father, may we rest comfortably with the mysteries and ways of God. Amen.

Day 473 — Job 37: I Stand Amazed in the Presence

> "Pay attention to this, Job. Stop and consider the wonderful miracles of God!" Job 37:14 (NIV)

Observation
Elihu continues his final speech to Job, describing, very vividly, the power and majesty of a storm. He points to God's presence and power. He reminds Job that the storms of God blow to give both correction and kindness. Elihu describes the work of God, expressed through nature, in both the seasons of winter and summer. Because of God's power and majesty, people should fear God and put away their pride. His words once again seek to address Elihu's perception of Job's behavior towards God. He closes with an invitation to Job to allow God to speak. And as the next chapter opens, God does begin to address Job, speaking to him during a literal storm.

Application
When I wrote this devotional thought, Nashville was experiencing winter's chill. When I awoke that morning, the thermometer read 2° F with a wind chill in the negative numbers. In fact, most of the country was caught in the grip of a huge blast of artic air. As you might imagine, a lot of folks were posting videos online of the various things affected by the extreme cold… frozen fountains, streams, and lakes, huge piles of snow on the roadways, cars that wouldn't start, and many other things. One of the more intriguing videos I watched was of a soap bubble, blown in the extreme cold. Within seconds, the moisture in the bubble began to crystalize, leaving a beautiful frozen sphere that would rival any delicate ornament on a Christmas tree. It was a reminder to me of God's majesty, creativity, and attention to detail in the world around us.

In our focus verse, Elihu challenges Job to stop and consider the wonderful miracles of God. That challenge should certainly find a place in our hearing as well. I wonder if we take the time often enough to stop and consider the splendor of God's creation all around us. Do we marvel at the colors in the foliage of the fall? Do we see the explosion of color in spring? Do we stop to consider all the hues of green on a June afternoon? Even in the cold, do we see the beauty of freshly fallen snow or ice crystals on the windowsill? Such things should remind us that God really is a God of creativity who longs to show off. God creates beauty for us to enjoy, delicately crafting the details of nature to give us a glimpse of God's splendor. It is evident that the world around us has not been created by random chance, but by the very deliberate hand of a creator. So even this day, stop and consider the miracles of God.

Prayer
Father, thank you for the creativity that you share with each of us. Amen.

Day 474 — Job 38: Who Do You Think That You Are?

> "Have you ever commanded the morning to appear and caused the dawn to rise in the east? Have you made daylight spread to the ends of the earth, to bring an end to the night's wickedness?" Job 38:12-13 (NIV)

Observation

This chapter begins what is arguably the most intriguing section of the Book of Job. God begins to challenge Job's assumptions, questions, and accusations. Over the course of months, Job has become worn down physically, emotionally, mentally, and even spiritually. His pressing God for answers reveals an attitude of distrust, and maybe even insolence. God, through more than 60 rhetorical questions, begins to pull Job's thoughts into a proper perspective of both the omniscience and omnipotence of God. Because Job had previously stated his desire to "plead his case before God," this dialogue becomes very much like a "day in court" for Job. Throughout this chapter, God uses "general revelation," (meaning a revelation of God evident to all through the observation of nature and its ways) to address Job's arguments, accusations, and questions. Job will quickly be humbled before God, reducing him to silence. God will reveal to Job that as a mere man, Job has been ignorant of God's plans and purposes, and especially in this case, he has been ignorant of God's conversations with Satan.

Application

From time to time, some representatives from Jehovah's Witness will knock on my door, armed with questions, pamphlets, and warm smiles. (Although I certainly don't accept all their doctrinal or theological positions, I do appreciate their zeal at taking their message to the masses by a door-to-door approach. They've got spunk. Give them their due.) And typically, when they arrive, I politely tell them of my theological education and ministerial experience. I try to graciously convey that I am comfortable in my faith positions and that I am not currently interested in learning more about their message. I just want them to know with whom they are dealing. Admittedly, I am not the average person they will encounter at the door. And although I never claim to have all the answers, nor claim an infallibility of wisdom, I do tend to pull out the "I've been a minister for nearly four decades" card. We part as friends.

Sometimes it helps to know with whom you are dealing. Job quickly discovered that he was in dialogue with the creator God, whose wisdom, power, strength, and abilities were far more superior that anything that he could bring to the table. Let's take a positive spin from his experience. If we really understood with whom we were dealing, how much encouragement it could bring, how much peace, and how much affirmation, to know that such a God cares for us.

Prayer

God, in your majesty, thank you for caring about the smallness of our lives. Amen.

Day 475   Job 39: The Ways of Nature

> "Do you know when the wild goats give birth? Have you watched as deer are born in the wild? Do you know how many months they carry their young? Are you aware of the time of their delivery?" Job 39:1-2 (NIV)

Observation
This chapter records the second part of God's rhetorical questioning of Job. God focuses on the animals of the earth, interrogating Job about his relationship to and his knowledge of the ways of the animals. God mentions lions, ravens, wild goats, wild donkeys, wild oxen, ostriches, horses, and birds of prey. It is impossible for Job, or any other human being, to know all of the details about the skills, behaviors, and instincts of these animals. The point is that God knows all there is to know about each one of them. Not only does God know about them, but God also displays goodness towards each one of them. Obviously, the message that God longs to drive home is that Job's wisdom and understanding are limited at best. He will ultimately have to trust in God, whose knowledge and wisdom far exceed that of his own.

Application
Like most of you, I try to manage my health. I consider diet, exercise, and rest. When something goes wrong, I do what we all do… I get on the internet to diagnose and treat my illness. But, from time to time, I require a little more in-depth observation or assessment. And so, I visit my doctor, Daniel. I trust his judgment. He knows more about medicine than I do. He has expertise. He has degrees. He has experience. It just makes sense to trust in someone whose knowledge and wisdom exceeds that of my own.

It's the same way with life. There are a lot of bumps in the road. We encounter all kinds of problems, stress points, and difficult moments. In those moments we have to admit to ourselves that our understanding is limited, and our wisdom is fleeting. Doesn't it make sense, therefore, to place your trust in the God who knows all things? And, in the God who displays goodness towards all of creation? Take a moment to remember that nothing is a surprise to God. Nothing. God doesn't awaken one day and say, "Man, I wish I had known that was happening today…." God's knowledge about us is infinite, we must trust that God's dealings with us are always perfect, always what can draw us closer to God. We might be surprised by the twists and turns, but God isn't. So this day, rather than lean on your own understanding, put your trust in God and allow God to direct your paths. It's a better way to live, I promise.

Prayer
God grant us the common sense to follow your lead throughout this day. Amen.

Day 476 — Job 40: Knowing When to Keep Silent

> "Then Job replied to the Lord, 'I am nothing—how could I ever find the answers? I will cover my mouth with my hand. I have said too much already. I have nothing more to say.'" Job 40:3-5 (NIV)

Observation

As this chapter opens, Job offers a very brief response to God's first speech. The reader may recall that Job had accused God of dealing with him unjustly (10:2, 23:6). But God had reminded Job that Job was deficient in his knowledge of the ways of God. He was incompetent to control the universe. As a human, Job was inferior to God and had no right to question God's ways. In response, Job wisely chooses silence. He realized that he had already said too much, knowing his insignificance in comparison to the majesty of God. The second part of the chapter begins God's second speech to Job. Again, speaking from the whirlwind, God reveals to Job that Job is powerless to take on the role of deity. He even challenges Job to run the universe for a while. God mentions an animal, "Behemoth," an animal so large and powerful that a mere human is unable to control his behavior or actions. Scholars have offered several possibilities while attempting to identify this animal. Some suggest an elephant, a buffalo, a hippopotamus, or some great creature that is no longer present on the earth.

Application

One of my favorite sitcoms is *Everybody Loves Raymond*. It features a character named Ray Barone who has a knack for getting himself into trouble with his words. Sometimes, he just doesn't know when to quit. Rather than choose silence, he offers one or two more comments that inevitably lead him into trouble with his wife, Debra. It's the same trap that captures all of us from time to time… we just don't know when to be silent, or when we have said enough.

Job's problem was that he had said too many foolish things either to God or about God. Relying merely on his human intellect and experience, Job found himself often judging God's ways and timing, as though it was his place to do so. I wonder about our practice of faith and the ways in which we communicate with God. Are there times when we should "cover our mouths?" Are there moments when we have "said too much already?" Let's remember that God is certainly big enough and broad-shouldered enough to take on our questions, our complaints, our doubts, and even our anger. God longs to hear from us and to know the depths of our hearts. However, let's caution ourselves against an over-familiarity with God that assumes we have right to question God's ways or usurp God's wisdom.

Prayer

God may we know both humility and hope with each conversation we have with you. Amen.

Day 477 — Job 41: A Tiger by the Tail

> "If you lay a hand on it, you will certainly remember the battle that follows. You won't try that again!" Job 41:8 (NIV)

Observation
In this next-to-final chapter, God continues speaking to Job, confronting him with God's superiority contrasted against Job's weakness. As in the previous chapter, God once again points to a large animal named Leviathan. In fact, the entire chapter is devoted to its description. The problem is that no interpreter really knows what it is. Some suppose a whale, or maybe a huge crocodile, or even a dinosaur! But even those possibilities do not fit all the descriptive words God uses. (Harry Potter may think of a dragon!) The point is that only God can control such a beast with enormous power. Job, along with any mere mortal, lacks the greatness and power that God possesses. Job again realizes that he is unable to stand in the presence of such majesty and therefore his only defense is apologetic silence. God reminds him that "everything under heaven is mine." So, Job meets God's challenge with contrition and regret that he had even dared to question God's ways.

Application
There are some battles, foolishly engaged, from which we emerge wiser, but wounded. At times, we bear the scars of our conflict. To use the words of the Book of Job, "we will certainly remember the battle that follows and we won't try that again!" We regret some battles as soon as we enter the fray. (I once tried to give a cat a round of oral antibiotics. Ever try to give an angry cat a pill? To quote one of my favorite singer/songwriters, Dan Fogleberg, "Lessons learned are like bridges burned, you only need to cross them but once.")

Job learned not to question the authority or judgment of God. He quickly remembered the superior wisdom, strength, and power of God. The battle was overwhelming, and the experience was forever seared in his mind. What sleeping tiger have you foolishly awakened? What angry bear have you poked? Think in terms of spirituality. Sometimes we wrestle with God's authority in our lives. Sometimes we question the goodness of God's heart. Sometimes we throw our angry words in God's direction. Our doubts are not indicative a weak faith, nor do our questions unsettle God's heart. What we must never attempt however, is to deny for a moment whose world in which we live and who alone controls each moment.

Prayer
God forgive our foolish insolence and grant us a desire to love you more. Amen.

Day 478 — Job 42: Living a "Full" Life

> "Job lived 140 years after that, living to see four generations of his children and grandchildren. Then he died, an old man who had lived a long, full life." Job 42:16-17 (NIV)

Observation
In the words of the late Paul Harvey, here comes "the rest of the story." There are two main sections to this final chapter of Job. The first six verses recount Job's repentance before the Lord. He takes on the posture of repentance. His struggles have given him a first-hand experience with the Almighty. His "head knowledge" of God has turned to "experiential knowledge." He recants all his sins and confesses his insolence. He sits in dust and ashes to show his repentance rather than wallowing longer in his grief. The question of "why" had been answered in response to the question of "who." He completes his saga with a reaffirmation of absolute trust in God and in God's ability to seek the good in us.

The final portion of the chapter is devoted to Job's deliverance. First, God expresses anger towards Eliphaz and the two other friends for their false representation of God's ways and purpose. They have not spoken "accurately" about God and for this they must repent. They are instructed to offer a burnt offering and have Job pray on their behalf. The Lord then restored and doubled of Job's fortunes. He is blessed with sheep, oxen, camels, and donkeys. And as a crowning gift of restoration, Job fathers seven more sons and three more daughters.

Application
Pay attention to the final verse that sums up the ending of Job's life... "Then he died, an old man who had lived a long, full life." It is important to note that to live a full life, Job had to live a life that contained both sorrow and joy. The fullness of his life was caused by the rich depth of his experiences. I think that's what brings fullness to our lives along with depth, perspective, and even joy. Fullness is not found in a pain-free, trouble-free, emotion-free life, but rather in a life that takes on all with the knowledge that in every moment and trial God is present. Our lives are made full by God's presence, watch care, and fulfilled promises. It is not that a full life means an easy life... it is that a full life means a victorious life that has overcome all adversity and pain because of God's continual embrace. It is a life bound to a daily connection to God. It is a life that trusts fully in God even when the days are uncertain, the journey unclear, and the pain all but unbearable. When your life story is written, I pray that it will be said of you as a person of faith, that your life was long and meaningfully full.

Prayer
God, walk with us through each day, reminding us constantly of your nearness. Amen.

Day 479 — Psalm 1: Quiet Murmurings

> "But his delight is in the law of the Lord, And in His law he meditates day and night." Psalm 1:2 (NASB)

Observation
The Book of Psalms was written by multiple authors over a 1000-year period, from the time of Moses to the post-exilic period. Although 73 of the psalms are credited to David, others were written by Solomon, Asaph, the Sons of Korah, and even Moses. Forty-three have anonymous writers. Though the dominant theme throughout many of the psalms is praise, themes like prayer, sorrow, remorse, repentance, are also present. The book is the Bible's longest book with 150 chapters and is the highest in word count. It contains both the longest (Ps 119) and the shortest (Ps 117) chapters in the Bible. Psalm 117 is also the midpoint of the Bible with 594 chapters before and after.

Psalm 1 describes the need to develop the habit of walking with God through a constant connection with God's law or instruction. David, the writer of this psalm, makes an important connection between the blessings of God and the faithful person's willingness to delight constantly in the meditation of the law.

Application
According to this psalm, the righteous person is one who "delights" himself/herself in the law (instruction) of the Lord. Rather than becoming mired in dangerous wickedness, the righteous person finds true delight in meditating on God's word. The word *meditate* means, "to mumble," or "speak to oneself." The word bears the image of muttering the law of God under our breath. It is a quiet and consistent recitation of God's Word throughout the experiences of daily life. Those who remind themselves constantly of God's Word find strength, hope, comfort, and deep joy. As David describes, "they are like a tree deeply planted by the water's edge" (v. 3). On the other hand, those who delight themselves in the tedious, mundane, and foolish things of this world find little stability for their lives. So, in what do you delight? If others could hear the quiet murmurings of your heart, what would they hear? Is yours a reflection on the instruction of God or have your thoughts drifted to some other place? Something always fills the void in our minds. Every free moment and unencumbered pause is quickly filled by a word, a thought, a daydream. Have we made a place in our minds for the wisdom of God? Do we let God's instruction saturate our thoughts? Do we murmur God's words under our breath? If you are prone to talking to yourself each day, why not remind yourself of God's promises to you?

Prayer
Holy Father, fill our minds and even our reflective moments with your Word. Amen.

Day 480 — Psalm 2: Foolish Hearts, Foolish Nations

> "Why are the nations in an uproar and the peoples devising a vain thing? The kings of the earth take their stand and the rulers take counsel together against the Lord and against His Anointed, saying, 'Let us tear their fetters apart and cast away their cords from us!'" Psalm 2:1-3 (NASB)

Observation

In the Hebrew mindset, opposition to God and God's people typically proceeded from pagan nations whose leadership challenged God and those God put in authority. If you read this second psalm through the lens of that ideology, the theme of God's superiority over all the nations emerges more clearly. The nations of the earth "take their stand" like Goliath once did when he taunted the armies of King Saul. Yet despite earthly opposition to God's ways, God is in complete control over all the earth and "scoffs" at the foolish behavior of those who oppose it. This psalm speaks of God's ultimate victory through the work of the promised Messiah. When the Messiah is given voice in this psalm, he states that God has "begotten" him. This word does not refer to God giving birth to the son because the son is both uncreated and eternal in nature. It refers, rather, to Kingship and the moment at which all authority is granted to the son. The psalm ends with a challenge for the kings of the earth to receive God's truth and obey.

Application

The choices we make define us. When we choose well, we find prosperity, success, and health. Whenever we choose poorly, we discover the exact opposite in our lives. The psalmist challenged all nations of the earth to choose obedience to God rather than rebellion. He wanted them to know that whenever someone chooses to defy the absolute authority of the universe, bad things are going to result. Choose God and find success. Defy God and discover ruin.

Let's talk a moment about some of the choices you are making. Are you surrounding yourself with those who encourage you, challenge you, and make you better? Are you paying attention to the disciplines of good diet, good rest, and good exercise? Are you making sound decisions that help you to live within your means and plan for a successful future? Are your choices in how you spend your energy making a positive impact on your life or are you wasting a lot of valuable time? The choices are yours to make. Are you willing to make the difficult, but rewarding, decisions? Pay attention to your life and ask God to help you choose well.

Prayer

Holy Father, give us wisdom in every choice we make. Amen.

Day 481 — Psalm 3: Rest Amid Chaos

> "I lay down and slept; I awoke, for the Lord sustains me. I will not be afraid of ten thousands of people who have set themselves against me round about." Psalm 3:5-6 (NASB)

Observation

This psalm, ascribed to King David, has a unique feature. It is tied to a specific incident in King David's life that is recorded in 2 Samuel 15. In that narrative, David is fleeing from his own son, Absalom, who has committed treasonous acts against him. For an extended period, Absalom stood at the gate of Jerusalem and promised legal counsel and justice to those coming to the king for answers. Many began to put their trust in him. Over time, he "stole the hearts of the men of Israel." Absalom methodically set a coup in place and David had to flee from the city. Set in the context of that moment, this psalm reflects both lament and a confession of trust in God's ability to deliver him. David proclaims that God will be his shield, his glory, and will raise his head in victory. Verse 5 mentions David's ability to find rest amid all the happenings in his life at this time.

Application

There is not a person on the planet that hasn't spent a restless, sleepless night in worry, anguish, or fear. We have all done it. The problems of the previous day or the worries of the next have awakened us in the night from our rest. Our minds race, our rest flees, and our bodies thrash about on our beds. And in those moments, it becomes very difficult to tamp down the fears and anxiety and get back to sleep. Consider King David's plight for a moment. He had been betrayed by his own son. He had been ousted from his palace. He was being pursued by his enemies. He was on the run. And yet, he was able to lay down and find rest. How is that even possible? It was not that he was exhausted, it was that he was confident… confident in both God's presence and in God's ability to defend and sustain his life.

Surely you have tried both tricks and medication to regain your sleep in the middle of a restless night. Most of us have counted sheep or blessings or breaths while we watch the hands on the clock on our bedside table spin like a top. We take a pill to relax our bodies or read a book to relax our minds. But maybe a better strategy is to take David's counsel… what if we go to bed at night confident in God's presence and in God's ability to provide for our needs? The scriptures teach us, "Be anxious for nothing, but in everything by prayer and supplication, with thanksgiving, let your requests be made known to God; and the peace of God, which surpasses all understanding, will guard your hearts and minds through Christ Jesus" (Philippians 4:6-7 NASB). Ready for a better night's sleep? Rest confidently in the arms of God.

Prayer

Dear Father, may we find rest, comfort, grace, and peace in you alone. Amen.

Day 482 — Psalm 4: Anger That Robs of Us of Rest

> "Tremble, and do not sin; Meditate in your heart upon your bed,
> and be still." Psalm 4:4 (NASB)

Observation
The theme of this psalm is much like the one that precedes it. It is of finding peace while experiencing physical and emotional pain, that those whose trust is in God will find the ability to rest and even sleep in the midst of life's most disturbing moments. This psalm is the first of many to be subscribed to the "chief musician," meaning that this psalm was intended to be used in worship as a song of praise. The chief musician was the conductor of a company of priestly musicians and singers who led in worship. There are three themes contained in the eight verses. First is the petition for deliverance that David prays (v. 1). Next, David addresses the wicked to encourage them to turn away from their falsehood (vv. 2-5). Finally, David affirms that only God can provide great joy, peace, and rest to those who trust in God (vv. 6-8). In addition to speaking of the rest that God can offer, David also emphasizes the great joy that God gives. The joy is greater than the joy felt at harvest when the crops are abundant.

Application
Anger is also mentioned in this psalm. The New American Standard Version translates the Hebrew word, "*ragaz*," as "tremble." Most readers are probably more familiar with the translation "anger," as in, "be angry and do not sin." The Apostle Paul quotes this verse in Ephesians 4:26. This Hebrew word, *ragaz*, means, "to be so agitated that one quivers or shakes with anger." Therefore, David counsels tempering one's anger so that it does not interfere with one's ability to relate to God nor interrupt the worship of God.

You've been there, haven't you? We all have. Sometimes we let our anger with people, situations, and circumstance so overwhelm our lives that it robs us of sleep, threatens to destroy relationships, and even interferes with how we relate to God. Have you ever been so angry that you couldn't even pray? Ever sit in church with so much anger that you couldn't even pay attention? It happens. Anger can be a destructive force in our lives. It is an emotion that we must honestly claim if we are going to have any hope of taming it. Claim and tame. Sometimes we deny our anger and we allow it to slowly churn away in our lives until we create an explosive moment. At other times, we lash out in our anger and say and do things that we later regret. Anger is a human emotion. The key is to handle it effectively and carefully. When anger starts to build, begin immediately to diffuse its power in your life.

Prayer
Dear Father, in our anger, may we not sin against you or others. Amen.

Day 483 — Psalm 5: How to Speak with God

> "In the morning, O Lord, You will hear my voice; In the morning I will order my prayer to You and eagerly watch." Psalm 5:3 (NASB)

Observation
According to the instructions that precede the actual text, Psalm 5 is written by David, subscribed to the choir director, and is to be accompanied by a flute when read. In our focus verse, David offers two insights about praying effectively. First, David emphasizes praying in the morning. For David, having moments with God before the day begins to spin out of control is important. There is a calm, an assurance, a peace that is afforded those who begin their day in the presence of the Lord. Second, David suggests that we who pray must wait expectantly once the requests have been made. Why, in fact, would we take the time to ask for God's involvement in our lives if we don't expect God to respond? Prayer is not a meaningless exercise. Our morning prayers should remind us that God will both hear our petition and bring answers to our needs.

Application
Like the early disciples that once asked Jesus to teach them how to pray, most of us struggle with how to pray effectively. We long for God to offer us insights into how we can make our prayer time more fulfilling. We wonder about when to pray and what to pray. We may at times wonder about the role of faith and its effect on our prayer life. Are our prayers answered or not answered based on the amount of faith we have in God's ability to act? At times, we wonder about certain words or phrases to use… if our prayers are too long or too short, too specific, or too generalized. Admittedly, there is still much we need to learn. But listen again to what David invites us to do. Pray early in the morning. Obviously, we can and should always pray. Paul teaches us to pray without ceasing. But David's point is that there is great value in praying as our day begins. Such prayers bring prioritization to our days. They order our lives and remind us of our reason for being. Prayer reminds us to align our will with God's each morning. It's a great way to start the day.

We must also learn the value of expecting God to answer. God loves to dialogue with us. God longs to be revealed to us in clear ways. So, let us offer our prayers and listen for God's response. That response could come through a moment of meditation, from a passage of scripture, or through the words of a messenger. We really should look and listen for God's answers to our prayers. To know that God responds should compel us to a greater discipline of prayer. So right now, before the day gets crazy, pray to your God, and listen throughout the day for God's response.

Prayer
Father, thank you for listening this morning. Speak and we will hear. Amen.

Day 484 — Psalm 6: Tender Mercies

> "Return, O Lord, rescue my soul; Save me because of Your lovingkindness."
> Psalm 6:4 (NASB)

Observation

Psalm 6 is written by David in a moment of great distress. Apparently, he is suffering from a grave, physical illness, from which he is fearful of not recovering. He confesses that he is being punished by God. He is fearful of God's wrath. Therefore, he calls on God during this period of great distress. (This is a common theme in the psalms of lament.) Whenever a God-follower dies, his or her voice is lost from those who sing praises in temple worship. So, David makes the point that if God still wants to hear his voice in worship, then God must deliver him because, "in the grave who will give You thanks?" (v. 5) The last part of the psalm reflects the joy of David's answered prayer. God has healed and restored him. The enemies of David will be silenced and troubled by his recovery.

Application

I read one of John Grisham's latest novels about lawyers, courtrooms, and hard-to-defend criminals. In this narrative, a man had been arrested for driving more than 80 miles per hour in a 45 MPH zone. He was looking at some jail time and a big fine. The lawyer, whose name was Mark, was able to do a little behind-the-scenes work, make a few promises, and manipulate the system. The man got off with a slap on the wrist and a small fine. He couldn't believe his good fortune. He thanked his lawyer profusely for his savvy and expertise. (What he didn't know at the time was that his lawyer was practicing without a license!)

Most of us have experienced a moment of mercy when we didn't receive the punishment due for our transgressions. Maybe it was something as simple as a teacher's forgiveness when an assignment was turned in late, or something as serious as a judges' dismissal when we deserved to be punished. We have all experienced grace and forgiveness. And we are told that as proud recipients of mercy that we should extend it to others whenever we have the opportunity. But let's talk for a moment about your past, your mistakes, your disobedience before God. Surely your punishment is deserved. Surely your guilt should make you squirm a little at the thought of God's wrath. And yet because of God's lovingkindness, God's mercy, and God's overwhelming love for you, God chooses to redeem rather than condemn, forgive rather than punish, embrace rather than shun. You are loved more than you can comprehend and forgiven more than you can imagine. This day, take a moment to thank God for these tender and powerful mercies.

Prayer

Father, thank you for not giving us what we deserve for our sinfulness. Amen.

Day 485 — Psalm 7: Rise Up!

> "Arise, O Lord, in Your anger; Lift up Yourself against the rage of my adversaries, And arouse Yourself for me; You have appointed judgment."
> Psalm 7:6 (NASB)

Observation
Psalm 7 has a couple of unique features. First, the inscription written at the top of the psalm reads, "A Shiggaion of David, which he sang to the Lord concerning Cush, a Benjamite." This is the only place in scripture where the word "shiggaion" is used and its meaning is unclear. Most translators believe the word means something like, "to be exhilarated." If so, then, this psalm is to be sung with a loud and excited tone by those leading in worship. Second, notice that the subject of the psalm is a Jewish man named Cush. This is the only reference to him in the Bible. The best guess is that he is one of Saul's soldiers, sent to kill David when Saul once sought David's life in 1 Samuel 24. In this psalm, David cries out to God for deliverance. David ponders why he is experiencing such difficulty and acknowledges the possibility that some of his actions may have kindled God's anger. If so, David is willing to take on such chastisement because he wants to be made right with God. The psalm ends with a declaration of God's right to act against those who do not repent of their iniquities.

Application
I read a quote that suggested the overall theme of the Book of Psalms is two-fold. First, God is good. Second, life is difficult. The quote suggested that the life of faith is lived between these two realities. Perhaps it is. We struggle with the goodness of God in the juxtaposition of the difficulties of life. We wonder about such things as pain, persecution, suffering, and injustice. To be honest, we often verbalize the same prayer of King David when he said, "Arise, O Lord, in Your anger; Lift up Yourself against the rage of my adversaries." We ask God to rise from the royal throne and actively engage the perils that plague us. Or to put it in another way, "Get up, God, and do something about our problems!" We long for God's involvement and rescue and wonder where God has gone when our prayers seemingly go unanswered, and our situations remain unresolved. We long to stir God into involvement and compassionate acts. We forget that we are already the objects of God's infinite love and matchless grace. Even now, this very day, God is actively engaged in our lives, arranging people, place, and circumstance to God's glory. What we need is not a better, more engaged God, we need a greater trust in God's presence and a greater wisdom to understand God's ways. Rise up, O Lord, and teach us, save us, rescue us again.

Prayer
Father, thank you for your unending commitment to us as your children. Amen.

Day 486 — Psalm 8: Majesty Restored

> "What is man that You take thought of him, And the son of man that You care for him? Yet You have made him a little lower than God, And You crown him with glory and majesty!" Psalm 8:4-5 (NASB)

Observation

Psalm 8 is one of the more familiar psalms and is cited four times in the New Testament, usually in reference to the work of the Messiah. Notice that this is a psalm of David to be sung while accompanied by a "gittith," some type of stringed instrument used in worship. Typically, there are two ways to interpret and use this psalm. One is as a nod to the coming Messiah who would be crowned with majesty and glory. The Son of Man reference is a royal designation, used by Christ himself. Thus, the psalm describes the majesty of the coming Savior in whom God has placed authority. The other way to interpret the psalm is to think more universally in terms of God's desire to have created humankind as the crowning glory of God's creative action. The Greek Septuagint (ancient Greek translation of the Hebrew Old Testament), translates verse 5 as, "You have made him (humankind) to lack little of God." In other words, humans were created to reflect the majesty of God. They are given dominion over all the earth and the creatures of the earth. The majestic God is reflected in the people whom God has made.

Application

To be honest, there are few days when I feel like a "majestic creation of God." I understand that human beings are the supreme expression of God's creative acts. I understand that God has given us limited dominion over all the earth. I understand that nothing is more important to God than people. But I also understand that we are flawed, fragile, and feeble in our attempts to reflect the majesty of our creator. We are a perversion of the majesty that God intended. We rage with jealousy. We lash out in anger. We lust. We rob. We hold grudges. We trust in ourselves and not in our God. When people view our lives, they are prone to say, "Look at how bad human beings have become," rather than saying, "Look at how great God must be to create such wonderful beings."

But there is a very important, redemptive word to offer. God has never been satisfied to let his creation languish in sin, in shame, and in the poverty of poor decisions. According to 1 John 4:14, "...the Father sent the Son to be the Savior of the world" (NLT). In Christ, we recover our majesty. Through the grace, love, and mercy of Jesus, we become the people that God wants us to be. Because Christ lives in us, we begin the transformation from brokenness to new creation. Even this day, something of God's majesty can be displayed in your life.

Prayer

Father, may we reflect more and more, the majesty of our Creator. Amen.

Day 487   Psalm 9: When the Enemies Are Forgotten

> "You have rebuked the nations, You have destroyed the wicked; You have blotted out their name forever and ever. The enemy has come to an end in perpetual ruins, And You have uprooted the cities; The very memory of them has perished." Psalm 9:5-6 (NASB)

Observation
Psalm 9 is a psalm of David, subscribed to the choir director to be sung in worship. It is to be played on a "muth-labben." This is the only occurrence of this word in scripture and the meaning is unclear. It could refer to a musical instrument, or to a hymn tune. The words literally mean, "death of the son." It may have been a tune composed when David pondered the death of his son Absalom as described in previous psalms. This psalm is a prayer for deliverance and thanksgiving. Originally, it may have been combined with Psalm 10 as a single unit. Ten of the initial verses of Psalm 9 form an acrostic from the Hebrew alphabet and seven of the verses in Psalm 10 follow the same pattern. Both psalms carry the same theme as well. Notice that David insists on praising God "with his whole heart" (v. 1). Real praise is never half-hearted. David praises God for both name and works. Also notice that when David describes his enemies, they are unnamed. Surely this reflects a confidence that God is in ultimate control over all the enemies of God's Kingdom. Even the names of the enemies will be forgotten one day, but the name of the Lord will endure forever. In the later verses, David asks to be spared from death so that he may continue to praise God in the Temple.

Application
Most of us have a few enemies, don't we? Not the flesh and blood kind of enemies, but the enemies of the soul, mind, and spirit that diminish our lives and rob us of the life that God intends. We face the dark enemies of the soul… like anger, jealousy, envy, selfishness, hatred, greed, and lust. Even human nature becomes our enemy as we face the constant battle between obedience to God or enslavement to our human tendencies and motivations. And… it may well be that some of us do, in fact, have those flesh and blood enemies. None of us get through life unscathed. And try as we might to be pleasant, decent, compassionate, and forgiving, there are still some folks with whom we just can't seem to forge a relationship. Maybe you can name someone who just seems to have it in for you… an enemy that attacks you at work, or in the social circles in which you run, or in the involvements in your community. You try to avoid them, but they seem to be a constant irritant, no matter how hard you work at reconciliation and relationship. Our focus verse speaks of how the names of the enemies of God will one day be erased forever. Even the memories of them will perish. In terms of our enemies, their power over us will one day cease, and the hurt they bring will fade away forever.

Prayer
Father, give us patience in our struggles, knowing that one day peace will come. Amen.

Day 488 — Psalm 10: Living in the "Mean" Time...

> "O Lord, You have heard the desire of the humble; You will strengthen their heart, You will incline Your ear to vindicate the orphan and the oppressed, so that man who is of the earth will no longer cause terror."
> Psalm 10:17-18 (NASB)

Observation
Whoever authored this psalm (not identified in the title) obviously did so in an atmosphere of great oppression and fear. He cries out to God praying for the overthrow of the wicked. He prays that the day will come when all evildoers will be judged because of their actions. Through his words, he offers a "why do the evil prosper" kind of thought. The psalm turns towards the end and declares the justice of God. It ends on a triumphant note as the oppressed will gain freedom and the helpless will find hope.

Application
We all long for justice. We look forward to the day when things will be set right... when the innocent will find mercy and the evildoers will find justice. Let's admit it... we have all been passed by that speeding motorist on the interstate and quietly wished that he or she would be caught. We would just love to see them pulled over to the side. But go beyond that simple illustration. We long for the day when the greater offenders of our culture find punishment.

I love the sense of resiliency and victory in this psalm. Notice our second focus verse, "You will incline Your ear to vindicate the orphan and the oppressed, so that man who is of the earth will no longer cause terror." There is a promise in that verse. God is a God of justice, and the day will come when all our fears are driven away by God's power and will to set things right. Typically, our greatest fears come from "mere" people. We fear those who have power over us. We fear an overbearing and abusive spouse. We fear a harsh and unkind boss. We fear a group of students at school. We fear the work associate that seems to have it in for us. Understand the promise... those who oppress us can only oppress us for a while. Those who insult us can only insult us for a while. Those who belittle us can only belittle us for a while. Those who abuse us can only abuse us for a while. God knows the hopes of the helpless. God will hear their cries and will bring comfort... even to us. Those who mistreat you, accuse you falsely, and show little regard for the difficult circumstances of your life will one day be held accountable for their harsh actions. People will not "get away with their sins." The God who sees all things, is also the God who will one day make things right. So this morning, pray for patience, pray for comfort, and pray that your own heart will never be darkened by the difficult people who sometimes invade your life. God will hear and God will bring justice.

Prayer
Father, grant us courage and patience in the midst of all persecution. Amen.

Day 489 — Psalm 11: Flee Bird

> "In the Lord I take refuge; How can you say to my soul, 'Flee as a bird to your mountain;'" Psalm 11:1 (NASB)

Observation
This is a psalm of David that expresses great trust in God while experiencing tremendous adversity. Though historical context is not provided, it is apparent that David is being pursued and challenged by wicked people. The imagery is interesting. In our focus verse, David makes reference of taking refuge in the Lord. This seeking of refuge is like a small bird seeking refuge beneath the wings of his or her mother. In mocking contrast, the wicked advise David, "to flee as a bird to the mountain." They view David and all others who are righteous as being helpless birds who flee to the protection of their mountain homes. What they fail to realize is that the mountain home is the protection of God. And even though the wicked have readied their bows to shoot arrows at the righteous, God's foundation of authority and control will not be defeated. In contrast, God "will rain snares" (verse 6) on the wicked. The Hebrew word for snares literally means "bird trap." So, in response to the wicked who challenge the righteous to flee like birds, God will capture the wicked as though they are the fragile birds waiting to be collected in a snare.

Application
I was a teenager in the mid-to-late '70s and was influenced by the classic rock and roll of the time. I was a Lynyrd Skynyrd fan and loved their ballad, "Free Bird." To this day, I can hum every note and vocalize every lyric. Even now, there is something liberating and exhilarating when considering a flight toward the freedom from a situation, a job, or a hardship. But notice the title of this devotion… it's not Free Bird, but Flee Bird. Clever, right? David felt the security and protection of placing his life into the powerful wings of God Almighty. He knew that in God's protection, there was rest, security, and serenity.

You may not picture yourself a frail, small bird, needing the protection of your mother's wings, but if the truth be told, we are all a little frail and small and vulnerable to the adversaries of this life. We have our enemies. We have our pressure points. We have dangerous influences surrounding us, which seek to destroy our lives. To what place do you flee to find safety, security, and peace of mind? Ultimate refuge is not found in any person, nor in anything created by the hands of men. Our hope and security rest only in the strong arms of God who longs to shield us, defend us, and nurture us. So, if you are feeling a little overwhelmed this morning, consider your refuge point. Where have you placed your trust? Who's guarding your life? As David suggests, our trust must be in the Lord alone.

Prayer
Father, even today, keep us safe and secure from those who conspire against us. Amen.

Day 490 — Psalm 12: The Best Words

> "The words of the Lord are pure words; As silver tried in a furnace on the earth, refined seven times." Psalm 12:6 (NASB)

Observation

This psalm of David is characterized, along with many other psalms, as a psalm of lament. Such psalms begin with an introductory cry of distress. In this case, David writes, "Help, Lord, for the godly man ceases to exist…" The psalm begins with an emphasis on the power of the wicked as they assault the righteous with idle and destructive words. By contrast, the psalm ends with the assertion that God's words are just the opposite… they are powerful and truthful. David wonders as he writes these words if there are any righteous people left. He points to the many wicked men of his day, who think they can say anything without consequence. In response to David's musings, God speaks through the words of the psalm declaring that God will rise and intervene. God will judge the speech of the wicked while establishing God's justice.

Application

Some of you will remember the destructive battles that took place within the Southern Baptist Convention during the mid-to-late '80s. The conflict focused on the distance in thought and practice among ultra-conservatives and moderates within the convention. There were some who argued that the Convention was becoming too liberal both in theology and in the role of women in ministry. Others argued that the convention was being directed into a very narrow, limited, overly conservative viewpoint that, at times, attempted to thwart the leadership of the Spirit by denying both the Priesthood of the Believer and the autonomy of the local church. It became nasty and divisive. During the heart of that struggle, my father offered me a wise word. He said that one of the problems that the moderate side faced was that of language. He said that the fundamentalist group had taken all the good words… words like "Bible-believing, conservative, historic Baptists…" He was right. Sometimes words make a huge difference in trying to sway a position or direct the thoughts of culture and time.

David writes in our focus verse that the words of the Lord are "pure words." They are the kind of words that heal, redeem, build, reconcile, love, and extend grace. The words of the wicked are the opposite. They offer words that divide, harm, abuse, and belittle. In the midst of a million words that swirl around in our time and culture, let us be careful to distinguish the good from the bad, the godly from the wicked, and let us be fervent in our quest to offer only those words that God has ordained.

Prayer

God, may we long for the pure words of your heart and not the distorted ones of culture. Amen.

Day 491　　　　　　　Psalm 13: Our Bounty of Blessings

> "I will sing to the Lord, because He has dealt bountifully with me."
> Psalm 13:6 (NASB)

Observation
This, too, is a psalm of lament. It is an impassioned cry by David to God for help. The psalm breaks into three parts. First, there are words of lament because David feels a little forsaken. Then there are words of petition for deliverance. And finally, there are words of praise as the psalm concludes. The sentiment follows a common theme that is found in many of the psalms of lament: "I am hurting. You have forgotten. The enemy is winning." David pours out his anxiety four times by saying, "How long, O Lord?" His fear and persecution are so real that David feels the closeness of death. He prays for God to intervene. Finally, the psalm turns to hope as David resolves to sing the praises of God based on the assurance that God will deliver him. David closes this psalm with the words, "I will sing to the Lord, because He has dealt bountifully with me." As he pauses to consider all that God has done in his life, he finds great hope and assurance and breaks out in song.

Application
Music often gives expression to the emotions of the heart. Depending on mood and circumstance, our minds can select a song to play, much like pushing the right buttons on an old jukebox. When our spirits are lifted, we choose happy, upbeat songs. When our day is going a little rough, we might hum a song that fits that emotion. Sometimes, like King David, as we consider the blessings and activity of God in our lives, we are compelled to break forth in glad adoration. I grew up in a church that placed a lot of value in the great hymns of faith. To this day, I can easily fit the lyrics of a song into some emotion that I am feeling. In fact, I recently took one of those online surveys where you try to name the title of a hymn by reading through a few of the lyrics. I scored a perfect 10! (Thanks Kenneth and FBC, Rome.) So at times, rather than filling my mind with one of those new-fangled, 3-note, 2-word, praise songs, an old hymn bubbles to the surface.

All of us, should be so mindful of God's "bountiful" blessings in our lives that we desire to breakout in song. You don't have to sing a song today, but you should take a moment to realize your blessings. The fact that you have a book in your hand or a computer on your desk puts you way ahead of much of the world. Though you may or may not feel materially blessed, you are. And not only has God provided things like a car, a house, or a set of clothes to wear today, God has also surrounded you with people who love you and a savior who constantly forgives and redeems you. You are blessed beyond measure. You just may want to sing.

Prayer
God, fill our hearts and lives with endless praise for your blessings in our lives. Amen.

Day 492 — Psalm 14: Ignorance Is No Excuse

> "The fool has said in his heart, "There is no God." They are corrupt, they have committed abominable deeds; There is no one who does good."
> Psalm 14:1 (NASB)

Observation

This psalm of David speaks about the foolishness of men. It is sometimes referred to as a wisdom psalm, and this psalm closely parallels Psalm 53. David speaks of the "foolish" who are living as though there is no God. The "fool," who says in his heart that there is no God, refers to someone who is morally and spiritually insensitive. Such a person practices a "practical atheism." He or she thinks, "Even if God does exist, it really doesn't matter to me. It makes no difference to my life." David states that such people are "corrupt." The Hebrew word for corrupt literally means, "to go to ruin." Or as one writer suggests, "it is the image of soured milk." Failing to believe in God sours the life of an individual to the point that their morality continually declines until they willfully do evil. David also paints the picture of the Lord looking down from heaven. It is the image of God's knowledge of all things, particularly God's ability to see the hearts of all men. No one escapes God's scrutiny, and no one is found to be innocent. There is a depravity within the human condition. Sin is present in the life of every individual. The answer is to seek refuge in God who will redeem all of those who are faithful.

Application

Let's pretend that you are seated at your desk at work. Suddenly, you discover that your printer is out of paper and that your shelves are empty where you normally keep a little extra. You're in the middle of a project and desperately need to complete your print job. So you walk over to the next office and grab a ream of paper from an absent co-worker's desk. Later, when confronted about taking the paper, you offer the excuse, "Well no one told me that it would be a problem. I didn't know that it was wrong."

Stupid answer, right? But is it really any different from the lame excuses we sometimes give to God? "Sorry, God, because I can't find any specific rule in the Bible about this activity or issue, I just assumed it was okay to act poorly." Being ignorant of the ways of the Lord is no excuse for poor behavior. God's standard of righteousness is not on a sliding scale dependent on our knowledge or lack of knowledge. We can't plead ignorance and expect to get a free pass. God is revealed to us in many ways… through nature, through scripture, through the Spirit, and through the counsel of the godly. We are left without excuse for poor behavior. That's bad news. But the good news is that we are not left without a redeemer. Through the love of Christ we can be forgiven when we have acted poorly.

Prayer

God, give us an awareness of both our sinfulness and our acceptance in Christ. Amen.

Day 493   Psalm 15: Standing Where You Have No Right to Be...

> "O Lord, who may abide in Your tent? Who may dwell on Your holy hill? He who walks with integrity, and works righteousness, And speaks truth in his heart." Psalm 15:1-2 (NASB)

Observation
David describes those who become citizens of Zion. He speaks of the qualifications needed to stand in the presence of God. When he writes about God's "tent" and God's "holy hill," he is describing the place where God sits enthroned. His rhetorical question is of who can enter the presence of God. And the answer is simple… those with a pure heart… those who lead blameless lives, who do what is right and speak the truth. God requires much of those who will worship in God's presence.

Application
Times have certainly changed. I remember the day when Sunday morning worship meant looking your best and wearing your finest. Back in the sixties, women wore dresses and maybe even a hat. They carried a purse and wore gloves on their hands. Men wore suits and ties. Shoes were polished, shirts were starched, and ties were pinned in place with a tie-tack. No one would have ever thought of wearing jeans to worship. No one would have worn flip flops. No one would have dreamed of being untucked, unshaven, or unprepared. It was a different time and quite honestly, I miss some of the formality of worship. Something about looking your best in the presence of the king still resonates with me.

But this psalm is not speaking about clothing styles or worship services. It is talking about the guidelines needed to truly stand in the presence of God. Let's admit it… it's a tough set of conditions that David outlines. Ask us, "Who may worship in your sanctuary?" and we would have to answer, "None." In the eyes of God, who is blameless, who always does what is right, and who speaks the truth with sincerity? Not me… and not you. How would we ever hope to stand in the presence of God? Why would we ever think that our lives would bring honor and glory to God? Here's the secret. We've got a helper who tips the scales in our favor. His name is Jesus Christ. Truthfully, none of us can stand in the presence of God. None of us are worthy. None of us fit the criteria described. But all of us can gain access. It is the love of Christ, expressed through his sacrificial death on the cross, that suddenly makes us worthy. Christ died to remove our sins, to make us pure and holy, to wash away any hint of iniquity's stain. We can worship, not because of what we have done or have failed to do, but because we have been claimed by Christ. It is no small thing that you are invited to stand in the place you have no right to be. Even this day, you can stand in the presence of your Father and feel welcomed, embraced, and wanted.

Prayer
Father God, thank you for the joy of standing in your presence this day. Amen.

Day 494 — Psalm 16: A Piece of the Pie

> "The Lord is the portion of my inheritance and my cup;
> You support my lot." Psalm 16:5 (NASB)

Observation

Though this psalm of David is a psalm of lament, it offers a very powerful and promising vision of the work of God's coming Messiah. The prophetic undertone in the psalm parallels many of the prophecies about the Messiah, especially some of those that are offered in the suffering servant motif of Isaiah 53. David employs some of the same language of refuge he used in Psalm 11. Here again is the image of a small bird seeking refuge under his mother's wing. David finds refuge through his complete trust in God. He acknowledges in this psalm that all good things come from the Lord. Notice in our focus verse that David mentions that the Lord is the "portion of my inheritance." You may recall that after the time of the conquest, that all the tribes of Israel received a portion of the land, except the priestly tribe of Levi. Their inheritance was in the Lord and in the provisions that the other tribes were commanded to offer them. Though David had both an ancestral inheritance and royal holdings, he reflected that his greatest inheritance was in his relationship with God. It was that inheritance that would provide his escape from ultimate death and place him on "the path to life" (v. 11).

Application

Ever wonder what you will one day inherit? My brother and I sometimes discuss "who gets what" when both of our parents are gone. It's not a morbid conversation, but one that insures each of us will receive an appropriate piece of the pie. (Now let's be honest… we are not talking about massive amounts of gold and silver that will one day make us filthy rich.) We are talking about family heirlooms, pieces of furniture, or keepsakes that we want to one day claim. With us, it's not going to be an ugly argument. Relationships are always more important than the "stuff." It's more about having something to remember the lives of our parents and in both the tangible and the non-tangible, we have been richly blessed. The "inheritance" will be meaningful.

Beyond all earthly inheritance, my brother and I will also claim a lasting inheritance, a permanent inheritance, a faith inheritance. Our parents provided us with the "path to life" that King David described. They told us the story of Jesus and how to find true meaning and purpose in a pursuit of him. So yeah, we've already got a piece of the pie. We share in the glorious, eternal riches of God's Kingdom. And if we do it right, our kids will get the same inheritance as well. Live a life of faith and pass it along to the next generation.

Prayer

Father God, thank you for the lasting inheritance we have through Christ. Amen.

Day 495 — Psalm 17: The Complete Make-Over

> "As for me, I shall behold Your face in righteousness; I will be satisfied with Your likeness when I awake." Psalm 17:15 (NASB)

Observation
In this psalm, David pleads for God to protect him from those who oppress him. He calls on God to vindicate him because, as God knows, David is innocent in his suffering. (There are times in the psalms where David fully confesses his sins and acknowledges that he certainly deserves the upheaval in his life because of his poor actions and choices. This psalm, however, reflects a different mindset. David believes that he is experiencing undeserved suffering and so he appeals to God's lovingkindness to provide relief.) David claims that his is a "just cause." He even invites God to test his heart and examine his life. There is an interesting image in this psalm of David imploring God to "incline His ear" to David's prayer (v. 6). It is the image of God bending close from the heavens to listen and to consider David's plea. The psalm ends on a statement of resolute faith. David knows that when the righteous are raised up from the sleep of death, that they will be perfected into the image of God. David affirms that the day is coming when he will behold the face of God and that his own likeness will more closely reflect it.

Application
You hear a lot these days of people or structures getting a "complete makeover." In fact, the television industry makes a good profit by airing shows that deal with some great transformational change in someone's life or in someone's home. To get a complete makeover, people tend to lose weight, change their diet, cut their hair, or select better clothing. You've seen the "before and after" images on those shows. Sometimes it's a house that undergoes a radical transformation. Walls get torn down, new floors are installed, fresh paint is applied, and landscaping is radically changed. The old is transformed into something fresh, and new, and exciting.

In terms of faith, our call to discipleship is a call to radical transformation. We are called to be "conformed to the image of His Son" (Romans 8:29 NASB). This transformation begins the moment we first embrace Jesus through a faith experience. It is not an immediate, nor complete change. The transition takes time. Gradually we become more like Jesus. Step by step we embrace his heart, his Spirit, and his priorities. Slowly, but surely, we begin to look more like him and less like ourselves. And King David is right, it is only through death and resurrection that the complete transformation will be revealed. We will one day perfectly reflect the image of Christ. But until that comes, let us be steadfast in our pursuit of change.

Prayer
Father God, help us this day, in ways great and small, to be more like Jesus. Amen.

Day 496 — Psalm 18: Inner Strength

> "For by You I can run upon a troop; And by my God I can leap over a wall." Psalm 18:29 (NASB)

Observation

This psalm of David is a lengthy hymn of celebration, the lyrics of which are also found in 2 Samuel 22. David opens with the words, "I love you, Lord." There are only two places in all the psalms where such a phrase is used, here and in Psalm 116:1. The word translated for love conveys a very deep compassion. In fact, it is similar to words meaning, "in the womb." David's use of this word describes a very intimate love for God like that of a mother for the child she has carried in her womb. Other language in the psalm is very familiar to words that David often repeats in his songs. He speaks of God as a rock and refuge, strong like a mighty mountain fortress. Such words were particularly meaningful for David who often sought refuge from his enemies in the mountains. This psalm extols God as a protector of the righteous. David gives a vivid description of the ways that God will use the elements of nature to deliver God's servant.

Application

When I was kid, one of the shoe companies that had carefully marketed their product to children, was the brand known as P.F. Flyers. Remember those canvas shoes with the rubber soles? They were manufactured by the B.F. Goodrich rubber company. The company claimed that their shoes made a person, "run faster and jump higher." What kid wouldn't want those results on the playground at recess? It begs the question, "What energizes your life? What motivates you to perform well and run passionately?" The sport drink companies would like for you to think that the right amount of Gatorade or Powerade will help you to perform at a peak level. Others argue that energy bars, or protein snacks are the way to go. Coffee makers would argue for a good shot of espresso.

But King David wrote about how the Spirit of God would motivate his steps and give life to his weary feet. "For by You I can run upon a troop (team of soldiers); and by My God I can leap over a wall." David recognized that "If God is for us, who can ever be against us?" (Roman 8:31 NLT). Let me remind you this morning, that the Spirit of God indwells your life at this very moment. That Spirit longs to guide you and correct you, but also longs to inspire you, encourage you, and strengthen you. Barriers that you face are not insurmountable. Enemies you face are not undefeatable. Fears that you face are conquerable. You can surely face the challenges of this day through God's power and strength. Take courage for the journey. The God who once delivered David is surely at work in your life this day as well.

Prayer

Father God, teach us a comforting, empowering reliance upon you. Amen.

Day 497 — Psalm 19: The Secret Self

> "Let the words of my mouth and the meditation of my heart be acceptable in Your sight, O Lord, my rock and my Redeemer." Psalm 19:14 (NASB)

Observation
Psalm 19 is a beautifully and powerfully written poem of King David. It is categorized as a psalm of wisdom. It is a celebration of God's mighty creative acts, the purity of God's law, and the heart needed by those who truly long to seek the heart of God. In the psalm, David speaks of the ways in which all of creation reveals the glory of God… "The heavens declare the glory of God" (v. 1). The vast expanse of the heavens bears powerful testimony to the greatness of God. Even the sun, worshipped by pagan religions as a god, is viewed by David as an entity created to celebrate its creator. Obviously, David longs to please God. In light of his description of God's nature and perfection, David is forced to consider his own imperfections and hidden faults. He asks God to deliver him from any transgression.

Application
Our bodies contain a lot of secrets. I'm not describing the secrets that you hold in your mind that someone has passed along to you… instead, I am describing the medical secrets that are hidden in your bloodstream, muscle tissue, and DNA. I just completed my annual physical. As a part of that process, my doctor orders a very complete blood profile. He looks at cholesterol, triglycerides, iron content, liver and kidney function, and thyroid numbers. He wants the "secrets" to be revealed so that he can do a good job in monitoring my health.

In his psalm, David prays that the "mediation of his heart" would be acceptable in the sight of God. He is inviting God to look at the "secret self." He is asking God to examine even the unexpressed thoughts that roll around in his mind. I wonder if we are bold enough to beg God to consider the meditation of our hearts. Sure, we tend to acknowledge that in the infinite wisdom of God, that God can see and judge our thoughts. But do we really invite God to do so? Are we willing to open the pages of our thoughts so that God can scrutinize all that is written there? There are a lot of things that I might be tempted to say that decorum and good sense would never allow me to say. I have enough self-control at times not to verbalize what I may be thinking. But are unexpressed thoughts any less sinful or damaging to our lives just because we don't say them out loud? No. Every thought is significant. Thoughts lead to action. Thoughts shape the psyche and alter the mind. It takes conscious effort to rid our minds of wayward thoughts. Though we may not be able to always control the first thought, we can surely choose how long we will allow such thoughts to rattle around in our minds. May our thoughts be acceptable…

Prayer
Father God, may we honor you with even our secret selves. Amen.

Day 498 — Psalm 20: Misplaced Trust

> "Some boast in chariots and some in horses, But we will boast in the name of the Lord, our God." Psalm 20:7 (NASB)

Observation

This psalm, attributed to King David, is a psalm of trust in which David admonishes all people to put their ultimate and lasting trust in God alone. The tone of the psalm is one of blessing, most likely set in the context of David's prayer over his army on the eve of some battle. He mentions the "day of trouble." This is perhaps a reference to the upcoming battle, although certainly the petition holds true for any moment of hardship that we might face. David also mentions that God will help from God's sanctuary. This refers to more than the Temple in Jerusalem. It most certainly refers to heavenly realms where God sits enthroned. David asks that God would remember the offerings and sacrifices of God's people. Again, this is most likely in reference to the impending battle. Soldiers would have confessed sin and sought the protection of God through their acts of worship. David affirms them by saying, "May the Lord fulfill all your petitions" (v. 5). David ends with a note of assurance, suggesting that the (Great) King will answer when the people call out.

Application

Nations are not the only entities that boast in their "chariots and horses." Most of us do as well. Oh, we don't brag about having the best chariots and the fastest horses, but we do boast in our "stuff," believing that our stuff somehow makes us superior and will somehow bring us deliverance. It's a foolish thought. Ask a man dying of cancer how well his money protects his life. Ask a student with the latest social media access how well her electronics build quality relationships. Ask a businessman how well his fancy car will chase away depression. Ask a single mother how the money from her divorce settlement helps her to raise sweet-spirited, well-adjusted kids. You get the point. People trust in a lot of things, none of which gives meaning to life or even a sense of lasting protection. Our trust must be in something greater, something stronger, something more vitally important. Our trust must be in our God. King David knew this secret. That's why he built a relationship with God that influenced his decisions and provided wisdom for his leadership.

God longs to do such things in our lives. When our faith and trust are ultimately in God and not in ourselves, then we go from self-sufficiency to God-dependency. We find unparalleled strength, lasting joy, and meaningful hope. Where is your ultimate trust? Is it in the things you found under your Christmas tree this past December? Is it in your portfolio? Is it in your educational experience? Is it in the position you hold at work? Where is it?

Prayer

Father God, may we place our trust in nothing else but your provision. Amen.

Day 499 — Psalm 21: Room to Breathe

> "O Lord, in Your strength the king will be glad, and in Your salvation how greatly he will rejoice!" Psalm 21:1 (NASB)

Observation

In the previous psalm, David offered prayers for his army. In this psalm, David writes with the assurance of God's blessing in his own life as the king. (Both are royal psalms.) Most ancient rulers would have found joy and strength in his or her own power and wisdom. But David underscores the fact that a wise king would have found pleasure in God alone. David acknowledges that all power comes from God. In our focus verse, David writes about the salvation of God. This is the Hebrew word, "Yeshuah," the same word translated as "Jesus," whose name means, "God is salvation." An additional translation of the Hebrew is this phrase, "room to breathe." In other words, God's salvation allows the recipient the space to find peace from one's enemies. God had given David a release from the pressures and restraints that had bound him. Therefore, David acknowledges that God is the source of all his blessings and that the greatest of all blessings is life, both now and forever more. The psalm ends with a shout of joy as David calls the faithful to join in praising God.

Application

Think about an oppressive time in your life. Consider a moment in time when you were overwhelmed, overworked, overstressed... maybe overtired. We have all had such moments. Life can be overwhelming at times. And it does seem that our troubles seem to hit from all directions. It's like the childhood game of "pile on," when someone tackles a playmate and suddenly all the other kids join in on the pile. You never wanted to get stuck at the bottom. Sometimes life hits us the same way. We feel like we are at the bottom of a huge pile of problems, stresses, and dilemmas. In our desperate state, we cry out for help, for relief, for comfort. It is this sense of relief that King David describes. God had given him room to breathe from his enemies and he reveled in the joy of a moment's peace.

Let's admit that it is sometimes hard to find a moment's peace. It's hard to discover a moment of grace in the midst of a very arduous chapter in our lives. We sometimes wish for just a day away from our troubles, or just a few moments to relax on a crazy day. David is right in suggesting that our ultimate salvation is in God. In God alone will we find our ultimate room to breathe as God delivers us from sin, shame, and even death. Our enemies are put to rest and we, too, revel in the joy of God's peace. But what about today? Maybe you need a few moments of rest and calm. Consider taking a recess. Carve out a 15-minute stress-break for yourself. Take a walk. Read a book. Listen to a song. Schedule a moment to be alone.

Prayer

God, as you provide us with eternal rest, teach us to find a moment's rest today. Amen.

Day 500 — Psalm 22: Hope in the Midst of Suffering

> "My God, my God, why have You forsaken me? Far from my deliverance are the words of my groaning." Psalm 22:1 (NASB)

Observation
Even a casual reader of the psalms will recognize these words. They are, of course, the last words spoken by Christ on the cross, and they are often misunderstood. It's important to understand the full intent of David's words as he writes this song of both praise and prophecy. (One side note... notice in the psalm's header, that it is to be played upon Aijeleth Hashshaha. The meaning is a little uncertain. The literal translation is "the deer of the dawn." Scholars suggest that this phrase could be a description of an instrument, not familiar to modern readers, it could reference a song tune to which the words would be sung, or it could refer to the time of day at which David suggests it should be sung... maybe at daybreak, or the beginning of the day.) It is vital to note that the psalm begins with lament but ends with praise at God's triumphant deliverance. Although these words were written by David in the context of his own experiences, he writes by the guidance of the Holy Spirit. His words are very prophetic as they have both clarity and exacting details of what happens to Christ on the cross, an event that is still 1,000 years away. David's words express a painful sense of being separated from God during a time of great turmoil. (Jesus quotes the psalm in Matthew 27:46, and Mark 15:34.) Yet David is reminded that God has been faithful to each generation and will continue to be faithful to those who call upon God. Verse 9 is instructional as David writes, "You make me trust...." Instead of doubting God in the midst of suffering, we are reminded to continue to offer our lifelong praise for surely God will deliver. The psalm ends with a note of triumph reminding the reader that the Gospel will speak to those "yet not born" (v. 31). So rather than thinking Jesus abandons all hope and feels totally rejected by God, we must hear his words through the mind of one who knows how the story of redemption will end. By quoting the first line of this well-known psalm, the faithful at the foot of the cross, would know that his suffering would lead to great triumph.

Application
Ever been there? Ever felt like you have been abandoned by God? If so, you need to remember the words and message of this psalm. Even when we feel separated from God, He is as close as our next breath, bringing purpose and plans into fruition. Our feelings of abandonment have absolutely no bearing on God's nearness to us. What we must remember, expressed through the experience of Jesus, is that in those moments of lonely separation, God is still near, and an experience of great joy and triumph is but a moment away.

Prayer
Father, even on our worst days, may we be reminded that you are still in control. Amen.

Day 501 — Psalm 23: To Catch One's Breath

> "He makes me lie down in green pastures; He leads me beside quiet waters. He restores my soul;" Psalm 23:2-3a (NASB)

Observation
This psalm is, of course, the best known and most often quoted psalm of David. It features the image of "Shepherd" God who watches carefully over the flock. David had been a shepherd boy in his early life and therefore he knows well the business of tending sheep. The psalm is not only a look at the ways God watches over us, but also speaks of the role of a good king (David) and the way he is to watch over Israel. The imagery of the psalm is rich and powerful. David expresses an abiding trust in God. He has no fears or concerns because it is the Lord God Almighty who watches over his life. Sheep cannot lie down in rest or peace unless they feel fully secure. The Good Shepherd gives protection and abundant care that brings a sense of calm. David writes about the dark and difficult valleys we all experience whenever the distressing times of our lives cause us to have a sense of our own mortality. David reminds us that God will walk with us through those moments. In fact, God prepares a banquet meal of abundance in the face of the enemies of heart, mind, and soul that cause us to suffer. David ends the psalm by reminding the reader that "goodness and mercy" will follow the sheep. It is a reminder that we will not be pursued by enemies, nor wild beasts, but by the shepherd and God's protective gifts of mercy and goodness.

Application
Whenever I read this familiar psalm, I am always intrigued by the line, "He restores my soul…." One of the ways to think about the soul is to think in terms of the breath of God within us. It is God's breath, according to Genesis, which calls us to life. "And the LORD God formed man of the dust of the ground, and breathed into his nostrils the breath of life; and man became a living soul" (Genesis 2:7 KJV). So, substitute the word "breath" in this verse for the word "soul." It reads like this, "He restores my breath…" or better yet, "He allows me to catch my breath." Do you see the image of a weary, tired, and desperate person, having a moment to rest, reflect, and catch his or her breath? We all need those moments. Let's be honest, most of us race through our days at a quick pace. Life is hectic, chaotic, and a little dizzying at times. We rarely take a moment to relax, find a moment's peace, or even reflect on where our lives are going. The promise of this psalm is that God longs to provide us with such moments. It is when we remember God's watch care, provision, and protection over our lives that we can find a minute to relax and refresh. We need the "still water moments" to gain perspective, insight, and wisdom. I pray that this day, you will find a moment of peace that God provides.

Prayer
Father, free us for a moment, from the pressures, pains, and problems of this day. Amen.

Day 502 — Psalm 24: Raise the Roof!

> "Lift up your heads, O gates, And be lifted up, O ancient doors, That the King of glory may come in!" Psalm 24:7 (NASB)

Observation

This psalm of David is another example of a royal psalm. This psalm describes the Lord's entrance into the Holy City of Jerusalem. It is very likely that this psalm was sung as David brought the Ark of the Covenant back to Jerusalem, an event described in 2 Samuel 6:15. The song answers the question of who is fit to come into the presence of the Lord. The response comes in verses 3 and 4 as David replies, "he who has clean hands and a pure heart, who has not lifted up his soul to an idol." For David, the ability to stand in the presence of the Lord comes with both the purity of one's actions and the purity of one's heart. (From a New Testament perspective, the reader will know that no one is made righteous except through faith in the King of Glory, even Jesus our Lord.) David proclaims early in this psalm that God is sovereign over heaven and earth. There is no adequate response to his rhetorical question, "Who may stand in His Holy Place?" The idea being that only those whom God invites may stand in that place. It is interesting that David speaks to the gates and doors of the city as though they are capable of praise. He challenges them to raise their drooping and weary archways to welcome God's coming.

Application

Let's talk home improvement for a moment. Whenever a house has stood for more than a few years, there are little items of improvement that need to be addressed. Maybe the front door was not sealed well and there is some water damage to the floor. Maybe there are a few drywall "pop outs" here and there as nails have pushed their way through the drywall. Maybe the deck needs painting. Maybe an appliance needs to be replaced. It happens. Every home needs a little propping up, fixing up, or cleaning up.

Our lives experience the same issues of aging. Over the course of the years, the sands of time tend to wear us down a little. We get a little defeated, a little discouraged, maybe even a little jaded. We don't always walk in hope, live in joy, and dream with bright anticipation. Maybe we need to hear the voice David in our lives reminding us that the King of Glory has come to dwell within us. It is the Spirit that gives life to our mortal bodies and refreshes our immortal spirit. Imagine the edifice of an old house, with sagging doorframes and crooked shutters suddenly springing to life again when the king arrives like some cartoon. Now imagine the discouragement and dismay of your life being lifted as the King of Kings comes to reign in your life once again. Lift your head... the King is here.

Prayer

Father, may we find grace, peace, and joy knowing that you dwell within us. Amen.

Day 503 — Psalm 25: Shame vs. Guilt

> "To You, O Lord, I lift up my soul. O my God, in You I trust, Do not let me be ashamed; Do not let my enemies exult over me."
> Psalm 25:1-2 (NASB)

Observation
Though this is classified as a psalm of lament, it is unique in that David petitions God to forgive him. Also unique is its construction in the original Hebrew text. It contains an acrostic. Each poetic line of the psalm begins with a successive letter of the Hebrew alphabet. A careful reading of the psalm will also reveal an opening and closing appeal to the Lord to not let David be ashamed before his enemies. Shame would reveal a character flaw and would make David seem weak as a leader. In the psalm, David describes "waiting on the Lord." Waiting on the Lord means to hope in the Lord and in the Lord's provision. David also pleads for the forgiveness of the sins of his youth and the transgressions of adulthood. The psalm closes with a plead for God to forgive and to redeem the nation of Israel, just as God has done with David.

Application
Let's talk for a moment about the difference between guilt and shame. Surely all of us have experienced both. Guilt occurs when a good person makes a bad choice… when a righteous person makes a mistake. We feel guilty in such a moment because we know that we have failed to act responsibly, godly, or obediently to the vows that define our lives. Shame, on the other hand, occurs when good people become so burdened by their guilt, that they move to the point in their minds when they no longer see themselves as being good, as being loved by God, or as being usable in the Kingdom's work. Shame tells a person that he or she is bad, flawed, beyond redemption and grace. It is vital to understand that because of the grace, forgiveness, and sacrificial love of Jesus, that shame no longer needs to rule in our lives. We need to forbid shame to enter our lives, redefining both self-worth and self-definition. Shame is conquered through the redemptive work of Christ. We stand in the presence of God as innocent and welcomed children. Guilt, therefore, becomes a more positive entity in our lives. Guilt is an indication of where we have gone wrong. Guilt reminds us that there are areas in our lives where we are not fully obedient to the purposes of God. Guilt should tell us that we are stepping on the pathway toward shame… that we are headed in a direction that is not God's purpose for our lives.

So, let me ask a hard question this morning… What are you feeling guilty about? Your guilt is a warning that you need to repent and embrace the forgiveness that Christ offers you this day. Guilt is a warning signal that some pattern of behavior needs to be altered.

Prayer
Father, may guilt point us toward redemption, so that we don't experience shame. Amen.

Day 504 — Psalm 26: Open Book

> "Examine me, O Lord, and try me; Test my mind and my heart."
> Psalm 26:2 (NASB)

Observation

In this psalm of lament, David offers a prayer for divine scrutiny and redemption. He prays to be "vindicated" in the eyes of the Lord. He wants to be declared righteous. His prayer is one of a forgiven sinner, who lives within the restraints of godly boundaries. He asks God to consider, or judge, his integrity. David insists that he has trusted God without wavering. He claims not to sit with sinners nor idolaters. He has made the choice to continually seek the heart of God. David affirms that God can discern those who have responded to His grace and those who have not. So, he willingly seeks the examination of God, knowing that he will be found innocent.

Application

Ever been through an IRS audit? I have. It's not a pleasant experience, nor is it one that I ever hope to repeat. Once summoned to the IRS office, you take all your receipts, statements, and documentation and lay your financial life bare before the examiner. He or she carefully examines your records and renders a decision. It's a little frightening to be that fully exposed before an authoritative entity.

Consider the almost arrogant request of King David. He begs the scrutiny of God. He pleads with God to examine his life, believing that he had lived righteously, nobly, and innocently before God. I wonder if any of us would dare to challenge God in such a way? Notice the wording of our focus verse... "Test my mind and my heart." The mind was the center of knowledge and thought. The heart was the center of emotion and feeling. David was asking God to examine both his actions and thoughts. For most of us, it's not the day-to-day actions that take us out of compliance with God. We can normally control our actions in a civil and respectful way. It's that "thought life" that tends to get a little crazy. We let our minds drift, our thoughts wander, and our desires go a little too unbridled. We play with the possibilities. We think the impure thought. We imagine the yet unexplored emotions. It's as though we think that our thought life is somehow blocked from the scrutiny of God. I'm not sure we guard our thoughts, protect our intentions, and govern our desires. It's a bold prayer that David prays... test my mind and my heart. If you are willing to pray such a prayer, be ready to respond to what God may reveal. Seek God's forgiveness. Welcome God's redemption. Practice intentional repentance. We cannot always control the thoughts that race into our minds, but we can control what we allow to linger within. Bad thoughts lead to bad actions. Guard yours and ask God to help you root out those that are destructive.

Prayer

Father God, may we come to you with pure hearts and minds. Amen.

Day 505 — Psalm 27: A Saving Light

> "The Lord is my light and my salvation; Whom shall I fear? The Lord is the defense of my life; Whom shall I dread?" Psalm 27:1 (NASB)

Observation
This psalm is a powerful declaration of trust. In it, David affirms that his trust is in the Lord and in the reality of God's presence in his life. He expresses his desire to live in the presence of God continually. He refers to God as his "light and salvation." David recognizes that God is his only true source of deliverance from darkness, meaning the presence of evil around him. David speaks of the wicked attempting to "eat his flesh." It is the image of wild, ravenous beasts who long to destroy his life. In response to the threats of his enemies, David longs to dwell or remain in the house of the Lord forever. He longs to walk in the assurance of God's daily presence. He closes this psalm with the challenge to wait on the Lord. Waiting should not be viewed as a passive activity or even inaction. Waiting on God is the willful and deliberate choice to depend on God and trust in God's provision. It is to patiently wait upon God's timing and actions.

Application
Years ago, while waiting with my grandfather in a parked car while my wife and grandmother were shopping, my grandfather told me a story of his childhood. It seems that he, along with some friends, were exploring some woods a few miles from his home. The young men, maybe in their early teens at the time, became a little disoriented and lost their way. For a few moments, there was a sense of fear and panic. The sun was starting to sink into the late afternoon horizon. Suddenly one of the boys said, "Let's follow the sun!" knowing that it would set in the west and give them a directional guide. They stayed on course and soon came to a country lane that they recognized. In reflecting on the story, my grandfather said, "Just keep walking toward the light and it will bring you home."

Surely the same sentiment is reflected in the heart of David as he declares, "The Lord is my light and my salvation." David saw in his relationship with God, a saving light. It was a light, a direction, a hope… that would give David the assurance needed to walk amid uncertainty and danger. Most of us need a saving light as well. We tend to stumble around in the darkness of hopelessness, uncertainty, fear, and doubt. We need a light to illumine our path… to give us assurance, hope, and promise. Jesus declares in John's Gospel that He is the "light of the world" (John 8:12 NASB). What assurance we can find, what hope we can harbor, and what joy we can imagine because God's light continually illumines our path. Whom indeed shall we fear? Whom shall we dread? Keep walking in faith… the light will lead you home.

Prayer
Father God, thank you for the light of the Gospel that instills endless hope. Amen.

Day 506 — Psalm 28: Caught in the Tide

> "Do not drag me away with the wicked and with those who work iniquity,
> Who speak peace with their neighbors, While evil is in their hearts."
> Psalm 28:3 (NASB)

Observation

This psalm of David is a very emotionally worded prayer in which David pours out his heart to God from the depths of his distress and anguish. He begins his prayer with the affirmation that God is his rock. He acknowledges that God is the source of his protection and shelter. He pleads to be heard by God… "Do not be silent." Perhaps David is awaiting a specific word from God through a prophet or priest. Without a response of delivery from God, David fears that he will go down to the "pit." The pit is an image for death. David wants deliverance from death so that he can live to praise God. In a posture of prayer, David lifts his hands before the Lord. He longs to distinguish himself from the wicked around him so that he will not be swept away with those of his culture who have no appreciation for the things of God. As the psalm draws to a close, David has heard from God, and he rejoices. The psalm ends on a note of praise.

Application

A few years ago, I was vacationing with my wife in the Georgia Coastal City of St. Simons. It was one of those picture-perfect days… the sun was bright and clear, the temperature was warm, and the sea was calm. All along the beach families played in the surf. There were children on rafts, dogs chasing Frisbees, and picnic blankets on the ground. One family waded out from the shore and discovered a sandbar about 50 yards out. The water was only knee deep, even though the distance from the shore was considerable. And then it happened… a large, rogue wave suddenly washed over the sandbar, catching the young family completely off-guard. One of the children was inundated by the wave and carried along in the current. His parents never saw him again. After three days of search and rescue, the lifeless body of the young boy was found. The current had simply been too strong, and it swept him away.

In his prayer, David prays that he will not be swept along in the wickedness of his culture. "Do not drag me away…" was his plea. He understood that sometimes, when the consequences of evil pour over a culture that many will be caught in the relentless, churning current. He longed to be spared when the wicked were destroyed. As Christians, we have a choice to make. Either we will influence our culture or we will be influenced by our culture. Unfortunately, many who could stand up and make a difference are being swept away in their compromise with culture. May we guard our lives so that we stand firm in the dangerous tide.

Prayer

Father God, may we stubbornly cling to our values in difficult days. Amen.

Day 507   Psalm 29: Thunder in the Mountains

> "The voice of the Lord is upon the waters; The God of glory thunders, The Lord is over many waters." Psalm 29:3 (NASB)

Observation
This is a psalm of worship in which David extols the sovereign reign of God. He instructs the "mighty ones" (a reference to those spiritual beings who are in the presence of God) to give glory to God. And then David picks up on some imagery borrowed from the Canaanite culture of his day. The Canaanites worshiped Baal, the god of the storm. They believed that by praying to Baal, he would respond with rain. In response to the worship of that pagan deity, David declares that the storms of nature are directed by Almighty God. David insists that the sound of thunder is the voice of God. He repeats the phrase, "The Voice of the Lord," seven times in the psalm. It almost sounds like the rapidly succeeding peals of thunder in a storm. The storm that David describes has movement to it. It travels from Lebanon in the north to Kadesh in the south. Nothing can stop the advancing storm. God is displayed by its intensity and strength.

Application
For a season, my family and I enjoyed living in the Great Smoky Mountains. We were residents of Gatlinburg, where I pastored the First Baptist Church for five years. I have a lot of great memories and friendships from those days. One of those memories is the sound of a thunderstorm in the mountains. It's different. When a thunderstorm rolls through the region, the thunder tends to echo off the mountains. It reverberates over and over again as though each mountain catches the sound and throws it back across the valley towards an opposing mountain. It is an impressive sound. Obviously, one not soon forgotten.

When David describes the voice of the Lord in the mighty thunder of a storm, he gives great life and imagery to the power of our God. David is right when he calls even the angels in heaven to give glory to God's name. Let me suggest that God longs to be revealed to us. He does so in the great and mighty voices of nature and through the still quiet voices of a gentle night or lazy afternoon. I find God present in both the powerful rumble of thunder and in the quiet stillness of the night. This may seem a little weird but try doing something this morning… take one minute to sit in silence. Close your eyes and listen to all the sounds around you. Strip away the manmade sounds of machine and system and listen for the sounds that can only be produced by the world God created. Listen to the wind, the birds, the gentle splashing of rain. Remind yourself that even on this day, God is being revealed.

Prayer
God, thank you for being present in our world and reminding us of your presence. Amen.

Day 508 — Psalm 30: Choosing to Live Again

> "You have turned for me my mourning into dancing; You have loosed my sackcloth and girded me with gladness, That my soul may sing praise to You and not be silent. O Lord my God, I will give thanks to You forever."
> Psalm 30:11-12 (NASB)

Observation
Psalm 30 is of thanksgiving expressed from David's heart for God's deliverance from death. It is apparent from his words that David suffered from a near-fatal illness. He describes death as a great pit into which a person drops into the darkness of the unknown. In the psalm, David describes the way in which God has heard his prayer for safety, and how later, when David became arrogant, God humbled him to remind him that his strength was bound up in God's provision for his life. The psalm ends on a very triumphant note as David praises God for taking away his grief and turning it into joyful dancing.

Application
You don't have to live for very long before you will feel the sting of grief. For most of you reading this thought, there has been some type of significant grief in your life. You have felt the despair, the loneliness, and the "sadness of soul" that grief brings to your doorstep. It is a painful, gut-wrenching experience. But may I remind you that grief is a natural response, a God-given emotion, that comes to us when we experience great loss? Grief is necessary. It allows us to cope. It heals the heart. It empties us of some of the anguish and hurt. To fail to grieve, is to fail to be human. We grieve because someone we love is now separated from us. In fact, the greater the love, the greater the pain of grief. But here's the problem with our grief… it can linger so long that it affects our ability to move ahead with life and regain the "joy of the Lord" that we once knew. Though it cannot be rushed, there should be a context for our grief from which we will eventually escape. Though we will always miss those we love, the moment must come when we begin the journey out of mourning and back into life. It is a long, slow process, but a necessary process. How is it even possible? It is only possible by the grace of God and through the strength He provides. It is one of those journeys that begins with a single step and then another, and then, another.

There are some of you who need to turn your mourning into joyful dancing. There are some of you who need to start the process of recovery. You need courage, you need strength, and you need the support of others. Pray to God to grant you those things. God always has much for us to accomplish. Our lives don't end when the lives of our loved ones do. So, place your hand in God's this morning and let God help you to find joy again and re-establish your life. Claim hope in the promise of resurrection and pray for patience while you wait.

Prayer
God, as we struggle through the pain of grief, may we find renewal and hope. Amen.

Day 509 — Psalm 31: Things Said in Haste

> "As for me, I said in my alarm, 'I am cut off from before Your eyes';
> Nevertheless You heard the voice of my supplications when I cried to You."
> Psalm 31:22 (NASB)

Observation
Psalm 31 is classified as both a psalm of lament and a psalm of trust. The first 18 verses describe David's lament while the final verses offer words of praise, spoken in the context of his lament. One of the more familiar lines of this psalm is contained in verse 5, "Into Your hands I commit my spirit." These words, which reflect a complete dependence upon God, were spoken by Jesus on the cross (Luke 23:46 NASB), and by Stephen as he was being martyred (Acts 7:59). As David offers these words, he is declaring that his life is in God's hands. Later in the psalm, David admits that he is in trouble and turmoil. His sorrow is perhaps caused by some physical illness that has made him repulsive to others. He petitions God for deliverance with the words, "let Your face shine on me." He is asking God to "smile" in favor of his situation.

Application
Ever said something in anger or pain that you wish you hadn't said? It happens, right? Sometimes we experience a moment when our emotions overtake our self-control and we blurt out something that we will later regret. Maybe we yell at our spouse or say something derogatory to our child. Or maybe in anger you have yelled, or texted, or posted something online in the heat of the moment that you later regret having said or written. James reminds us that the tongue can be a "restless evil, full of deadly poison" (James 3:8 NIV). Notice our focus verse… David confesses to God that he said something to God "in his alarm" that he regrets saying. Some translations use the word, "haste," as in, "I said something in haste." But notice the response that David felt. "Nevertheless You heard the voice of my supplications when I cried to You." I wonder if we have ever committed the same infraction. Ever yell at God in a disrespectful way? Ever shout at God in anger or anguish? Ever accuse God of acting like an uncaring tyrant? Sometimes we say things in haste that we later regret. And yet… God loves us beyond our words or our angry outbursts. God understands our emotions and the pressures we face, along with the childish ways we sometimes respond. And rather than punish us for our insolence, God holds us even closer as beloved children. Your anger, your words, your outbursts, and your lack of understanding do nothing to change God's affections. But let's learn the lesson of David and admit our words said in haste and seek the forgiveness of God. Part of the fruit of the Spirit is self-control. Maybe we need to pray for more of that when our humanity sometimes takes over our words.

Prayer
God, forgive our sometimes-angry outbursts as we lean into your grace. Amen.

Day 510 — Psalm 32: How Do You Spell Relief?

> "How blessed is he whose transgression is forgiven, Whose sin is covered! How blessed is the man to whom the Lord does not impute iniquity, And in whose spirit there is no deceit!" Psalm 32:1-2 (NASB)

Observation

Psalm 32 speaks of the joy of forgiveness. Like Psalm 51, it has its origin in David's response to God following his infamous affair with Bathsheba (2 Samuel 11). It is interesting that scripture is willing to offer a look at both the low moments and days of triumph in the life of key characters. Certainly David's great transgression is not hidden from the Biblical narrative. David opens this psalm with the words, "How blessed…" The phrase literally translates, "how happy, how relieved, how filled with joy." It is the image of a person whose sins have been erased and thus his guilt has been removed. David admits that when he kept silent about his sins, he extended the length of his suffering. In the latter part of the psalm David speaks about the sorrows of the wicked contrasted by the joys of a forgiven sinner. The point is clear… confession brings about the forgiveness of sin. Forgiveness restores the joy to a broken life.

Application

An antacid company once had an advertising campaign that asked the question, "How do you spell relief?" Their answer, of course, was R-o-l-a-i-d-s. Rolaids might work for stomach pain, but it can't begin to touch some of the other stress in our lives. Each day as I drive home from work, several ads play on my radio. One talks about debt relief. Another promises delinquent tax-payment relief. Still another talks about getting out from under student debt. Whenever something is oppressive, heavy, or hard to bear, we long for something that will give us a little relief.

David experienced the same longing in his life. Because of his sins, David labored under the extreme weight of guilt and shame. Guilt robbed him of his rest. It snapped his vitality. It caused his body to waste away. But then he found the relief that only confession can bring. He went from the darkness of shame to the joyful light of grace. All it took was confession. Confession is one of those good spiritual words that we like to throw around a lot. It simply means to, "agree with God about the disruptive nature of our sinful actions." Confession causes us to admit both to God and to ourselves that we have erred and need a sense of relief. Take a moment to consider under what oppressive weight you are now living. What is the sin that you have failed to confess? What is the infraction that you don't really want to own? David was right. The longer you wait, the longer you prolong your suffering.

Prayer

God, teach us the discipline of forgiveness that we might know the joy of grace. Amen.

Day 511 — Psalm 33: The Sovereign God

> "For He spoke, and it was done; He commanded, and it stood fast."
> Psalm 33:9 (NASB)

Observation
This psalm is one a few in the collection that is anonymous. The author writes to invite all people to join with the faithful believers in Israel in praising God and trusting in God's goodness. The hearer of the psalm is invited to praise God with both song and instrument. Both the lyre and 10-string harp are mentioned specifically. The psalmist reminds the godly to look beyond the confusing evil and suffering of the world to see the goodness of God in the countless ways God's goodness is manifested each day. He also speaks about God's ability to control the seas. He speaks of the shaping of the oceans at creation, when by speaking, God created the sea and the dry land. The psalmist also mentions the ways in which the eyes of the Lord are continually on the earth, giving careful watch care. The psalm ends with a plea for God to allow mercy to be upon all those who trust in God.

Application
Depending on one's level of authority, a voice can create great change. For example, the owner of a well-trained dog can control the actions of the animal with just his voice. A parent of a well-taught child can control the actions of that child with just her voice. A boss of a company can set direction and policy by just speaking instructions. The leader of a country can dictate policy with just the spoken word. Again, those who have authority can manipulate thought and action with just a few verbal instructions. In this passage, the psalmist reminds his readers, that because of God's ultimate and all-powerful authority, God can create, define, discipline, and bless. When God speaks, all the created order listens and responds. Even the mighty waters of the earth were gathered into oceans and seas by the power of God's voice.

Doesn't it stand to reason, that if God has the power to control all things, then certainly God has the authority to direct our actions? One interesting aspect of God is the willingness to motivate us by love, rather than by force. God invites us into God's presence, joyfully offering grace. God willingly presents Jesus as a sacrifice for our sins. We are invited, not forced, into a relationship with God. However, make no mistake about God's ultimate authority. The world spins at God's command. The sun rises at God's instruction. If we force God's hand through our inattention and disobedience, God can surely force God's will and way upon us. But that's not God's way and it's not the way of grace. God loves us and desires that we would be obedient in response to God's affection. Let us this day, acknowledge both God's authority and love.

Prayer
God, may we know both your power and your infinite love for us. Amen.

Day 512   Psalm 34: Living in the Bubble

> "The angel of the Lord encamps around those who fear Him, And rescues them." Psalm 34:7 (NASB)

Observation

This psalm, written by David, is both powerful and rich in imagery and assurances. Like other psalms, this psalm is an acrostic in the Hebrew language with each verse beginning with a letter of the Hebrew alphabet. It is interesting to notice the inscription at the beginning of the psalm. It states, "A psalm of David when he pretended madness before Abimelech, who drove him away, and he departed." This is a reference to an experience that David once had in the Philistine city of Gath. Abimelech was the king of Gath and, according to 1 Samuel 21:10-15, David could have easily lost his life but escaped by pretending to be insane. (Sometimes it pays to act a little crazy!) David invites the reader to join with him in offering praise to God. In fact, he speaks of the practice of offering continual praise (v. 1). God is to be praised for the deliverance that God provides. In an image similar to the experience of Moses on Sinai, David insists that those who look to God will have a radiant look on their face. Later in the psalm, David offers the invitation to the pagan world around him, "to taste and see that the Lord is good." He wants others to experience what it is to be in relationship to the Living God. In another key verse, David reminds his reader that "God is near to the broken-hearted and will save those whose spirits are crushed" (v. 18).

Application

On several occasions, while traveling to far away mission points, I have felt the protection of tall walls, iron gates, and 24/7 vigilant defenders. In places like Haiti, the Dominican Republic, and more recently, in the nation of Honduras, I was housed in a compound, surrounded by strong walls and watchful guards. I must admit that I slept well. There was no fear of thieves breaking in or wild animals entering the compound. There is something to be said about a safe and secure defense.

So, look again at our focus verse. David declares, "The angel of the Lord encamps around those who fear Him." (Often in Biblical literature the reader can substitute the words, "angel of the Lord," with the very presence of God. This is one of those places.) Therefore, David is affirming that God encamps around us. I like that image. I like the feeling of being protected, monitored, and kept safe. What a joy and privilege it is for all of us who have placed our faith and trust in God, to know that God constantly surrounds our lives. God knows every moment that we experience and waits to rescue us from all our enemies, even those of fear, anxiety, and peer pressure. Even this day, God is watching over your life.

Prayer

God, thank you this day for your vigilant watch care over our lives. Amen.

Day 513 — Psalm 35: Total Praise

> "With every bone in my body I will praise him: 'Lord, who can compare with you? Who else rescues the helpless from the strong? Who else protects the helpless and poor from those who rob them?'" Psalm 35:10 (NLT)

Observation
In this psalm, David places an unusual emphasis on the role of his enemies. He prays for their destruction, believing that his enemies are also the enemies of God. This is an example of an "imprecatory prayer." An imprecatory prayer is one in which the person offering the prayer, invokes judgment, calamity, or curses on his enemy. It's the kind of prayer we have often thought about praying but know that we probably shouldn't… "God, I hope you zap my enemies into oblivion!" Something about loving our enemies and praying for those who persecute us, doesn't seem to match-up with that kind of praying. In his psalm, David expresses the fact that he has been wrongly attacked. He prays for God to defend him. He even asks God to take up weapons like a soldier to fight for him. Another interesting feature of this psalm occurs in verse 23 where David tells God to "Wake Up!" as though God needs to be alerted to David's plight. As the psalm concludes, David realizes and rejoices that his help is always in the Lord.

Application
This morning, I want to pick up on that opening phrase from our focus verse, "With every bone in my body I will praise Him." If we made such a promise to God, what would such a promise resemble? What if every bone in our bodies truly offered God praise? What about the bones in our hands? Does everything we touch bring glory to God? Does the work of our hands honor God? And what about the bones of our feet? Do our steps… our daily journeys take us to places that bring God glory? What about our skulls which house our brains? Do we protect our minds from evil thoughts? Do we guard what we see and hear so that our brains are filled with that which honors God? And what about our breastbones? Do we protect our hearts? Do we keep them pure and focused on sharing the compassionate love of God with all whom we encounter? And what about our spines… do we have enough backbone to stand for what is right and oppose that which is wrong in our culture? It really is quite a prayer to offer… this idea of saying that "every bone in our body will praise God." It implies the totality of our lives will be offered daily to God, for God's service and for God's praise. It implies that what we do, where we go, and how we speak really does make a difference. We can praise God and honor God through our actions, or conversely, we can bring shame to God's Kingdom. So how will you spend your day? Will every bone in your body praise God?

Prayer
God, may our actions, words, thought… all of it, be acceptable in your sight. Amen.

Day 514 — Psalm 36: The Whisper of Sin

> "Sin whispers to the wicked, deep within their hearts. They have no fear of God at all." Psalm 36:1 (NLT)

Observation
This psalm is another example of a wisdom psalm of David. In this psalm David will contrast the nature of sin with God's unfailing love and goodness. David seems to write with prophetic insight into the nature of wickedness. Those who are wicked have complete disregard for the reality of God in their lives. They live as though God does not exist. The wicked are egotistical. They flatter themselves. They deceive themselves. In contrast to the depths of wickedness among the people of the earth, David describes the expansive nature of God's love and mercy. He mentions that God's love is taller than the mountains and deeper than the seas. God's salvation and mercy are like a "fountain of life," from which the living water that sustains life flows. There is an interesting verse in this psalm for those who are pet owners. In verse 6 David writes, "You care for people and animals alike, O Lord." Certainly David is correct in declaring that God cares for all of creation.

Application
"Sin whispers to the wicked, deep within their hearts..." In most cases, the voice of temptation in our lives is indeed like a gentle whisper... a clever, relentless, persistent whisper. Temptation seldom screams its arrival. It comes at the key moment, the vulnerable time, the second our defenses have been lowered. It whispers in ways that catch our attention. It lures us into playing with the possibilities. It deeply embeds within our hearts. And because it is a quiet whisper, we often ignore the force it carries and soon we are undone. Recently I had to replace the faucet in our bathroom sink. You know how those things go... it began with a very small drip... the kind that you just couldn't quite shut-off. But it's such a small drip... not worth the effort or expense to fix, or so we say. And then the drip becomes steadier and the effort to twist the knob a little harder, increases. Finally, the drip becomes more of a trickle, which gives way to a steady stream and suddenly a trip to the hardware store gets placed on the agenda. You've been there. You try to ignore that which seems insignificant, until a real problem is created. That's the nature of sin and temptation. It's the quiet whisper that we ignore. We think we can control the influence the whisper exerts in our lives. But in our refusal to close our ears and block the pathway to our minds, the temptation finds a place to land and once it takes root, it's hard to stay strong. I want you to take a moment to listen very closely to the noises in your life today. Is there a voice, a whisper perhaps, that is consistently attempting to get your attention and alter your judgment? Pray for strength and for wisdom to quit listening.

Prayer
God, remind us that even the gentle whisper can powerfully control our thoughts. Amen.

Day 515 — Psalm 37: Fully Invested

> "Commit everything you do to the Lord. Trust him, and he will help you."
> Psalm 37:5 (NLT)

Observation
This is another wisdom psalm written by King David. It is a call to maintain patience in the midst of troubles. David affirms that God's people can persevere because the eternal reward they will inherit far surpasses any temporal struggles they may face. The theme of the psalm is contained in the opening verse in which David says, "Do not worry." The faithful are not to worry as the wicked seem to prosper. A patient dependency upon the Lord will bring lasting results whereas the wicked and their prosperity will quickly vanish. David reminds the listener that God knows the circumstances of their lives and will reward, sustain, and bless those who are righteous. In fact, David suggests that there are always life choices to be made… the vital choice is to pursue God or to pursue evil. In verse 27, David clearly states, "Depart from evil and do good."

Application
I have to admit that I am in a slightly different role in my current job than I have experienced over the past three decades. When I was serving as the lead pastor in several churches, I occupied the seat of authority. I made many decisions. People came to me for final approval, advice, and direction. Here at Belmont, I work directly under the President of the University. The decisions I make, the plans I outline, and the direction of the program necessarily fall under the authority of the President. Before I venture too far down any path or direction, I seek his approval. I make sure that my vision and plans are in line with his thoughts for our program.

Listen again to what David writes in our focus verse… "Commit everything you do to the Lord." His advice is simple, make sure that everything you do is done under the authority of God. Commit every aspect of your life, your work, your relationships, your activities to God's scrutiny. Look to God for wisdom, encouragement, and approval. It's a simple plan for success. All that we are, all that we do, all that we say, all that we think, should somehow bring honor to God and build the kingdom that God longs to establish on the earth. So we commit to God. We ask for God's approval, God's nod, God's smile, God's encouragement. We constantly seek God's guidance. And let's be clear… God is not vague about God's purpose nor is God flippant about our righteousness. If we truly seek God's counsel, God will direct our paths and illumine our thoughts. So as you begin this day, commit everything that you will do to the Lord. Ask for the guidance, wisdom, and blessing that God longs to give.

Prayer
God, may each of us commit the full scope of this day to your lordship. Amen.

Day 516   Psalm 38: Troubled Soul

> "For I confess my iniquity; I am full of anxiety because of my sin."
> Psalm 38:18 (NLT)

Observation

This is a psalm of lament written by David in which he displays a penitent heart for the sins he has committed. In it, he pleads desperately for God's mercy. The instructions that headline the psalm insist that it is to be played as a memorial. It is believed that this psalm may have been used in worship on Rosh Hashanah, the celebration of the Jewish New Year that is said to be a memorial. If this is true, it would offer a calling to repentance and renewal at the start of the new year. There are two primary concerns listed in this psalm. First, David is worried about the distress and turmoil in his life that is a result of his sin and God's resultant discipline. His second concern is the extent of his painful remorse. He admits that his sins have overwhelmed him, and that God's wrath may be too severe in his life. In verse 4 he mentions the weight of his guilt... "For my iniquities are gone over my head; As a heavy burden they weigh too much for me." So difficult is the guilt and shame of his sinfulness, David fears that even those closest to him will abandon him. He closes his thoughts by confessing his sins before God and praying for forgiveness and restoration.

Application

Most of us know the experience of having a troubled soul. When something about our life is not set right, we fret, we worry, we pace, we live in turmoil. Such anguish can be the result of any number of things. For example, if there are too many bills and too few dollars to pay them, a person can spend an anxious night in worry over how to make ends meet. Or suppose that a husband and wife have a sharp disagreement. The lack of marital cohesion can certainly knock both partners off-stride until some resolve has been reached. Maybe there is a problem at work that is far too worrisome. Again, when something about our lives is not set right, we experience the troubled soul. For David, the cause of his troubled soul was the sin in his life. Though, as readers we are not told what sins led to this great turmoil, it is clear that David's heart and mind are consumed with wanting to work pass the guilt and the shame that have overwhelmed him. He finally finds some solace in the confession of his sins and in the assurance that God will forgive him and set things right again. Obviously, that message needs to reach our ears. How often do we struggle with the anguish of unconfessed sin? We know that something is just not quite right. We feel the oppression of our guilt. We feel the tension and awkwardness when our sins cause brokenness. It is when the guilt begins to overwhelm that we must reach out to God and offer the full and honest confession of our sins. It is the first step towards healing.

Prayer

Father God, may we know the relief of honest confession and restoration this day. Amen.

Day 517 — Psalm 39: Because Life Is Short

> "Lord, remind me how brief my time on earth will be. Remind me that my days are numbered—how fleeting my life is. You have made my life no longer than the width of my hand. My entire lifetime is just a moment to you; at best, each of us is but a breath." Psalm 39:4-5 (NLT)

Observation
This is an interesting psalm written by David that reflects some of the language and sentiment that Job experienced in his suffering. It is apparent that David is suffering, and it is his belief that his experience is a result of God's discipline in his life over sins that he has committed. The pressure of discipline is great and David muses on the experience in the words of this psalm. Notice that it is inscribed to Jeduthun, the chief musician. Jeduthun is the father of one of the three families of Levitical singers. Obviously, this psalm was intended to be sung in worship. Rather than speaking loudly in the presence of his enemies as he often does, David indicates that he will remain silent before them. His silence is so that he will not speak foolishly before his enemies while he is under the pressure of God's discipline. He also speaks about the brevity of life and its fleeting nature. David recognizes that his only chance of deliverance is in God and so he cries out for God's help. Yet, in very unusual language, he asks God to leave him alone if God is not going to relent from the discipline. Obviously, he writes these words while on the edge of despair.

Application
I've done a little fishing in my day, mostly in lakes and ponds. And most of my success is trial and error. But some days you get just the right bait at the right moment and life is good. For example, if you want to have some luck in the late spring of the year, wait for the mayflies to make their appearance. At times there can be thousands landing softly on the surface of a quiet lake, late in the afternoon. And the fish go absolutely crazy. Throw in a lure that resembles a mayfly and hang on! I remember one late afternoon in Southern Alabama when the mayflies were everywhere. Fishing alongside of a friend, we reached our limit in minutes. But here's the thing with mayflies… they only live for about 24 hours. Their entire lifespan from birth, to reproduction, to death all happens in a single day. So time your fishing trip carefully.

Not to be obsessed with the thought of a limited lifespan… but we need to recognize as David did that our lives do have a beginning and an all-too-soon ending. It's what we do in the days we are given that matters. We can choose to live selfishly and play the game of acquiring wealth for the sake of a sense of security or happiness… or, we can choose to invest our lives in things that matter… the lives of others who have needs we can solve.

Prayer
Father, because the days are short… let us live well and love with extravagance. Amen.

Day 518 — Psalm 40: Count the Blessings

> "O Lord my God, you have performed many wonders for us. Your plans for us are too numerous to list. You have no equal. If I tried to recite all your wonderful deeds, I would never come to the end of them."
> Psalm 40:5 (NLT)

Observation
This is a psalm of declarative praise in which David describes the way in which God has lifted him out of despair and rescued his life from the ungodly. He begins his reflections with the words, "I waited patiently for the Lord." David is not describing a quantity of time but a quality of time. To wait on the Lord is to have a confident trust and faith in God's salvation. David thus, waited with great anticipation and trust that God would deliver him. He speaks of God's inclining ear to David. It is the image of God leaning in to hear the prayers of both David and all those who are helpless. God directs attention and thoughts towards those who cry out in the midst of their struggles. David also declares that God has "put a new song in his heart." David is refreshed and strengthened by the nature of God's salvation. He also speaks about the understanding he now has concerning what God cares about the most… even beyond sacrifices and burnt offerings. God cares most about having the hearts of God's people and the attention of their lives.

Application
We would do well to act as David has done, in recounting all the wondrous deeds that God has performed for us. David describes how the wonders of God are too numerous for us to list… that the list of God's blessings would never come to an end. Remember the old hymn "Count Your Blessings?" We don't sing it much anymore, but the message of that song reflects David's thoughts in this Psalm 40. The refrain of the old hymn goes like this… "Count your many blessings name them one by one, count your many blessings see what God hath done. Count your many blessings, name them one by one; count your many blessings see what God hath done." Here's the point. It's simple human nature for most of us to spend our time complaining about what we don't have, rather than thanking God for what we do have. The blessings of God in our lives really are too numerous to count. To list our blessings would require more pen and ink than we possess. And yet I fear we offer such little praise for what we have. In fact, most of our praying finds us asking God for even more. "I need this, and I need that… please give me this and answer my prayer." You get the point. What if you took the time this morning to list just five of your blessings… just five? And then take the time to spend a few reflective moments thanking God with a grateful heart. Try it. Name five blessings and thank God, who has provided those gifts in your life.

Prayer
Father, as we daily enjoy the blessings you provide, fill our hearts with gratitude. Amen.

Day 519 — Psalm 41: Poor, But Not Impoverished

> "The Lord nurses them when they are sick and restores them to health."
> Psalm 41:3 (NLT)

Observation
This is another psalm of David that has elements of both praise and lament. Specifically, this psalm speaks of the plight of a person suffering from some serious physical illness. No doubt David is in the throes of an illness that he fears could take his life. He begins with an acknowledgment that God is the source of all blessings and blessed will be the person whose trust is in God. When David writes about the poor, he is writing about more than those who lack money. He is describing those who suffer illness or misfortune from no fault of their own. He speaks of those to be pitied because of their plight. In verse 5, David mentions that his enemies ridicule him in the midst of his illness saying that the day will come when even his name would perish... meaning that no one would even remember that he existed. He describes the way his enemies visit him on his death bed, not to offer support but to simply gain gossip to spread about him. Verse 9 is directly quoted by Jesus in reference to Judas in John 13:18, "But this fulfills the scripture that says, 'The one who eats my food has turned against me'" (NLT). The psalm closes, however, with a triumphant note as David revels in the knowledge that God has spared his life.

Application
My wife does not have a degree in nursing, but she probably should after what I put her through. A couple of years ago, I had double-knee replacement surgery. Foolishly, I assumed that I'd be back on my feet in no time and breeze my way through rehab. Well... it was a little more than I had expected. Therapy lasted for four months, pain pills for 90 days, sleepless nights, and two months out of work. But through it all, my wife was a trooper. She drove me to therapy. She kept me on track with my meds. She made sure that I was eating and drinking properly. She checked on me through many long nights. By her efforts I was restored to health. In referring to those who are sick and impoverished, David affirms the Lord nurses them when they are sick and restores them to health. The poor, the sick, the downcast often find themselves in moments of desperation, anxiety and perhaps fear. But they never find themselves without hope, nor without access to God's grace, nor without representation. That is because God constantly watches over us. God's presence is constant. God's compassion is never ending. Add to that, the fact that God's knowledge is all encompassing. So even this day, if you are struggling physically, emotionally, or even spiritually, take heart, you are not alone... God is with you. God will nurture your spirit, restore your body, and renew your mind.

Prayer
Father, may we find a gentle and healing grace for this day. Amen.

Day 520 — Psalm 42: Sacred Spaces

> "These things I remember and I pour out my soul within me. For I used to go along with the throng and lead them in procession to the house of God, With the voice of joy and thanksgiving, a multitude keeping festival."
> Psalm 42:4 (NASB)

Observation

This psalm marks the beginning of Book 2 of the collection of Psalms, which includes Psalms 42 through 72. The main theme of the psalms contained within this portion of the psalms (42-72) is that of God's fatherly care. This psalm is subscribed to The Sons of Korah. These men were the faithful servants of God who were not swallowed up by the earth for rebelling against Moses in Numbers 26:10-11. These men and their generations became the Levitical singers who led in worship. Originally, Psalms 42 and 43 may have been a single poem. Psalm 43 contains no subscription in the heading and repeats the refrain verbatim from Psalm 42. They were probably divided to use in temple worship. The author (unknown) speaks of his thirst for God while in trouble and in exile. He is obviously cutoff from Jerusalem and the worshipping community. He feels the distance and longs for closeness with God. He speaks of "panting" for God, which implies a very deep thirst. He desires to be in Jerusalem with the multitudes praising God, for in that time and moment, the only true place to worship God was in the Temple. He reminds himself that one day, he will once again experience the presence of God in that place and therefore he finds hope in his present circumstances.

Application

Most of us understand that God can be worshipped in any place. God is present everywhere. Worshippers can gather and offer their praises in great cathedrals, mountain-top retreats, a grassy hillside, or the basement of a neighbor's house. Maybe you have worshipped God while enjoying the solitude of a solo hike, or during a walk on a deserted beach. But notice the two elements for which the psalmist longs... he seeks to be in the Temple, the place where God is consistently found, and he seeks to be in the presence of the multitude. He wants to know the power and volume of corporate worship. This morning, I want you to reflect for a moment about the special places and moments of worship where you have felt the presence and power of God. I want you to think in terms of a sanctuary dedicated for such a moment. I want you to think about a time when the room was filled with eager worshippers, all raising their voices in unified praise to God. I have a lot of fond memories of the churches I have served, sanctuaries filled with those moments of extraordinary worship, like an Easter resurrection service or a Christmas Eve candlelight service. As you reflect on a special memory of worship, may you thirst for yet another.

Prayer

Father, thank you for exciting and meaningful moments in worship. Amen.

Day 521 — Psalm 43: Led by the Light

> "O send out Your light and Your truth, let them lead me; Let them bring me to Your holy hill and to Your dwelling places." Psalm 43:3 (NASB)

Observation
This is a continuation of Psalm 42. The psalmist (unknown) seeks vindication from God. It is as though he longs to proclaim his innocence. He feels that he has been wrongly attacked. More hurtful than the words of his enemies is the sense that God has rejected him. And so, he asks for God's deliverance. He affirms that the true light of God will save him from the darkness that surrounds him. As he expressed in the previous psalm, he desires to rejoin the worshipping community in Jerusalem. He urges himself to continue to believe in the power of God. He ends his thoughts with a hopeful refrain… "For I shall yet praise Him…." He expresses the assurance that he will, in fact, one day return to the Temple where he will join others worshipping God.

Application
Years ago, I pastored a central Kentucky church that was located near a large lake. Many of our members lived on the water and occasionally my wife and I were invited to enjoy a cookout and usually an evening of playing Rook. We were fond of one elderly retired couple who had a beautiful home on the lake. There was a long, winding pathway that led from their back porch to their dock. It had been carefully landscaped and was illumined by a series of accent lights. I still recall how the lights led the traveler down the path and to the water's edge. Without the light, the pathway would have been treacherous and a bit frightening.

Go back to the days of creation and consider God's first act of creation. "Let there be light." Light was God's first gift to the created order. It brought illumination to the chaos. It gave perspective. It was certainly for humanity's benefit and was a symbol of God's redemptive work as the light of goodness pierced the darkness of the world and its influence. Even today, the light of God illumines our path. It points to the salvation we have in Christ. It points to the Spirit embedded into each of us, giving us direction and insight. It gives wisdom for each day and certainly offers bright illumination of the steps we are to take. The psalmist begged for God's light to draw him once again to the place of worship. Surely, we echo the same thought. "God, send out your light once again. Give us hope in uncertainty, illumination in our darkness, and clear direction in our chaotic journey." It's a dark, scary, and treacherous world out there… the light of God will show us the path needed to navigate it successfully.

Prayer
Father, thank you for providing the Light of your counsel and salvation. Amen.

Day 522 — Psalm 44: What Did Your Father Tell You?

> "O God, we have heard with our ears, Our fathers have told us the work that You did in their days, In the days of old." Psalm 44:1 (NASB)

Observation

This is an interesting psalm that describes both the former deliverance of God and the contemporary suffering of God's people. The lament of the community is expressed. It is a "collective sigh" of the people of Israel as they ask for God to once again help them in a time of great national stress. The psalm begins with a reminder of God's great deeds in the Exodus event. God's deliverance was certainly a vital memory in the narrative of Israel's history. As every generation told the story to the next, it was not merely a recitation of history, but a description of God's loving character demonstrated to God's chosen people. God had certainly favored the nation and given them victory over former foes. But with verse 9, the psalm turns in a different direction. Suddenly there are words of lament for the current condition of the nation. The people express their frustration, speaking about their loss as if God had "sold" them to their enemies. They protest that they have not forsaken God, and they beg God to "buy them back." They stretch out their hands in prayer, not to a pagan deity, but to the one true God.

Application

In the opening verse, the psalmist describes the way in which former generations spoke of God's work. They carefully told the redemptive history of God to each new generation. The psalmist declared that "We have heard with our own ears...." In the world of Biblical studies, scholars often speak of the "oral tradition" of the Israelites. Before the invention of mass-produced books or even the development of written word, fathers carefully told the stories of God to their children, who carefully told the stories to the next generation. We get that. All of us have those family stories that we pass along from one generation to the next. In fact, with today's technology, we can write the stories in a journal, type them into a word processor, or even record them in audio and video file formats. We can ensure that the great stories don't get lost to the sands of time. But here's the problem... the great stories can't be preserved if they are not told. I wonder if we are careful to tell the stories of God at work in our own lives, to our children and grandchildren. Do we take the time to make certain that the "faith stories" are woven into the narratives of our family histories? Most of us can remember a few tales that we have picked up along the way from our parents and the experiences of their lives. But can we remember the stories of how their faith impacted the living of their days? We can't remember that which we have never heard. Share the stories of your faith so that future generations will remember the great work of God.

Prayer

Father, may we have the discipline to teach the stories of our faith. Amen.

Day 523 — Psalm 45: The Oil of Joy

> "You love justice and hate evil. Therefore God, your God, has anointed you, pouring out the oil of joy on you more than on anyone else."
> Psalm 45:7 (NLT)

Observation
Psalm 45 is a royal psalm… a royal wedding song that celebrates human marriage in such a grand manner that the New Testament writers applied it to the Great King Jesus as well (Hebrews 1:8-9). Notice in the subscription that it is set to "The Lilies," which likely indicates the melody or tune to which these words are to be sung. The imagery of the song seems to place the setting of the described wedding in the opulence of an ancient eastern royal court. Both the bride and the groom are splendidly dressed for the occasion. Our focus verse describes the blessings of God that have been poured out upon the groom. He has obviously found favor in God's eyes for his love of justice and his hatred for evil. The bride is encouraged to forget both her own people and her father's household so that she can live fully into her role as a wife to the king.

Application
I like the descriptive words of our focus verse, "Therefore God, your God, has anointed you, pouring out the oil of joy on you more than on anyone else." Ever know someone who seems to have the "oil of joy" poured out in their life? Some people are that way. They have an inner joy, a delight, a satisfaction, and contentment with life that is seemingly drawn from some deep inner well. Not only are they seldom defeated or downcast, but they have an infectious spirit that brings joy and gladness to the people around them. Such people have obviously discovered a wonderful truth… they have found the source of strength and peace for their lives. That source of joy comes only through a relationship with God… not a casual one, mind you, but one that is growing, vibrant, and deep. Here's the key: Those who center their lives on loving God passionately and who attempt to live in accordance with God's will, find a joy, a peace, and a contentment that surpasses all human understanding. That's not to say that everything that happens in that person's life is a joyful thing. But it is to say that they have learned the value of trusting in God in each moment and in that sense of trust they have found a sustaining joy. Such people light up a room. They leave happiness in their wake. They offer comfort in moments of uncertainty. We long to be in their presence because their joy is so contagious. Here's some good news: God is not selfish with the "oil of joy." God's flask is always filled to overflowing. God is waiting to pour out a little in your life today. So if you are a little downcast, feeling defeated, or just a little out of sorts, ask God for a few drops of that oil. Receive the grace extended and find the peace that God offers.

Prayer
Father, may our knowledge of you bring to each of us a lasting joy. Amen.

Day 524 — Psalm 46: When the Earthquakes Come...

> "God is our refuge and strength, always ready to help in times of trouble. So we will not fear when earthquakes come and the mountains crumble into the sea." Psalm 46:1-2 (NLT)

Observation

A very familiar psalm, Psalm 46 speaks about God's deliverance of God's people. The powerful imagery of God as a place of refuge and strength inspired the writing of Martin Luther's reformation-era hymn, "A Mighty Fortress Is Our God." The subscription states that it is to be sung by Alamoth, which is a reference to soprano voices. Clearly the psalmist wants to describe the impenetrable defense that God establishes to protect God's people. In any battle, conflict, and even natural disaster, God provides refuge and strength. Unlike the strong walls that surrounded cities in the Middle East, God's defenses could never become breached or scaled. The psalmist mentions a river in Jerusalem that "gladdens" the city. This may be a reference to Ezekiel 43:1-12 where the prophet describes a river that will open up just below the altar of God, bringing life and healing with its flow. He also speaks of the fact that God is in the city. It is a reminder that God will always be with God's people. God is not an absentee deliverer. The psalm also offers the familiar phrase, "Be still and know that I am God." It is a call to "cease striving," or to "relax," secure in the knowledge that God is always with us and remains our eternal stronghold.

Application

"We will not fear when the earthquakes come and the mountains crumble into the sea." Ever experienced an earthquake? I have only felt the rumble of a minor quake on a couple of occasions, nothing big, mind you, but enough to get my attention. One occurred in my hometown of Rome, Georgia, when I was a kid. I was at the barbershop just off Broad Street with my dad when we noticed our chairs began to shake. It was interesting, but not frightening. But for others around the world who have experienced a major quake, I'm sure the moments are agonizingly slow and tremendously fearful. Imagine the collapse of walls and the upheaval of streets. I'm sure it is terrifying.

Though many of us may not have ever experienced the trauma of a severe earthquake that rattles our windows and destroys our homes, we have experienced a different kind of quake that uproots our lives and destroys the very foundation of our experience. There are earthquakes of illness, death, grief, broken relationships, and financial instability. We have all lived through many of those and know that more may come. So how do we survive? We recognize that God remains our eternal refuge and source of strength and in God alone we place our trust.

Prayer

Father, teach us to fear less and trust more, even in the quakes. Amen.

Day 525 — Psalm 47: Joy in Worship

> "Come, everyone! Clap your hands! Shout to God with joyful praise!"
> Psalm 47:1 (NLT)

Observation
Psalms 47 and 48 are closely connected. Both focus on Divine Kingship. This psalm focuses more on the King and the following psalm will focus more on the city of the King. This psalm describes the grand ascent of the King of Kings to the royal throne. The psalmist is inclusive of all people and nations, suggesting that they all clap their hands and shout to God with the voice of triumph. The clapping of hands and the raised voices were often associated with the crowning and recognition of a king. They are both signs of joyful adoration. Included in this psalm is the title, "Most High God." This title underscores the greatness and transcendence of God over all creation, absolute in power and authority. The psalmist declares that the nations are subdued before God. This speaks of the ultimate and complete victory of God's people "whom He loves." Literally, God has "made His choice in Israel." The rulers of the earth will gather with Abraham's descendants to honor God.

Application
When I hear "Give God a big hand clap!" I wince a little. I don't think our worship of Almighty God has to take on the element of a sideshow where a prompter attempts to stir everyone up into a frenzy. My fear is that often, such leadership in worship is more about creating a false sense of excitement than it is offering authentic worship before God. I grew up in a very traditional worship environment. Our services were punctuated with the great hymns of faith, organ and choral music, the reading of scripture, and solid, Biblical preaching. It had a sense of reverence, contemplation, and very often, the movement of God's Spirit. It also had a sense of excitement that was the natural outflow of participants and leaders all putting their very best efforts into the moment. Obviously, worship trends have changed a great deal over the past few decades. Things are less formal, less traditional, and more casual. Choirs are morphing into praise teams and suits and ties are transforming into skinny jeans and untucked shirts. It's not all bad. In fact, some experiences I have had in contemporary settings have been very moving. Whenever worship is genuine, authentic, and welcoming, surely God is pleased.

When the psalmist invites everyone to clap and shout with joyful praise, I don't think he is being prescriptive, nor manipulative. I think he is inviting all of us to give authentic expression in our praise and worship of God. Sometimes we need the reflective reverence of a quiet sanctuary and sometimes we need the loud shouts of praise. Authenticity is the key.

Prayer
Father, may we offer you the glad adorations of our hearts each time we worship. Amen.

Day 526 — Psalm 48: My Hometown

> "Walk about Zion and go around her; Count her towers; Consider her ramparts; Go through her palaces, That you may tell it to the next generation." Psalm 48:12-13 (NASB)

Observation

This psalm is sometimes referred to as a "Song of Zion" because of its emphasis on Jerusalem, the Holy City of God. Rich with meaning, this psalm was recited by the Levites during the daylight hours of Sabbath during the period of the 2nd Temple (530 B.C.—70 A.D.). Jerusalem was a special city because the presence of God resided in the Temple, in that inner courtroom known as the "Holy of Holies." The psalmist speaks of the beauty of the city, wanting the reader to make the connection that it is the presence of God in the city that brings its beauty. To praise the city is to praise the God who dwells there. In our focus verse, the reader is encouraged to walk about Zion and ponder its structures, fortresses, and splendor. The words probably refer to a worship processional in which pilgrims would, in fact, circle the city in a reflective mood, contemplating not only the greatness of the city, but the greatness of God.

Application

Most of us are not in the habit of walking around the cities in which we live. We tend to get in the car and drive from point A to point B with little or no reflection on the city itself. We see traffic, crowded sidewalks, construction cones, and the occasional dilapidated building. But there is something to be said about walking in the city. Walking allows us to see more than we usually notice, to observe things our minds might have missed, to feel emotion that we seldom give our hearts the space to know. It's been a long time, a very long time, since I walked around my hometown of Rome, Georgia. In fact, this day I can only walk through the streets of memory and imagination to recapture a feel of that city. But if I did walk around a bit, I would pass key landmarks like the old clock tower, my still-standing grade school, Central Primary, the old post office, the Carnegie library, and the sturdy columned-structure of First Baptist. I could walk along Broad Street and maybe eat at the Partridge Restaurant.

But the psalmist is asking for more than a stroll down memory lane. He is challenging us to engage in a "worship processional," one that would require some reflective thinking to consider all the ways that God has blessed a community. We should see churches and schools and civic buildings. We should view the places where people have lived their lives and spent their working years. We should praise the God who has created both the city and the people who dwell within it. Maybe when the weather is nice, you should do a little stroll in your city. Walk about and look at the places where God has been at work.

Prayer

Father, we thank you for our city. May you be present within it as you are present in us. Amen.

Day 527 — Psalm 49: Can't Take It with You

> "They trust in their wealth and boast of great riches. Yet they cannot redeem themselves from death by paying a ransom to God. Redemption does not come so easily, for no one can ever pay enough to live forever and never see the grave." Psalm 49:6-9 (NLT)

Observation
Psalm 49 is a wisdom psalm, which carries the tone of an extended proverb. It calls the wise person to realize that there is ultimately nothing to fear from the oppressing rich people of the land. The rich, just like the common animals of the earth, will share a similar fate and the grave will swallow them both, but the righteous will live forever. The opening verses call all people to listen to the wisdom that the psalmist is prepared to share. He warns against trusting in wealth. Riches can add nothing of lasting value in this life or in the life to come. Certainly riches cannot buy redemption nor salvation. Only God has the power to save. Death becomes a great leveler of sorts. The rich and the poor, the wise and the foolish all share the same fate. Death strips us of all but character and soul. We are wise, therefore, to invest in the things that matter most. The psalm offers an important note of encouragement as it reminds the reader that God will redeem the righteous from the power of the grave (v. 15).

Application
I dropped my smart phone on the pavement and the screen was shattered. I had to decide what to do: replace the screen or replace the whole phone. Because I have money, I could do either. Earlier, on the way to work, I stopped to fill up my car. I swiped my card and paid for the gas, because, again, I have the money to do so. I was planning to go out to lunch with a friend later that day. I was not worried about the cost of the meal, because, again, I have some money. I am not boasting about having great wealth, because I don't. But I do have enough that I don't worry so much about the day-to-day stuff. Sure, I could always use a little more, but haven't I already demonstrated too much reliance and trust in my wealth? We all get caught up in that game. We think that in our wealth, we have security, safety, and a good life. And yet, there are all kinds of storms that can rob us of our money and even of our ability to earn money. It's a fragile thing… this dependency upon wealth. And so the psalmist is right. Our trust, our reliance, and our hope must be placed in something more powerful, more dependable, more reliable, and more eternal. We don't take any of it with us… no wealth, no car, no house, no possession. That which survives the grave is the Spirit of God within us. Knowing God should consume the living of our days. Maybe it matters more what we give away, than what we try to hold.

Prayer
Father, we thank you for our daily bread, but more than that, our eternal life. Amen.

Day 528 — Psalm 50: Pleasing Your Father

> "Make thankfulness your sacrifice to God, and keep the vows you made to the Most High." Psalm 50:14 (NLT)

Observation

Psalm 50 is the first of 12 psalms attributed to Asaph, who was one of the musical leaders appointed by King David. It describes the distinction between the righteous and the wicked. In the psalm, God is portrayed as the great Judge. Out of Zion (Jerusalem), the glory of God radiates across the earth. His words of judgement are interesting. When speaking about the need for righteous acts, God mentions the sacrificial system described in Leviticus, where the meat of bulls and the blood of goats were offered for the sins of the people. The problem seems to be that the people failed to keep a godly perspective on the reasons for offering sacrifices. It was not to do God a favor. God is not hungry and therefore does not require the meat of animals to be sustained. God hungers for righteous behavior by God's people. Rather than their attempt to appease God by offering more and more burnt offerings and sacrifices, God instructs them to offer thankfulness and honest lives. What God truly desires is the allegiance of their hearts. As the psalm closes, God extends the opportunity for the people to repent and find forgiveness. God's desire is never to punish, but to save.

Application

Our focus verse reminds us to glorify God by doing two simple things. First, we are to make "thankfulness" our sacrifice to God. In other words, God finds delight in our genuine gratitude. Whenever we realize our state of "blessedness" and express our joy before God, God is honored. Thankfulness overflows in the life of one whose heart is full of gladness. Appreciation is worth more than the blood of some animal poured out in sacrifice. Giving thanks should be more than the simple spoken words we might offer in a quick prayer. Thankfulness should find practical expression in the deeds of daily life. "Because I am thankful to God, I will… feed the hungry, clothe the naked, heal the hurt, forgive the sinner, etc." We should look for ways to live out our thankfulness.

The second word of instruction is to the promises we make to God. Vows offered to God should never be taken lightly. Just as we expect God to keep all promises made to us, we should honor all the commitments we make before God. Our integrity, consistency, and honesty testify to our devotion to God. Because we reflect God's image, each time our words are true and our promises are kept, we bring God glory. Not only do the vows we make before God matter, so do the day-to-day vows we make to our neighbor.

Prayer

God, remind us that our integrity always indicates the level of our passion for you. Amen.

Day 529 — Psalm 51: Leave Your Bags Behind

> "Hide Your face from my sins and blot out all my iniquities. Create in me a clean heart, O God, And renew a steadfast spirit within me."
> Psalm 51:9-10 (NASB)

Observation

Psalm 51 is connected to one of the most difficult and unfortunate experiences in King David's life. It was written in the aftermath of his affair with Bathsheba. The story is told in 2 Samuel 11-12:15. When confronted by the prophet Nathan, David's immediate response is, "I have sinned against the Lord" (2 Samuel 12:13 NASB). His words reflect deep regret and shame, as well as his desire to be restored in the eyes of God. He calls out for mercy, which is the only appropriate request for a confessing sinner. A call for justice would certainly result in punishment. Mercy and forgiveness are God's gift to the repentant sinner. God's "unfailing love" is an indication of desire to redeem people. Speaking through the agony and guilt over his sin, David asks that God "blot out, wash, and cleanse" his life. He speaks of hyssop, which was used in a ritual act of cleansing described in the Law of Moses (see Leviticus 14:4). David asks to be re-created by the God of all creation. He longs to once again know the joy of a relationship with God, one that is not interrupted by the distance that sin creates.

Application

On April 15, 2010, a volcano erupted in Eyjafjallajokull, Iceland. (And yes, I spelled that correctly!) It spewed volcanic ash across western Europe. Air traffic was interrupted, and 10 million travelers were stranded in the various airports and cities across Europe. I was one of those stranded travelers. I was leading a mission team to Thessalonikki, Greece. Because of a weird set of circumstances, only a portion of our team made it all the way to Greece. Three of us, my son, daughter-in-law, and I, were stranded in Munich for more than a week. There was a mad scramble for hotel space. We finally found a small bed and breakfast in Allershausen, where we stayed for a week. One of the complicating factors for us was that we could not access our luggage. In fact, it made it all the way to Greece! So we were stuck for a week, with only the clothes on our backs and the small provisions we had in our carry-on luggage. But something about that circumstance became quite freeing. We were able to move about, travel, and enjoy ourselves without the worry and headache of wondering if our "stuff" was okay. We were not shackled to our baggage.

How freeing would it be, if you no longer had to carry around the "baggage" of your past mistakes and failures? How much better would your life be if you found complete forgiveness? What if God "re-created" you in way that offers complete absolution?

Prayer

God, may we know the joy of your complete forgiveness and restoration. Amen.

Day 530 — Psalm 52: Where Are You Rooted?

> "But I am like an olive tree, thriving in the house of God. I will always trust in God's unfailing love." Psalm 52:8 (NLT)

Observation

This psalm has an unusual subscription in its title. It reads, "A psalm of David, regarding the time Doeg the Edomite said to Saul, 'David has gone to see Ahimelech.'" The incident is found in 1 Samuel 22:9, 22. Doeg, an official of King Saul, spied on David when he fled to Abimelech, the priest at Nob, for provisions and guidance. This report to the king put David in great danger and distress. (The reader may also recall that out of anger for protecting David, King Saul had all the priests at Nob slain.) The bigger picture painted by this scenario is the eventual fall of the house of Edom at the hands of future King David. The theme therefore of the psalm is a strong judgment of David's enemies. It demonstrates the futility of boastfulness on the part of the wicked. The words of this psalm display a divine judgment on those who practice evil. The "boasting" in evil (v. 1) is the opposite of praising the righteous God. As the psalm concludes, David states that he is like "an olive tree, thriving in the house of God." It is an image of the success that David finds as he is firmly planted in the house of God, trusting in God alone for mercy and strength.

Application

Let's talk about olive trees for a moment. They tend to have a very long lifespan. If you visit the Holy Land and take a stroll on the Mount of Olives, a tour guide may tell you that some of the trees that are growing there may have been growing there as Christ prayed in the garden on the night of his betrayal. Is that even possible? Can a tree live for 2,000 years? Apparently so. In fact, there are some olive trees on Sardinia that date back almost 4,000 years. Contrast that with the Bradford pear trees that some developer thought would look nice in my neighborhood as it was being developed. Almost all of them have split apart and died in the first 15 to 17 years.

So what is David saying as he compares himself to an olive tree, thriving in the house of God? I think he is talking about longevity. David realizes that there is no more fertile ground, no more productive soil, no greater place to be rooted, than in the righteousness of God. Like the mighty olive tree, the person who is rooted in God's righteousness finds success, prosperity, peace, and longevity. So, consider for a moment where your life is planted. Into what type of soil have you placed the roots of your life? There's a lot of unproductive, shifting sand into which many attempt to place themselves. But the wise person roots firmly in the soil of God's Word, deeply watered by the inspiration of God's Spirit.

Prayer

God, may our lives this day be planted firmly in the soil of your grace and guidance. Amen.

Day 531 — Psalm 53: The Foolish Self

> "Only fools say in their hearts, 'There is no God.' They are corrupt, and their actions are evil; not one of them does good!" Psalm 53:1 (NASB)

Observation
Psalm 53 offers only a very slight variation of Psalm 14. The theme and most of the words are the same. As a reminder, the word fool does not refer to mental incompetence, but to moral and spiritual insensitivity. The fool is the person who acts as though God doesn't matter. His actions are corrupt, evil, and foolish. The psalm declares the corruptibility of humankind. No one has pursued God… all are corrupt. So darkened are the minds of the foolish that they "wouldn't even think of praying to God" (v. 4 NLT). The foolish offer no thought of God, no reliance upon God, and certainly no fear of God. And because of their corrupt ways, in the time of final judgement when God will come in power and glory, God will "scatter their bones." But, according to the final refrain, the righteous will shout with joy when God comes from Mount Zion.

Application
I'm amazed these days at how many things are "caught on camera." In the technological age in which we live, many of our daily actions are being recorded on a countless number of cameras that monitor nearly every step of our daily journey. Our driving is monitored on traffic cameras. Our progress in a store is under constant surveillance. Walk the hallways of a school, church or business and every move is recorded. Public parks have cameras. Airports have cameras. Most intersections in every major city have cameras. We must assume that "big brother" is always watching, and yet, many people, either forget for a moment, or just don't care, and so their actions are caught by the camera lens.

It's a little scary to think that someone is always watching. The wise person, who is aware of such surveillance, would hopefully attempt to live more responsibly, with greater accountability. This psalm reminds the reader that "God has looked down from heaven upon the sons of men…" (v. 2 NASB). Do we really believe that? And if we do, then shouldn't it affect our behavior, our thoughts, and our actions? My fear is that we default to practical atheism. We act as though there is no God. We act as though attempting to please God is not a priority nor a pursuit. We live according to our human nature and its continual pull on our lives. We forget that we are called to a higher ethic, a more noble pursuit, and a loftier standard of living. Not to scare you into submission, nor bully you this morning, but just maybe, the threat of God's worldwide vision and scrutiny should register with you and me. It is foolish to think that God doesn't matter, and that our actions bear no consequence. God's watching. Honor God.

Prayer
God, this day may we seek to honor you through action, thought, and deed. Amen.

Day 532   Psalm 54: Longing to be Heard

> "Hear my prayer, O God; Give ear to the words of my mouth."
> Psalm 54:2 (NASB)

Observation

This psalm of David, records both his petition to God and God's answer to his need. The extended title of the psalm gives the specific situation that gave rise to the poem. Twice, the people of Ziph had informed King Saul that David was hiding in their region (1 Samuel 23:19-23). The Ziphites were Israelite residents of Ziph, a city situated in the tribal region of Judah about 25 miles south of Jerusalem. Because they are citizens of the king, they felt obligated to report the presence of David, who was a fugitive at the time. In this psalm, David prays to be rescued. He calls on the name of the Lord, knowing the significance of God's name and of God's ability to provide help. Notice that David did not seek revenge on his enemies but acknowledged that vengeance was only in the hands of the Lord. David's prayer for help is answered by the end of the psalm. He joyfully declares that God has delivered him.

Application

Sometimes we long to be heard. We want our voices to count, our message to be delivered, and our presence to be felt. Think of the marches that have occurred across the country in protest of various situations, decisions, and policies that have recently come to the forefront. The women's movement, the March for our Lives movement, and others are all in response to people wanting their voices to be heard. Even as individuals, we sometimes need our voices to be heard and so we emphatically call out to the people whose attention we seek. Even my youngest granddaughter has learned the lesson that a loud cry can get her grandfather's attention!

I find it interesting in this psalm that King David longs to be heard by God. In fact, he begs God to hear his prayer and to give ear to his words. Obviously, spoken in a time of desperation, David eagerly and forcefully seeks God's attention. We've all had those moments as well. In a time of great distress, or grief, or peril, we have cried out to God, longing to be heard... longing to find some solace to our needs. Perhaps the emotional energy we expend at such a moment is a little "over the top." God is not far away and removed from our situation. God is not asleep and in need of being awakened. In fact, God hears every prayer we offer. God loves every child. God knows every situation of our lives. And so, whenever we call out to God, we can have the confidence that God is listening, and that God will respond. We are already the objects of God's mercy and grace. So plead with God in your prayers if that makes you feel confident, but just know, God is already listening.

Prayer

God, thank you for hearing this prayer and every other prayer we offer. Amen.

Day 533 — Psalm 55: Immediate Access

> "Evening and morning and at noon, I will complain and murmur,
> And He will hear my voice." Psalm 55:17 (NASB)

Observation
A careful reading of this psalm leads the reader to think that David wrote it with a heavy heart. It is written with deep emotion. Like other psalms, this psalm displays David calling out to God. His shock, however, is not that he is in distress again, or that he has a new enemy. His distress lies in the fact that his enemy is a close friend, confidant, and companion. He speaks of the "trembling fear" that has overtaken his life (v. 4). He longs to be at rest. Most troubling, perhaps, is the fact that this friend had once joined him in worship... stood with him in the house of the Lord. As David processes his emotions, he once again declares his trust that God will hear his petition. In the closing verses, David advises anyone who has experienced grief or desolation to "cast your burden upon the Lord and He will sustain you" (v. 22).

Application
We live in an age and culture that demands immediate access. We want to be able to take care of any business, find any information, and contact any individual at any time of the day or night. We demand smartphones that can efficiently and consistently connect us to the internet. We feel impoverished when the signal is poor or if no WIFI hotspot can connect to our devices. We want the ability to pay bills and check our accounts at any hour of the day. We are frustrated when a friend takes more than a minute to "text" a response. We want to search any question that comes to mind as soon as the thought hits us. We are conditioned to demand 24/7 responses to any need that we have.

Though the notion seems terribly modern, God has been providing such a response for centuries. Look again at the words of King David: "Evening and morning and at noon I will complain and murmur, and He will hear my voice." Talk about instant access... how exciting and comforting it is to know that God is there any time we call out, always listening, always present, and always responsive. In the darkest night, or on the loneliest path, or in the deepest need, God awaits our prayer. It has always been that way and will always be that way. We are loved by a God who is always on call, always listening for our cries for help. Take comfort today in the knowledge that help is always as close as your next breath. Evening, morning, and at noon, God will hear your voice.

Prayer
Father God, thank you for your continual watch care and listening ear. Thank you for patiently listening to every need of our hearts, and for the answers you provide amid our doubts and fears. Amen.

Day 534 — Psalm 56: Tears in a Bottle

> "You keep track of all my sorrows. You have collected all my tears in your bottle. You have recorded each one in your book." Psalm 56:8 (NLT)

Observation

According to the subtitle of this psalm, it is a psalm of lament sung to the tune of "A Silent Dove in a Distant Land." That's interesting because it was written by David when he was captured at Gath by the Philistines. He was himself, "as a dove in a distant land." In this psalm and in Psalm 34, David recounts the very devastating experience he suffered at the hands of the Philistines. He had been cut off from Israel and chased by King Saul. He had hoped to find shelter among the Philistines, but they turned on him. His only means of escape came about as he pretended to be insane (1 Samuel 21:10-15). In this psalm, David cries out to God through the overwhelming sense of loss during his time as a fugitive. He affirms, however, his trust in God and in God's ability to save him. This abiding confidence in God is reflected in the words of New Testament writer Paul in Romans 8:31. Our focus verse is expressive of God's continual watch care. David states that God has "collected all of his tears…" He is convinced that God remembers his suffering. Every tear shed evokes heartfelt empathy and compassion from God. The psalm ends with a report of David's deliverance.

Application

Consider for a moment the power of a tear. Tears move the hearts of men and women. They evoke sympathy. They stir others to action. They display the deepest emotions of the heart. They are contagious. It is difficult to see the tears of another and not be moved to join in their sense of grief or pain. When a young child weeps from pain or fear or hunger, are we not stirred to action? Are we not motivated to relieve the pain, calm the fear, or ease the suffering? Tears mirror the soul. They speak volumes. They reveal the deepest longings and the most profound pain. That's why David found comfort in knowing that God had seen his tears. He envisions God as "collecting his tears in a bottle." David knows that his tears are precious to God and that his pain is well remembered.

I find great comfort in the words of this psalm. I am reminded that God is careful to remember our tears, our pains, our deep longings. Our thoughts and emotions are important to the God who crafted us. When we suffer distress, devastation, and grief, it is comforting to know that our tears affect God, who is stirred to action on our behalf. God will relieve the pain, calm the fear, and ease the suffering. In case you fear that no one cares about your struggle, know that every tear is collected by God.

Prayer

Father God, thank you for your deep love and abiding compassion for each of us. Amen.

Day 535   Psalm 57: Hunker Down

> "Be gracious to me, O God, be gracious to me, For my soul takes refuge in You; And in the shadow of Your wings I will take refuge until destruction passes by." Psalm 57:1 (NASB)

Observation

According to the subtitle, this psalm is the first of four psalms to be sung to the hymn tune, "Do Not Destroy!" The others are Psalms 58, 59, and 75. The subtitle also indicates that it is connected to a particular event in David's life… "When David fled from Saul into the cave." Twice in David's life he was found hiding in a cave. Once he hid in the cave of Adullum, memorialized in Psalm 142. This psalm describes the moment he hid in the cave at En-Gedi, where he chose to cut a piece of Saul's robe rather than easily take his life (1 Samuel 24:1-7). In the psalm itself, David pleads for God to be gracious to him. He mentions that he will take shelter in the shadows of God's wings. This image is frequently used in the psalms. It is the image of resting or finding shelter in God like a young bird who finds shelter beneath the wings of a mother bird. David acknowledges that his enemies prowl around like lions looking for prey and yet he is confident that God will deliver him.

Application

David insists that he will take refuge in God, "until destruction passes by." Do you get the image? David will hide, crouch, hunker down until the destruction passes. Like hiding in a storm shelter till the fierce winds abate, David finds comfort and calm in the presence of God's protection.

In the technological age in which we live, we typically get good warning about impending storms. If unstable air moves in, or a thunderstorm heads our way, or a winter snowstorm is going to hit, we usually know about it far enough in advance to seek shelter. In fact, local TV stations will advise the wise person to go to a "safe place" to ride out the storm. It can save lives. I remember a story that my Grandfather Roebuck once told me about a tornado that hit Tuscaloosa several decades ago. The skies grew dark, and the winds started to rise. He heard the tornado, which sounded like a powerful train. He grabbed my grandmother and the two of them rushed into the garage of their home and got down in the seats of their automobile. My grandfather reasoned that the steel frame of the car might be their best protection. There was a lot of damage in their area, but they were safe.

Some storms are not as predictable. Some seemingly arise without much warning… storms of health, finance, security, and relationship. We would do well to take refuge in the shadow of God's wings until the destruction passes. There we will be safe.

Prayer

Father God, thank you for your protection in our storms. Amen.

Day 536 — Psalm 58: Broken Fangs

> "O God, shatter their teeth in their mouth; Break out the fangs of the young lions, O Lord." Psalm 58:6 (NASB)

Observation
The psalm has been categorized by some as an "imprecatory prayer," one that invokes judgment, calamities, or curses upon an enemy or an enemy of God. In this case, David may have been so viciously attacked by a group of evil men (in this case wicked judges), that he prays for the punishment of the wicked. Notice that the words of the psalm are directed towards these wicked men more than they are towards God. These judges act as though they possessed divine power and superior judgment. Their wicked actions and judgments have produced havoc in the land. The effect of their actions and the misuse of power has likened them to "poisonous snakes" who cannot be charmed. He further describes their judgments having powerful teeth which eat the righteous alive. David prays for God to shatter the teeth and destroy their power. He prays for justice.

Application
A friend of mine has an old dog that has lost all his teeth. Sometimes, when the dog feels threatened or feels aggressive, it will try to bite, but to no avail. His bark really is worse that his bite! But it's not always that way. Some of the enemies we face have real teeth, and they can inflict great harm and great destruction. I don't mean actual teeth that sink into flesh, but a meanness and evil, deep within some people that have the potential to harm with words, to ruin reputations, to belittle, to destroy one's self-esteem and outlook. These are the kinds of men that David describes in this psalm. Their words and judgments have devoured the flesh of many, and David prays for relief.

Most of us have "enemies" that seek to destroy our flesh and ruin our lives. Let's face it… there are some mean people in the world and some of them want to direct their energy in your direction. What should you do when they come at you with their teeth flashing and their claws extended? Well, you could try praying an imprecatory prayer… "God destroy them! Give them what they deserve!" That may help you with your emotions, but probably won't do much to facilitate change or usher in a sense of peace. Remember that peacemakers are called the "Sons of God" by Jesus because they act like the Father. Somehow, we have to pray that our swords of aggression and hatred become as a plow that plants seeds of reconciliation and kindness. Maybe the answer is not returned aggression, but compassion. Maybe it's our expression of grace that breaks the fangs of our enemies.

Prayer
Father God, teach us to love, not hate… to build and not destroy. Amen.

Day 537 — Psalm 59: Do We Sing Enough?

> "But as for me, I shall sing of Your strength; Yes, I shall joyfully sing of Your lovingkindness in the morning, For You have been my stronghold and a refuge in the day of my distress." Psalm 59:16 (NASB)

Observation
This psalm gives a word of strong assurance concerning the final judgment of the wicked. The subtitle of the psalm refers to the incident recorded in 1 Samuel 19:9-17, "Then Saul sent messengers to David's house to watch him, in order to put him to death in the morning" (v. 11a NASB). Recall that David escaped Saul's anger with the help of his wife, Michal, who was the daughter of Saul. Her bold actions led to a strained relationship with her father. In the two opening verses, David uses three different words to petition God, seeking God's support and salvation in this moment of peril. He asks for God to "deliver" him, which literally means, "to bring one out." He asks for God to "defend" him, which literally means, "to set out of reach of trouble." He asks for God to "save" him, which literally means, "to give room to… or provide space to breathe." Obviously, David seeks the rescue of the Lord. Also in the psalm, David speaks of the ways in which his enemies lie in wait to ambush him. He compares them to wild, scavenging dogs who roam the city. In a triumphant closure, David speaks of the Lord, "laughing or scoffing" at the wicked because of God's power over them.

Application
Feeling a sense of deliverance and relief from his enemies, David breaks out in song. In our focus verse, David promises to sing of God's strength and to joyfully sing of God's lovingkindness in the morning. The joy he felt in his heart, found expression in the song on his lips. It causes me to wonder… Do we sing enough? Do we sing enough as a way of expressing our thankfulness to God for continual action in our lives? Let's be honest… most of us don't wake up first thing in the morning and sing to the top of our lungs, "Oh what a beautiful morning! Oh, what a beautiful day," from the musical *Oklahoma*. Our spouse might think that we have finally gone over the edge! But certainly we should arise with a sense of gratitude in our hearts that God has kept us through the night and blessed us with the promise of a new day. And sometimes our sense of gratitude should cause us to break forth in song.

Singing is an important, but overlooked, spiritual discipline. Singing causes us to respond to God in ways that prayer, scripture reading, or meditation don't. It lifts the spirit. It fills the lungs with breath. It gladdens the heart. It strengthens the resolve. It joins us to others in the body of Christ as we sing the songs of faith. So give it a try today… somewhere, maybe far away from others, just sing your praises to God. It's a joyful noise in God's ears.

Prayer
Father God, teach us to sing your praises, with joy, gladness, and strength. Amen.

Day 538   Psalm 60: A Helping Hand

> "With God's help we will do mighty things, for he will trample down our foes." Psalm 60:12 (NLT)

Observation

This psalm of David is a lament over defeat in battle. According to the narrative recorded in 2 Samuel 8:3-8, the military campaign, led by David and Joab, failed to defeat the King of Zobah. The psalm expresses the feeling of bewilderment and loss experienced by the Israelites. The defeat sent the people reeling. They could not understand how God could abandon them to their enemies. An interesting aspect of the psalm is that God's voice is interjected into the poem. In verses 6 through 8, God speaks, affirming that God is in charge and that God will bring about ultimate victory. In his prayer, David cries out to God, knowing that "all human help" (v. 11 NLT) is of no value. David knows that unless God directs his path and even the steps of his armies, that all is in vain. He declares in the final refrain, "With God's help we will do mighty things."

Application

This past summer, a neighbor called late one night in desperate need of help. Water was dripping from the ceiling of an upstairs hallway. When I climbed into the attic, I quickly discovered the root of the problem. The pipe leading from her air conditioner's drain pan had become stopped up. To solve the problem, I had to take a flashlight and a shovel and dig out all the debris from the exterior end of the drainpipe. It had been clogged with too much dirt and mulch. As soon as I cleared away the debris, the water flowed easily, and the problem was solved. I tell that story, not to boast in my knowledge of air conditioning systems… I know very little about such things. But I tell the story to describe the way in which a helping hand can help a person through a crisis.

We all need a little help from time to time. Ever need someone to "jump off" your car's battery? Ever need a neighbor to hold a beam while you nail it into place? Ever need a little advice when making a big decision? Rarely do we triumph when we try to take on the challenges of life all alone. We need help. And as David discovered, our best help is in the Lord. Life's complexities are far too complicated for us to figure them out on our own. But with God's help, "we will do mighty things." Doesn't it make sense that if we long to find success in this life, that we should join our hearts, our lives, and our minds to the one who is greater than all our needs? You don't need to face life all alone. You have a heavenly Father who waits to help you in any moment of crisis and at any point of decision.

Prayer

Father God, thank you for coming to our aid each and every time we call on you. Amen.

Day 539 — Psalm 61: Safely Out of Reach

> "From the ends of the earth, I cry to you for help when my heart is overwhelmed. Lead me to the towering rock of safety, for you are my safe refuge, a fortress where my enemies cannot reach me."
> Psalm 61:2-3 (NASB)

Observation
This is another psalm of David that reflects elements of both lament and trust. From some distant place, David cries out to God, pleading for his prayer to be heard. David could be in a geographic location, far removed from Jerusalem, or he could be speaking from a place defined by spirit and emotion where he feels distanced from God. With a troubled heart he makes his prayer to God, confident that God will hear and rescue. He asks to be led to God's "towering rock of safety," that place high above the reach of his enemies, where he will find protection and security. He then pledges to abide in the presence of God forever. He shows a strong determination to center his life in the protecting grace and mercy of God. He closes the psalm with a note of triumph. He is confident that God has heard his prayers and will prolong his life.

Application
Ever long to be out of the reach of your enemies? Several years ago, I led a mission team to the Dominican Republic. The small dorm where we slept was an open-air structure. It had walls and a roof, along with bunk beds, but much of the structure had openings at the top of the walls to allow a breeze to cool the room. With no screens in place, we were susceptible to insects, mosquitos, and a whole host of creepy-crawly things. In fact, the day we arrived to put our stuff away, we had to chase three tarantulas out! We had been prepped before the trip to take along some mosquito netting. Once we made our beds, we carefully hung the nets and tucked them in and around our bedding. I'm glad to report that they did the trick! None of us experienced any kind of problems with bugs or spiders during the week. The nets provided us with a place of shelter where our "enemies" couldn't reach us.

What enemies are haunting you this morning? What soldiers are attacking your peace of mind and calm of spirit? What are the worries? The pressures? The concerns? Maybe you need to run to the "towering rock of safety" where your enemies cannot reach you. I'm talking, of course, about placing your life, with all its fears, anxieties, and enemies, into the safe arms of your Father. God longs to fiercely defend you against all that robs you of peace. He longs to offer forgiveness, grace, peace, assurance… Your role is to cry out to God knowing that God hears your pleas and will quickly come to your aid.

Prayer
Father God, thank you for protection and vigilant watch care. Amen.

Day 540 — Psalm 62: The Value of Silence

> "My soul waits in silence for God only; From Him is my salvation."
> Psalm 62:1 (NASB)

Observation
In this psalm, David expresses his silent confidence in the victory of God over all his enemies. He acknowledges that salvation is found only in God. As a side note, the subtitle of this psalm mentions that its public performance in worship is to be directed by Jeduthun. He is one of the directors of the choirs used in Temple worship. Throughout this psalm, David affirms that his complete dependence will be upon God who is his rock and refuge. He reminds those who attack him that they will soon be judged. His enemies are as a "leaning wall or tottering fence" that will soon fall (v. 3). (This interpretation is most clearly stated in the NKJV.) David goes further to instruct the righteous to put their trust and reliance upon God. One additional aspect to explore is the interesting wording of verse 11 in which David states, "God has spoken once, twice I have heard this." This is a conventional aspect of wisdom literature to use a number and then raise it by one. David had heard from God once, and now twice he has heard the same message. This simply means that David has heard the message with certainty.

Application
There is something to be said for waiting in silence to hear from God. In one of the undergraduate classes that I teach here at Belmont University, I instruct my students to sit in complete silence with eyes closed for two minutes. It seems excruciatingly long for these students. At the end of the two minutes, I ask the students to tell me what they hear during those two minutes of silence. They report hearing the ticking classroom clock, the buzzing florescent lights, the rush of wind from the air-conditioning unit, or the sound of someone walking in the hall. Some even hear birds chirping outside of the classroom window. I make the point that all these sounds swirl around us every time we meet for class. The reason we never hear them is because we are never silent enough to allow the sounds to register in our minds. The sounds are "drowned out" by the noises of everyday living. The same thing happens in our faith experience. My belief is that God speaks to us all the time, in many ways, but seldom are we silent enough to hear God's voice. We let the sounds of our busy lives drown out the still, small voice of God's Spirit. King David is on to something when he suggests letting his soul wait in silence for God to speak. When was the last time that you devoted a few minutes of silence before God as an act of worship? Today, find a favorite verse and read it a couple of times. Let the message resonate for a while. And then sit in silence inviting God to speak into that moment. You may be surprised by what you hear.

Prayer
Father God, give us moments of silent discovery. Amen.

Day 541 — Psalm 63: The Wee Hours

> "When I remember You on my bed, I meditate on You in the night watches." Psalm 63:6 (NASB)

Observation
This psalm is attributed to David while he is "in the wilderness of Judah." There is a portion of the subtitle that probably refers to the period recorded in 1 Samuel 22-24 when David is fleeing from King Saul. It is apparent that David is traveling in the desert wasteland, far away and removed from the Temple and the presence of the Lord. He obviously feels the distance saying that his soul thirsts for the Lord in a dry and thirsty land. Later in the psalm, he speaks of "praising" the Lord. Praise was a vocal and public act. He also mentions lifting his hands before the Lord. To "lift one's hands" was an expression of dependency and an acknowledgment of God's power, wonder, and majesty. Our focus verse indicates that David meditates on God while on his bed, during the watches of the night. (There were three watches each night.) This indicates that perhaps David is unable to sleep, perhaps worried about his life and his desperate run from Saul. But while he is awake during the night, he uses the moment for an occasion to worship. He fills his mind with the knowledge of God. This psalm ends on a triumphant note... David proclaims that God will uphold him with in God's right hand, the same image of power with which God delivered the Israelites out of the hands of the Egyptians.

Application
Admittedly, it doesn't happen too often, but occasionally I experience one of those nights when sleep is fleeting and no matter how hard I tell myself to go back to sleep, it doesn't seem to work. I'm not alone. We have all had those nights when we lay awake for hours watching the hands on the clock slowly move around the dial. Sometimes we reach for the remote and watch a little TV until we are drowsy. Or maybe we reach for a book, hoping that reading will make us sleepy. We count sheep in our minds or focus on taking deep, steady breaths hoping we drop off to sleep again. What if you took the interruption of a sleepless night and turned it into an opportunity for worship? I decided long ago, that if the Lord awakens me during the night, then someone I know must need my prayerful support. I think about the life situations of people I know and love and use the moments of quietness to carefully offer my prayers to God. I find a peace in doing so. I find a moment of intimacy with God that is usually hard to discover in the hurried pattern of my usual praying. I hope that you get a good night's sleep. I hope that the pressures of the day don't invade your night. But in case they do, you might want to pray.

Prayer
Father God, in our restless nights, may we find a gentle peace. Amen.

Day 542　　　　　　　　　　　　　　　　Psalm 64: Consequences

> "But God will shoot at them with an arrow; Suddenly they will be wounded." Psalm 64:7 (NASB)

Observation
This psalm of David is a wisdom psalm for in it, the ways of the righteous and the wicked are contrasted along with their destinies. In the opening verse David asks God to hear his voice as he, "complains, muses, or meditates." (The word used is dependent upon the various translations read.) In effect, David is asking God to listen as he gives meaningful contemplation about the plots of the wicked who seek to destroy him. The arrogance of the wicked as they scheme against the righteous is a continuing theme in the psalms. The wicked don't seem to care that God will see their actions and will repay them accordingly. By trusting in God, the righteous can rest secure in God's sovereign will for their lives. Concern about the future can be set aside because God has good plans for their lives.

Application
We understand the concept of crime and punishment. We, in fact, rejoice at the thought of justice… that the righteous will be rewarded and the wicked will fail. Even though we understand from a New Testament ethic that revenge and justice are not ours to enact, we at least rejoice in knowing that the ways of the wicked are seen by God and there will be consequences to pay for those whose sins are not erased through the grace of Jesus Christ. In this context, David has just spoken about the wicked and how they shoot their arrows of bitter words at the righteous. He turns the phrase to suggest that God will turn their wickedness upon themselves and they will be wounded by their own schemes.

For most of us there is a hypocrisy in our lust for justice. We want the evildoers to "get what's coming to them." We just don't want to get the punishment we deserve for our sinfulness. And so, is it right to wish for justice but exempt ourselves from it? We are challenged to be merciful as God is merciful to us. Does that mean that crime shouldn't be punished? Can we let those who break the law go free? I think the problem for us lies in how we view those who do wrong. We connect the person with the crime and thus label them as being evil, wicked, or bad. Would it not be better to see the good in all people while acknowledging that sometimes the sinful nature in each of us wins out causing us to do wrong? Take the woman caught in adultery in John 8. She had clearly broken both the law of God and the morality of her religion. And yet Jesus separated her from her sin. He saw worth and value while challenging her to sin no more. Instead of a bloodthirsty lust for punishment, let us pray fervently that the light of God within each of us, will win out over the dark.

Prayer
Father God, forgive us our sins and provide us with a lens of grace. Amen.

Day 543 — Psalm 65: There Is a Fountain...

> "Though we are overwhelmed by our sins, you forgive them all. What joy for those you choose to bring near, those who live in your holy courts. What festivities await us inside your holy Temple." Psalm 65:3-4 (NLT)

Observation

This psalm of David is a song of praise to God for God's abundant favor to man and to the earth. Written with great imagery, this song describes the lush beauty and abundant growth that covers the earth. David describes how the meadows are clothed with sheep and the valleys are covered with grain. All shout the joyful praises of God. David reminds the reader that every good rain and full harvest is a blessing from God showing delight in creation. Every time it rains, the event should be seen as the gracious visitation of God. In our focus verses, David is describing how God's favor rests on man, demonstrated by God's willingness to hear the prayers of the faithful and forgive the sins that have been committed. I also like the phrase, "what festivities await us inside your holy Temple." I think that sometimes we get so caught up in the day-to-day survival of this life that we fail to look forward to the joyous day when we are gathered in God's forever Kingdom. What festivities await us in that place!

Application

Great Bible truths are contained in these verses. The first is the acknowledgement of our sins. Indeed we are "overwhelmed" by how willingly and easily we allow ourselves to live disobedient lives. Sin is a very real problem... always has been and always will be. Is it not amazing how we can commit a sin, feel great remorse about having done so, beg God to forgive us, only to get up and commit the same sin the next day, and then the next? We really are overwhelmed sometimes. Sin lures us, tempts us, overpowers us, and ruins us, and we seem helpless against its constant onslaught. But notice the second truth contained in this verse... the forgiveness of our sins. David writes, "though we are overwhelmed by our sins, you forgive them all." At times it is hard for us to even fathom the depths of God's grace. The constant refrain of hope that threads its way throughout scripture is the promise that God will forgive our sins. It is as we confess our sins, pouring out our hearts before God, that we find ourselves forgiven, cleansed, and made new. Most of us would do well this morning to start fresh with God. In the quiet moments that bring calm and rest before the hectic pace of the day starts to spin out of control, why not take a few moments to confess the sins of yesterday, asking God to forgive you and to fortify your resolve to live better this day? Be specific. Be humble. Be cleansed. After all, there are some great "festivities" awaiting us in God's holy presence... why would we choose to let our unconfessed sins separate us from that moment?

Prayer

Father God, as unworthy recipients of grace, accept our gratitude this day. Amen.

Day 544 — Psalm 66: Keeping Your Word with God

> "I shall come into Your house with burnt offerings; I shall pay You my vows, which my lips uttered and my mouth spoke when I was in distress."
> Psalm 66:13-14 (NASB)

Observation

This psalm of David offers words of praise to God for God's awesome works. David stresses some of the important elements of Biblical worship, offering both "descriptive" praise and "declarative" praise. Descriptive praise occurs when the worshipper praises God for who God is and for what God does. Declarative praise occurs when the worshipper praises God for a specific answer to a prayer when the worshipper can declare his/her praise for a clearly apparent work of God. This psalm opens with a call for all the people of earth to join in the praise of the living God. All the earth should sing praises to God because God is pleased by music that uplifts God's name. Our focus verses center around an act of worship by David. David had once called out to God for deliverance in a time of peril. He promises that he will make good on the vows he has spoken. He will offer sacrifices out of a sense of gratitude for what God has done.

Application

Most of us have made a few promises to God somewhere along our life journey. Maybe we called upon God in a desperate moment when an illness was ravaging the life of a loved one. Maybe we cried out to God during a relationship upheaval. Perhaps we called upon God when we experienced job loss or financial stress. When we really want the attention of God, or need the mercy God can provide, we sometimes make a vow before God that goes something like this... "God if you will deliver me, save me from this moment, or solve this crisis, I will praise your name, I will give my income, I will attend church each week for the next 60 years!" Such a vow or promise is always a foolish endeavor because we are already the objects of God's grace and mercy. God wills what is best for us. God doesn't withhold God's blessings until we say the right words or make the correct promise. Even in this moment, God loves you with intensity and is working in the situations of your life to bring you hope, calm, and assurance. You don't have to talk God into being on your side. But here's the point I want to make this morning... if we make vows or commitments to God, whether out of gratitude or distress, let's at least try to keep them. In other words, if we have pledged greater fidelity to God's will, or promised faithfulness to worship, or made a commitment to serve the Kingdom in a greater way, then let's honor our commitment. One of the ways we express our gratitude to God for abundant mercy and grace is by our willingness to follow-through on the promises that we have made.

Prayer

Father God, may we be honest and faithful to the promises we make to you. Amen.

Day 545 — Psalm 67: The Smile of God

> "God be gracious to us and bless us, and cause His face to shine upon us—"
> Psalm 67:1 (NASB)

Observation
Psalm 67 is a psalm of praise written by David admonishing all nations to join with Israel in praising the God of all creation. The words translated in our focus verse as, "to shine upon us," are sometimes translated with the words, "to smile upon us." The Hebrew phraseology literally means, "to become bright." The psalmist is calling on God to smile on God's people. From the beginning, God has had a desire to bless all the nations of the world. Remember the Abrahamic covenant offered in Genesis 12:3? "And I will bless those who bless you, and the one who curses you I will curse. And in you all the families of the earth will be blessed" (NASB). God's desire has also been that the nations of the world would praise God as creator and provider. So in this psalm, David is reminding all the nations of the world of God's greatness, mercy, and care for all of creation. He even speaks of the earth "yielding her increase," as God continues to pour out blessings.

Application
Have you ever noticed the power of a smile? A smile has a way of communicating joy, blessing, or well-wishes. Even the smile of a stranger while walking down a crowded sidewalk can lift the spirit or brighten the day. What a joy it is when arriving home at the end of the day to see the face of a child or grandchild light up with joy as they flash a broad smile in your direction. Smiles are contagious. They give the gift of encouragement and calm to the recipient. Even the small, casual smile that you offer someone today can lighten the mood and gladden the heart of the one who receives it.

So how important is it for us to receive God's smile? In this psalm, David pleads for God to be gracious and to smile upon us. What an image that conveys… to think that Almighty God grins broadly in excitement to be in our presence. Most of us labor under enough guilt, shame, and remorse that we are like Adam and Eve in the midst of their sin who wanted to hide from the presence of God. And yet God seeks us out and delights in us. Rather than approach us with a furrowed brow and an angry spirit, God reaches out to us like a proud Father. God smiles at us and welcomes us. Talk about a contagious smile… shouldn't God's love for us overwhelm us? Transform us? Encourage us? Maybe even make us smile? I wonder what a simple smile on your face could mean to someone who is struggling today. Maybe becoming the presence of Christ in our world is as simple as conveying the joy and encouragement that a smile can bring.

Prayer
Father God, smile upon us and help us to smile upon others. Amen.

Day 546 — Psalm 68: The One Who Carries Our Burdens

> "Blessed be the Lord, who daily bears our burden, The God who is our salvation." Psalm 68:19 (NASB)

Observation
This psalm of David is a song that speaks of the great power of the glory of God. Parts of it are loosely based on the Song of Deborah contained in Judges 5. A very clear note is sounded in this song, indicating that the joy of the righteous will be great when there is an end to evil. David calls upon God to arise and bring God's judgment. In verse 4, he describes God as "riding on the clouds." In the culture of the day, the pagan deity named Baal was thought to be the god of the storm. Baal was known as the rider of the clouds. Here David strips the title from the pagan god and assigns it to the one true God who brings rain, and abundance to the land on which it falls. David also speaks of God's compassion, meeting the needs of the helpless by being as a father to the fatherless and a defender of widows (v. 5). David goes further to speak about the destruction of the enemy and calls once again, for the righteous to ascribe strength and honor to God. In our focus verse, he calls for God to be blessed as the one who daily bears our burdens.

Application
I have a friend who owns a decades-old pick-up truck. It's not pretty. It's not in good shape. It's not comfortable. But it is functional. And to his credit, he is generous to lend it out to dozens of us who occasionally need to "haul" something from one place to another. Personally, I have used it to carry items to the city dump, move furniture, and pick up a load of mulch. It's a modern-day version of a "beast of burden." It willfully carries the heavy loads that are forced upon it.

Though we don't choose to be, most of us are "beasts of burden." We carry around a lot of baggage. We strap on a load of remorse and guilt. We carry a lot of worry. We pack on a lot of fear. We carry the shame of our mistakes. And even though such things have no actual weight behind them, it doesn't take long for such burdens to weaken us both mentally and physically. Ever notice the slumped shoulders of a friend who is beaten down by life? It doesn't have to be that way. There is someone willing to carry all the baggage, one whom David calls the Lord who "daily bears our burdens." Most of us just call him our Savior. Remember his words? "Come to me, all you who are weary and burdened, and I will give you rest. Take my yoke upon you and learn from me, for I am gentle and humble in heart, and you will find rest for your souls. For my yoke is easy and my burden is light" (Matthew 11:28-30 NIV). So why are your carrying all that stuff when the Lord is waiting to relieve you?

Prayer
Father God, teach us to take our fears, our worries, and our pain to your throne. Amen.

Day 547 — Psalm 69: The Long Wait

> "I am weary with my crying; my throat is parched; My eyes fail while I wait for my God." Psalm 69:3 (NASB)

Observation
This psalm is a cry of distress from David as he offers a very urgent plea for help. He shares the image of drowning in muck from his extreme mental anguish. He is facing a difficult, unprovoked attack from his enemies who assault him with caustic words and rumors. He is absolutely weary from praying and crying before the Lord. Even his tears have given his enemies a reason to make fun of him. He writes that the elders of the various cities have looked upon him with disdain. In verse 29 he writes that he is, "poor and sorrowful." His spirit is broken. He has a sense of worthlessness caused by the assaults of the wicked. Yet through the midst of his sadness, he ends the psalm with a note of praise, confident that God will save him from his despair.

Application
David was experiencing a long wait on the Lord. He had prayed and cried and worried and languished, and then he prayed and cried and worried and languished some more. He says of his suffering, "I am weary with crying; my throat is parched: my eyes fail while I wait for God." Ever experienced a moment like that? A moment that seemingly lasts forever in which you pour out your heart before God in the midst a great struggle only to wait with frustration for God to act? You pray and you pray and you pray until you are tired of praying. And then you wait... you wait for a response, a reprieve, an answer that is so slow to come. I am not about to explain all the mysteries of God and the intricacies of prayer. I can't tell you why some prayers are answered almost as quickly as they leave our lips, while other prayers take decades to find resolution. I am confident of this however... that God hears every prayer that we make as soon as we make them. The delay on God's response has nothing to do with the fervency of our prayers, or the attitude with which we pray, or even the amount of love that God has for us. It has everything to do with God's unfolding plan for our lives and for the lives of others. There is a huge tapestry being woven that tells the story of God's redemptive work. The fabric of our lives is carefully stitched into that greater narrative. Remember that God "causes all things to work together for good to those who love God, to those who are called according to *His* purpose" (Romans 8:28 NASB). The long wait you experience... the long delay over which you agonize, is the intricate timing of God, who teaches us lessons with every event and who seeks to redeem every life possible. So the next time you have to wait on God, be thankful that God's timing is both perfect and redemptive, in your life and in others.

Prayer
Father God, may we pray with confidence and wait with patience. Amen.

Day 548　　　　　　　　　　　　　Psalm 70: Crisis Intervention

> "Please, God, rescue me! Come quickly, Lord, and help me… You are my helper and my savior; O Lord, do not delay." Psalm 70:1 & 5 (NLT)

Observation
This short psalm seems to be more of an introduction to Psalms 71 and 72. It does seem to link the petitions made in Psalm 69 with the two that follow this psalm. Nevertheless, Psalm 70 is another plea from David asking God to come to his aid. Obviously written at a time of great peril when David felt threatened by his enemies, he cries out to God in whom are his help and strength. It is interesting to note that David did not rely upon his physical strength, his powerful position, nor his personality to bring his deliverance. His strength of spirit and character were always drawn from his relationship with God. Notice in both the beginning and closing verses, David's urgent plea for God's intervention.

Application
Ever echo words like these of David in your own life? "Please, God rescue me! Do not delay!" The truth is that most of us have experienced those moments of desperation in which we have sought the help of God. The moment of crisis could have been one of financial woe, or a broken relationship, or even some awkward spot in which our poor decisions had placed us. We reach a moment of distress and so we cry out to God to "rescue us." We get to those moments when we realize that life is sometimes bigger than our ability to control it and so we seek divine intervention. And the good news is that even when we are the victims of our own poor choices, God brings us wisdom, grace, and peace of mind. But here's my point… it is not simply in the moments of crisis that we should seek God's heart. Imagine a friend who only comes to you at a point of desperation. Shouldn't relationships be built on more than crisis intervention? Shouldn't relationships have more of a give and take? More of a daily interaction and sharing of life?

In my ministry I have come to know a homeless man who struggles with alcoholism. His problems force him to make poor decisions that usually bring him to my door needing a little financial help. Duty compels me to help when I can, but I long for a better life for my friend. I wish that our relationship had more depth than it does desperation. I think it's the same with God. Yes, God is ready, willing, and able to help us in our times of need, but surely God craves a greater depth of relationship. Surely God would welcome daily interaction with us in which we would seek to know God's heart and experience the life that God longs to give us. Yes… call on God for the occasional rescue, but also call on God for the daily relationship.

Prayer
Father God, may we pray with confidence and wait with patience. Amen.

Day 549   Psalm 71: The Long Haul

> "Yes, you have been with me from birth; from my mother's womb you have cared for me. No wonder I am always praising you!" Psalm 71:6 (NLT)

Observation
In this psalm, David alternates between expressions of deep need and resolute trust in God. He describes himself as an old man who has trusted God for his entire life. Amid an old-age crisis, David is asking that he not be put to shame. His fear is that if he falters in his old age, that his enemies will ridicule both him and his God. However, David knows that trusting in God is never foolish. He prays that God will once again deliver him, or literally, "cause him to escape." The work of God in his life is described by David as being a "wonder," similar in glory to the great miracles of God. In this psalm, David declares that he will praise God with both lute (lyre) and lips. With his skills and with his words, David will offer praise to God. In the final verses of the psalm, David declares that it will be his enemies who will experience shame and not himself because of God's intervention in his life.

Application
My parents once owned a black and white cat named Pepper... or maybe Pepper owned them. For more than 20 years she was a part of their lives. At first, my dad wasn't really a cat person. Mom loved cats and dad tolerated them. But he soon shared in the experience of "cat love." Pepper came into their world as a kitten. She grew to become a beautiful cat and loyal companion. Once she did battle with a car and lived to tell about it. She had to undergo surgery and a long convalescence. But she made it and lived a very long life. On the day the decision had to be made to let her go... my dad cried all alone in his car when he got the news. It happens, right? We claim people, pets, and possessions for the long haul.

    Notice that David declares in our focus verse that God has been with him since birth. For all his life, David knew the love, nurture, and guidance of God. He had walked with God... prayed to God... cried out to God... sought the favor of God. And what he discovered at the end of his long life, was that God had always been with him. Hopefully that same discovery comes to all of us. God is in it for the long haul. When God creates us and chooses to bring us into family, it's a permanent relationship... set in in stone. God is a fan of us all. God cheers for us. God encourages us. God protects us. God loves us. From the moment we are formed in our mother's womb until God welcomes us into heaven, we are God's. We are a prized possession... a special child... a beloved son or daughter who is never far from God's heart. So whether you are living in the exciting days of youth or finding more grey hairs on your head each morning, just know that God is in it for the long haul.

Prayer
Father God, thank you for your constant devotion to us for all of our lives. Amen.

Day 550 — Psalm 72: Compassion for the Least of These

> "For he will deliver the needy when he cries for help, The afflicted also, and him who has no helper. He will have compassion on the poor and needy, And the lives of the needy he will save. He will rescue their life from oppression and violence, And their blood will be precious in his sight."
> Psalm 72:12-14 (NASB)

Observation

Psalm 72 is an interesting psalm for several reasons. First, it is the last psalm included in what is now referred to as Book 2 of the Psalms. According to the final verse, this is the last of the psalms of David, although according to the subtitle, it is a psalm of Solomon, one of two that he contributed. It is a royal psalm probably written by Solomon in praise of his father, David. It is also likely that this psalm marked the final psalm in an early collection of psalms. It is apparent that Solomon arranged the psalms of his father in their present order and added this final word of tribute to his father. In the psalm itself, Solomon calls for good leadership over Israel under God's blessing. The image of the psalm describes the future reign of God's mighty King over all the earth. Geographic references in the psalm had significance to the people of Israel. The mention of the "river" is likely a reference to the Euphrates River, where the Garden of Eden was to have been located. By suggesting that the reign of the King was from the river to the ends of the earth implied that all of earth was under the King's domain. The references to Tarshish and Sheba represented the most distant places known to Israel... places well beyond the imagination of Solomon. Clearly, Solomon wants to affirm that the name of the future Great King (Messianic description of Jesus) would be regarded as the greatest King of the universe.

Application

In his description of the Great King, Solomon suggests that the poor, needy, and afflicted will certainly gain the attention of the King. He will rescue them from oppression and violence. I am reminded this morning of what it was like to grow up in a Southern Baptist Church. I was a Royal Ambassador. That was the name given to a missions-awareness organization for boys. Even now I can recite the Royal Ambassador pledge and quote the motto drawn from a key verse undergirding that organization. It was 2 Corinthians 5:20a, "Therefore, we are ambassadors for Christ" (NASB). It makes sense to me that if, as believers, we represent the Great King, then His interests must become our interests. His priorities must become our priorities. And so we are called to champion the cause of the poor and needy. We cannot ignore their plight nor fail to share of our resources. It is as we care for the marginalized, the afflicted, and those who lack access, that we find ourselves representing our King.

Prayer

Father God, give us a faith that moves beyond piety to responsible action. Amen.

Day 551 — Psalm 73: The Green-Eyed Monster

> "But as for me, my feet came close to stumbling, My steps had almost slipped. For I was envious of the arrogant as I saw the prosperity of the wicked." Psalm 73:2-3 (NASB)

Observation
This psalm marks the beginning of the collection of psalms known as Book 3. Psalms 73-89 are included in this section; the primary focus being, "The importance and obligation of holiness." In this psalm of Asaph, the ways of the wicked and the ways of the righteous are contrasted. There is a very honest look at the psalmist's struggle with envy, doubt, and faith. Through his struggle, he learns, once again, the lesson of trusting in God. His dilemma is knowing that God is good to Israel but wondering about the success and wealth of the wicked. They seem to have no trouble. They are prideful and boastful of their accomplishments. They are apathetic towards God and yet they seem to prosper. According to verse 17, he has a moment of enlightenment while in the Temple. He remembers that their wealth will have no value in the next life. They are just a step away from disaster. All they possess will vanish in a moment. The psalmist then reflects a spirit of humility as he confesses his own foolish thinking and behavior about the wicked who prosper. He realizes that the righteous will have the privilege of living with God forever and the wicked will not.

Application
This question of "Why do the wicked prosper?" has been around for a very long time. We have pondered it. We are dumbfounded at times in our attempt to explain why bad things happen to good people and seemingly good things happen to the bad. Ever been tempted to just ask, "Why try to walk the straight and narrow path? Where does it get you anyway?" (Spoken like a true cynic.) Here's where it gets you… walking the straight and narrow path puts you in a pursuit of godliness that the world can't take from you. By being a person of distinct and active faith, not only do you influence the world around you in a positive way, but you also draw nearer to God. We live our lives piously, not because it makes God love us more than, but because it helps others see the goodness in God's heart. Because we are human, we sometimes long for and maybe even lust after the things the prosperous-wicked possess. We forget that our pursuit is about an eternal Kingdom and not the quickly passing decades we spend in this life. Maybe, like Asaph, we need to go to the Temple for a little attitude adjustment. Let's confess our foolish envy and shortsightedness. Rather than envy the wicked in their prosperity, let's mourn their short-sightedness.

Prayer
Father God, may our piety exceed our envy, and our faith exceed our jealousy. Amen.

Day 552 — Psalm 74: I've Got Your Sign

> "Turn Your footsteps toward the perpetual ruins; The enemy has damaged everything within the sanctuary. Your adversaries have roared in the midst of Your meeting place; They have set up their own standards for signs."
> Psalm 74:3-4 (NASB)

Observation

This is one of the 12 psalms written by Asaph. In it he expresses a desperate plea for relief from those who are oppressing the people and land of Israel. Perhaps written in the context of the Babylonian invasion (587 B.C.), the psalmist describes the devastation of Jerusalem and, even more jarring, the destruction of the Temple. The plea is that God's chosen people be remembered during great upheaval. He appeals to God's special connection to Israel by using such words as, "the sheep of Your pasture, Your congregation, Your tribe of inheritance." In verse 3, he begs God to walk in the perpetual ruins. He is calling on God to get up and walk around to see what is happening to the city. He then reminds God of the mighty acts of power during creation when the dark forces that ruled the universe were subdued and the seas and serpents were overpowered. The psalmist is hoping that God will once again remember God's people and defeat the enemies of Israel.

Application

In two separate places within this psalm, Asaph talks about "signs." He is describing actual banners, or placards that were once visible in and around the Temple. Our focus verse mentions that the enemies had put up their own signs and ripped down the banners that had once been placed throughout the city. Like gang graffiti that is sprayed on the walls of public places declaring turf and territory, the signs of the oppressors declared a new "ownership" of the city and its inhabitants.

I live in a portion of middle Tennessee that is experiencing rapid growth. It seems like every month a new construction project begins along the major roadways of our town. First, there is the evidence of new construction as excavators start removing dirt and debris. Next comes the steel framework. And then finally, the walls are built and the parking lot is poured. At first, you have to guess at what the new business will be. But somewhere along the process, a sign goes up... telling all who pass by that this site is the future home of a certain business. Recently a new building was well underway before I could tell what it would become. I was hoping for a fast-food restaurant, but it was a new dental office. Signs are important. They tell the story. They reveal the name. They proclaim ownership. Imagine if you were to carry around a sign today, describing your identity. Would people know to whom you belong?

Prayer

God, may others clearly see from our words and deeds that we belong to you. Amen.

Day 553 — Psalm 75: It's Time to Praise Talk

> "But as for me, I will declare it forever; I will sing praises to the God of Jacob." Psalm 75:9 (NASB)

Observation
This psalm of Asaph has been described as a "grand psalm of praise." It includes a lively interchange between the people, the psalmist, and the Lord. It is one of only four psalms in which the Lord speaks. (The others are 12, 87, and 91.) It begins with a word of public praise and thanksgiving offered by the people. There is a sense of awe knowing that God is ready to intervene on the part of God's people. There is also a sense of God's sovereignty as God speaks of choosing "the proper time" to judge the earth. God also reminds the people that even when the world seems to be falling apart around them, they are not abandoned and God has not relinquished authority. The psalmist offers a word of warning to the wicked, reminding them not to misinterpret God's delay thinking there will be no judgment. God is indeed the judge and God will judge the wicked when the time is right.

Application
In our focus verse, the psalmist declares that he will forever praise God. I wonder if most of us spend enough time praising God. When given the opportunity to speak in some public forum, maybe a worship service or when we share a devotional thought with a small group, most of us are pretty good at having a few good words of praise for what God has done in our lives. When given the opportunity, we offer our praises. But do we create opportunities to declare God's praises? I'm not talking about asking a pastor or worship leader to give you a spot on the program. I am talking about learning to praise God and tell of God's blessings in everyday conversations. Praising God for blessings and declaring God's glory should crop up in our daily dialogues. We should see every conversation as an opportunity to talk about faith and declare God's praises. Many of the people who need to hear it will never show up in our churches on Sunday or in our early morning Bible studies. They do show up in the hallway at work, the aisle of the grocery store, or the waiting room at the doctor's office. It is in those conversations—those everyday life-sharing conversations—that we should proclaim what God has done. Our spoken, first-hand testimony creates an atmosphere where the Gospel can start its transformation of someone else's life. Chances are you will have many conversations before this day is done. Will any of them be flavored with a word of praise about your God?

Prayer
Father, give us a grateful heart and a bold faith. Teach us to praise you in the everyday experiences of our lives. Amen.

Day 554 — Psalm 76: The Perfect Gift

> "Make vows to the Lord your God and fulfill them; Let all who are around Him bring gifts to Him who is to be feared." Psalm 76:11 (NASB)

Observation

This Psalm of Asaph is a psalm of praise in which Asaph advises the hearer to fear the awesome power of God. He declares that God alone is great and that God's name is known throughout the earth. In verse 2, he states that Salem is the location of God's tabernacle. The word Salem is an abbreviated form of the word Jerusalem. The idea of tabernacle is familiar to most Bible readers. The tabernacle, which was a temporary, tent-like structure that was the forerunner of the Temple, was said to be the "dwelling place" of the Most High God. The more literal translation of the Hebrew word used in this verse translated as "tabernacle" is actually the word for "lair," as in the dwelling place of a great lion. Thus, Jerusalem is pictured as the holy city were the great and powerful lion of God abides. The psalmist also describes the unsurpassed glory and beauty of God, saying that nothing in the universe compares. In verse 6, Asaph makes a reference to chariot and horse, which is a reminder of the defeat of Egypt and Pharaoh, a display of God's power. He also asserts that God is to be feared (v. 7). For the righteous, fear is awe, wonder, and adoration. For the wicked, the fear of God is the fear of wrath and judgment.

Application

Ever find yourself on a quest to discover the perfect gift for someone you care about? Maybe it's your anniversary or your spouse's birthday. Maybe you are trying to find just the right graduation gift or baby shower present. We have all been there. We think of the person we long to honor and we carefully search for just the right gift that will warm the heart and bring a smile to their face. In our focus verse, Asaph suggests that we make vows and bring gifts to God, who is to be feared. He is talking about dedicating our lives and making vows of praise, sacrifice, and faithful living.

What if we attempted to find the perfect gift for God? What would we get a God who already owns all things? We give God our hearts. We are created in a way that allows us to willingly offer our lives back to God. God does not force our love. God doesn't coerce us into relationship. God created us and then set us free to choose how we would respond to God. The gift God longs to receive is the gift of our hearts, the fidelity of our commitments, and the passion of our lives. I hope that on this day, you will intentionally offer your life to God.

Prayer

Father, may we offer you the passion of our lives and the loyalty of our hearts. Amen.

Day 555 — Psalm 77: The Reassurance of Memory

> "And I said, 'This is my fate; the Most High has turned his hand against me.' But then I recall all you have done, O Lord; I remember your wonderful deeds of long ago. They are constantly in my thoughts. I cannot stop thinking about your mighty works." Psalm 77:10-12 (NLT)

Observation
Another written by Asaph, this psalm reflects the heart of a troubled believer. He stretches out his hands before God in prayer throughout the night. What he knew of God contrasted what he was experiencing. Where was God's mercy? Where was God's compassion? He could no longer sleep… he cries out in anguish and despair. He asks in verse 9, "Has God forgotten to be gracious?" But then he makes a conscious decision to turn from his pain and focus on the person, work, and wonder of God. He recalls the redemptive work of God's liberation of God's people from Egypt. He considers the power of God who caused the waters to part and who controls the winds, the waters, and the skies. Lost in contemplation of the greatness of God, he allows the pain of his stress and despair to drift away.

Application
Sometimes, we just need to remember the past to gain hope, perspective, and encouragement for the difficult situations that we face. As Asaph moved through a dark period in his personal life, questioning his faith and wondering if God even cared about his plight, he chose to remember the powerful works of God… and in that recitation of God's history with God's people, he found hope, renewal, and encouragement.

Maybe we need to practice the same discipline when our lives get a little crazy. None of us are immune to the pressures, worries, and pains of daily living. Sometimes, while living in the "meantime," we cry out to God and when God seems silent, we feel abandoned. We allow seeds of doubt to sprout in our hearts and we question God's goodness. We know from experience that "God is great and God is good," but when our lives are in peril, we quickly forget some of our bedrock confessions. And so we need to cultivate a good memory. We need to recall the work of God in our lives at a previous moment or time. We need to remember the blessings, the answers, the guidance, and the liberation from the enslavement of our problems that God has provided. And then let us remember that God is consistent; the one who loves us, who is ever-present with us, is also mindful of our needs. Though we may struggle in the present moment to see God at work, let us remember that God is always at work.

Prayer
Father, even this day, may we remember your mighty acts and be encouraged. Amen.

Day 556 — Psalm 78: Angel Food Cake

> "He rained down manna for them to eat; He gave them bread from heaven.
> They ate the food of angels! God gave them all they could hold."
> Psalm 78:24-25 (NLT)

Observation
Psalm 78 is the second longest of the entire collection of Psalms. (Psalm 119 is the longest.) This psalm celebrates the history of the Lord's dealings with the nation of Israel. It has been referred to as a "contemplation," as Asaph reflects on God's kindness to the rebellious Israelites. It alternates reports of God's faithfulness and the people's rebellion. Asaph longs for the present generation of Israelites not to repeat the failures of so many past generations and so he offers these "parables" (v. 2). He identifies himself as one among them but stands over them as a teacher. His hope is that the wisdom of each generation will be passed on to the next... something that had not been done consistently. He speaks about the deliverance of Ephraim during the days of Jephthah and the deliverance of the Israelites from Egypt. He mentions the compassionate mercy of God along with the 10 plagues, the parting of the Red Sea, and the eventual conquest of the land of Canaan.

Application
Asaph describes the wonderful blessings of God in the wilderness as manna rained down from the skies, calling it the "bread of heaven." In our focus verse, he declares that men ate the food of angels. We sometimes err in thanking God for all the blessings God provides, including, as Jesus once mentioned, "our daily bread." This morning, I want to think in terms of the blessings of daily bread. Let's don't take the usual theme of thanking God for daily provision in our lives—the food we eat and the water we drink and the shelter we enjoy. Instead, let's describe the food of angels that we are sometimes privileged to enjoy. There are some meals and some dishes and some desserts that are so good, that surely the angels would love to feast on what we are eating. For example, is there anything better than a slab of ribs from Dreamland in Tuscaloosa, or a chili dog from the Varsity in Atlanta, or a Milo's burger from Birmingham? What's better than fried shrimp from Sea & Suds at Orange Beach? We all have our favorites... those meals that are so good, made with such flavor that even the thought of them makes us want to jump in the car to race down the interstate to get a taste. What about the biscuits your grandmother made? Or the steaks your dad grilled? Or the caramel cake your friend Bob created? Or the pumpkin bread that Linda makes at Christmas? Sometimes food is more than just taste, flavor, and spice. Sometimes it gets wrapped around a memory, a person, or a place. And yes, sometimes, it becomes the "food of angels" for which we must be grateful.

Prayer
Father, thank you for our daily bread, and especially, for the really good stuff. Amen.

Day 557 — Psalm 79: Judged by the Worst of Us

> "Do not hold us guilty for the sins of our ancestors! Let your compassion quickly meet our needs, for we are on the brink of despair."
> Psalm 79:8 (NLT)

Observation
This is a psalm of lament displaying the community's response to an attack on the city of Jerusalem and the sacking of the Holy Temple. This is most likely a description of the events that occurred when Babylonians destroyed Jerusalem in 587 B.C. It is obvious that the city is in ruins and the Temple has been all but destroyed. As Asaph writes these words, he is cognizant of the fact that God has allowed this to happen because of God's anger over Israel's disobedience. So the question that Asaph asks is of how long will God allow that anger to go forward? He then prays for vengeance on the enemies of Israel. This type of prayer is often found in psalms of lament. (See Psalm 137 for an example.) Asaph reminds God that if Israel is redeemed, the international reputation of both God and the nation will be lifted as God's power is demonstrated.

Application
In our focus verse, Asaph asks that God would not hold all of Israel guilty for the sins of her ancestors. That thought reminds me of a conversation I had with an Imam. I was hosting an inter-faith dialogue on campus. The Imam was joined by a Catholic priest and a rabbi. Over the course of the conversation, the Imam made a very important statement: "I would hope that people will not judge all of Islam by those who represent the worst of us." And I thought how the same sentiment should be applied to the Christians in the room. Who among us would want to be judged by the worst among our faith tradition? And then the thought hit me… I also do not want to be judged by my worst day, and you probably don't want to be judged by that criterion either. In the course of living thousands of days in which we make thousands of decisions, some of them are not going to be wise choices, nor are they going to reflect the nature of Christ within us. I hope that we will be defined, not by our worse days, but by the reputation we forge over a lifetime of seeking to follow Christ. And if I don't want to be judged by my worst day, then I should not be willing to judge others on their worst day either. I hope that makes sense. Rather than making the choice to see only blemishes in the lives of others, I hope that we could see the good and the positive… those moments when the better side of our nature shines forth. Consider the moment when Christ encountered the woman at the well. She had five previous husbands and was currently living with a man who was not her husband. Her sinfulness was not the defining aspect of her life. Instead, her life was defined by the grace offered by a loving Savior.

Prayer
Father, may we find grace as we are careful to offer it to others. Amen.

Day 558 — Psalm 80: Heard It Through the Grapevine

> "Turn us again to yourself, O God. Make your face shine down upon us. Only then will we be saved." Psalm 80:3 (NLT)

Observation

Written by Asaph, this psalm is a call for rescue. Asaph's hope is in the restoration of the nation that has been obliterated by the surrounding nations. Asaph pleads that God's presence be known in a saving manner. He specifically mentions the three tribes of Ephraim, Benjamin, and Manasseh. These are probably symbolic of the entire nation because Ephraim was in the north, Benjamin in the south, and Manasseh was east of the Jordan. Woven into the Psalm is a metaphor describing Israel as a grapevine. Asaph describes how the grapevine was first planted in Egypt and then spread to the land of Promise. He speaks of how the vine grew strong and produced fruit, only to be cut down and damaged by God's enemies. He acknowledges that the punishment received is the result of disobedience. And so in our focus verse, he pleads for God to once again "turn" the people to God, acknowledging that only then will the grapevine be restored. (One other interesting fact about this psalm is that it contains the only reference in the Bible for the Hebrew term for "vineyard," which literally means, "root-stock.")

Application

I find this image of God a bit disturbing. The psalmist asks God to turn toward God's people again, as if God has turned away from them. That's quite an image… God looking away, head turned, ignoring needs and struggles. Ever felt like that? Ever felt like God has surely abandoned you to deal with life on your own? The truth is that sometimes there is indeed quite a distance between God and ourselves. The distance, however, has not been created by God, but by us. God longs to dwell within us. God seeks a close and intimate relationship with each of us. But at times, we push God away with our disobedience, our selfishness, and our lack of attention to spiritual things. We treat God as unimportant and we wonder why the relationship deteriorates. Like the psalmist, let's acknowledge once again that only by God's presence will we be saved from ourselves and from the ills of our culture. Rather than asking God to turn God's face towards us again, let's challenge ourselves to turn our faces towards God. Knowing that God eagerly wants our presence, let's turn our hearts, our thoughts, and our attention in God's direction. There is joy to be found as we draw close to God. Let's make sure our "faces" are pointed in God's direction.

Prayer

Father, teach us this day to turn our faces towards you. May our thoughts, our attitudes, and our desires reflect what we see in you. Amen.

Day 559 — Psalm 81: The Gods We Worship

> "You must never have a foreign god; you must not bow down before a false god." Psalm 81:9 (NLT)

Observation
This psalm is of both praise and admonition in which the voice of the Lord is heard. Asaph mentions several instruments on which the praises of the Lord are to be offered. He mentions the timbrel, the harp, the lute, and the trumpet. (In case you were wondering... The timbrel or "tabret" was the principal percussion instrument of the ancient Israelites. It resembles the modern tambourine.) Voices and instruments together are to offer a joyful expression of worship. He goes on to mention the keeping of the New Moon festival. The regulations for this festival are recorded in 1 Chronicles 23:31. The basis for the festival was the salvation of Israel from Egypt. The people are to detest the history, culture, and language of Egypt and this festival was a celebration of their deliverance from that former life. In verses 8 through 10, God declares that the people will be admonished. There is a repetition of the first commandment to emphasize that no foreign god is to be worshipped in any way. The people's resistance to obeying God led to their punishment. Their stubborn hearts were the root of their problems.

Application
The scriptures are clear... the only God we are to worship, serve, and honor is the Lord God Almighty, creator of heaven and earth. But if we are honest, we have bowed to a few others along the way. In fact, there are probably several right now that are captivating your heart and diverting your attention. Here's a good litmus test to discern your level of pagan worship. Take a few days and log the number of hours you are spending on things like Twitter, Facebook, Instagram, or Netflix. Then log the number of hours you are reading the Bible, serving God's people, and pouring out of your heart in prayer. I know the argument... you are going to say that it's just not practical to spend all your time in your spiritual disciplines. You have to work. You have to commute. You have to keep up with your world. I am not denying that any of those things are important. However, we make the time it takes to chase after the things that are important to us. We make the time for social media. We make the time for television. We make the time for texting our friends. We do so because we value those activities. We don't create time for things that are not important. The things we casually consider to be non-invasive have a way of taking over our lives. Maybe it's time for a little "time assessment." Our gods may be more prevalent than we think. What will get the best of your time this day?

Prayer
Father, teach us to value the things that are of greatest importance. Amen.

Day 560 — Psalm 82: Intentionality

> "Give justice to the poor and the orphan; uphold the rights of the oppressed and the destitute. Rescue the poor and helpless; deliver them from the grasp of evil people." Psalm 82:3-4 (NLT)

Observation

This psalm, written by Asaph, is categorized as a psalm of wisdom. In it, God calls for all the judges of the earth to appear before the heavenly assembly. The wicked judges of all time are to appear before God and give an account of themselves and their wicked judgments. These unrighteous judges had perverted their calling to represent God who had called them to establish wisdom on the earth. Asaph declares that the defenseless should have a haven of justice in the courts, but instead, they are denied justice and often exploited. He suggests that wicked judges create an unstable land. The poor and the afflicted of all the ages cry out to God to help them. Their cries will not go unheeded. The great righteous God will come and will establish justice on the earth.

Application

There is an old expression that states, "It's not what you know, but who you know, that makes the difference." And whether you agree with that statement, you have to admit that it is true most of the time. Our relationships and connections open doors, grant favors, and work the system. I once lived in East Tennessee where the local sheriff was a member of my congregation. We once drove to a University of Tennessee football game together. On the way home, he instructed me to ignore the speed limit and "get on down the road." I was cruising along at a rather high rate of speed, and sure enough, it wasn't long before I got pulled over by a local law enforcement officer. When he peered into the car he said, "Oh, Sheriff Montgomery, I didn't know you were in the car! You are free to go." And off we went. It was about having someone who had authority and power in the car with me who could alleviate my condition.

Let's be honest… the poor, needy, and marginalized people in our culture remain oppressed and helpless because there are few willing participants to advocate for their causes. People who have status, power, and access can make a difference. People of privilege can affect change. They can mend broken systems, force legislation on corrupt laws, and provide relationships that link the poor and needy with the services that they need. But here's the key… intentionality. Those who are able to help have to be very intentional about becoming involved. They must see the poor man's plight as their own plight and work for solutions that bring change. We are to "give justice to the poor," not ignore their condition.

Prayer

Father, may those of us who have power and influence use it redemptively. Amen.

Day 561 — Psalm 83: A Little Trash Talkin'

> "O my God, make them like the whirling dust, Like chaff before the wind."
> Psalm 83:13 (NASB)

Observation
This psalm, written by Asaph, is another example of an imprecatory psalm, meaning the writer offers a curse against the enemies of Israel. An imprecatory prayer asks God to bring about wrath and destruction on those who oppose God's ways. Asaph's intent is to vindicate the work, reputation, and glory of God who has been disparaged by the surrounding nations. In the opening verse, Asaph declares, "Do not keep silent, O God!" His plea is for God to rise and root out all the evil in the land. Asaph is repulsed by the enemies of Israel and he wants God to cut them off. Many nations had conspired against Israel and in so doing, at least in the mind of the psalmist, they had conspired against God. In the culture of the day, remembering a person long after they were gone was extremely important. In our focus verse, Asaph prays that the memory of these enemies would be as whirling dust or windblown chaff. It is a strong curse asking God to completely erase even their memory.

Application
We all have our enemies, and at times, we almost want to pray a prayer asking God to "zap" them with some illness or misfortune. And yet the Jesus ethic in all of us makes such a prayer not only dangerous, but downright sinful. Didn't Jesus tell us to love our enemies and pray for those who persecute us? Didn't he remind us that love was the defining quality of our faith? So how do we reconcile the words of the psalmist with the words of Jesus? If both were inspired of God to say what they said, how can we join the two together? First, let's talk about our "enemies." Most of our enemies are those people with whom we have had some personal conflict. Maybe it's a neighbor who stirs up trouble, or a co-worker who gossips, or a businessperson who has cheated us, or maybe even a motorist that cuts us off in traffic. In our anger, we desire justice. We want such people to "get what's coming to them." Our human nature pushes us to offer a prayer asking God to curse them. But is that the response that God seeks from us? Isn't He a God that demands reconciliation, redemption, and forgiveness? I'm just not sure that God will honor our imprecatory prayers for vengeance against OUR enemies. Look again at the prayers of Asaph. He didn't pray for vengeance against HIS enemies, but against the enemies of God. And that's the difference. We should be angered by the things that anger God. We should pray about the ungodly injustices and systems of our day. And if we feel strongly enough to pray a prayer of vengeance, then we should be willing to use our energies to fight the good fight that such prayers demand of us.

Prayer
Father, may we forgive our enemies as we engage the battle against yours. Amen.

Day 562 — Psalm 84: No Place I'd Rather Be

> "A single day in your courts is better than a thousand anywhere else! I would rather be a gatekeeper in the house of my God than live the good life in the homes of the wicked." Psalm 84:10 (NLT)

Observation

Psalm 84 is a psalm of Zion, which celebrates the presence of God in Jerusalem where God's presence dwells in His Holy Temple. It is written by the Sons of Korah. (The reader may recall from earlier observations that the sons of Korah were a musical family which served as key leaders in Temple worship for generations.) The psalm declares how lovely is the dwelling place of God. Written from the viewpoint of a pilgrim who has made his/her way to Jerusalem, the psalmist declares how beautiful the courts of the Lord truly are. He even mentions a swallow who has made a nest near the Temple, finding a place of peace and safety just like the wearied pilgrim will do. The pilgrim, who has made his/her way to Jerusalem has done so, not out of obligation, but out of joy. And even though the journey may have been difficult, God's blessings have been evident all along the way, even through the Valley of Baca (which means weeping.) The joy of the arrival strengthens the soul and the pilgrim is blessed to take it all in. According to our focus verse, nothing in the experience of one's daily life routine can compare to a day spent in the presence of God at the Temple.

Application

If I were to ask you to name the one place you would rather be than anywhere else on the planet, where would that be? For some of us, it might be a physical location. My mind wonders from a Hawaiian beach, or main street in Disney World, to some wonderful mountain cottage in the Smokies during the fall of the year. For others of us, our thoughts might be centered around the company we keep. It doesn't really matter where we are as long as we are with the right people… the ones we love and cherish. But what if you could be in the right place, with just the right people? That sounds like heaven on earth, right? I think that was the experience of the psalmist as he wrote his words. He was in the right place with the right person. He was in Jerusalem in the presence of Almighty God. What could have been any better? In fact, he writes that a single day in that one spot would be better than a thousand other days anywhere else. There is something very satisfying, very rewarding, and very peaceful about being in the center of God's Will for your life. It's that place where moment, circumstance, location, and company all converge into a single "sweet spot" where you know you are in just the right place at just the righ time. To know that moment is bliss. To be anywhere else creates a longing to return to that spot. May you know the joy of being in that place.

Prayer

Father, lead us to the place where we will find you consistently present. Amen.

Day 563 — Psalm 85: Guilt Free

> "You forgave the guilt of your people— yes, you covered all their sins."
> Psalm 85:2 (NLT)

Observation
Psalm 85 is another psalm composed by the sons of Korah. (Korah himself was swallowed up by an earthquake but his sons were permitted by God to continue their role as musicians who led the people in worship.) This psalm is a prayer for restoration. The words of the psalm seem to concern the process of restoration of the people and land following some great crisis or calamity. It is perhaps written in response to the Babylonian captivity. The prayer itself includes a request for the revival of the people and the renewal of the land. In the process of renewal, the people still feel the aftereffect of God's wrath for their disobedience. They ask to be revived and renewed. They long for the sense of peace that comes when God's mercy and truth result in righteousness throughout the land.

Application
It is an amazing thing to realize that God has forgiven all our guilt and covered all our sins. But if the truth be told, most of us struggle more with lingering guilt than we do over the concept of being forgiven by God. More specifically, most of us have enough theology and faith to really believe that we can be forgiven of our sins. We cling to verses like 1 John 1:9 that reminds us that "If we confess our sins, He is faithful and just and will forgive our sins and cleanse us from all unrighteousness." What we struggle with is the erasing of our guilt. In fact, most of us continue, maybe even for a lifetime, to beat ourselves up for some indiscretion or poorly made decision. Forgiven? Yes. Guilt-free living? No. Let's remember that lifetime guilt is not God's design for us. In fact, our guilt is the result of our own inability to forgive ourselves. Guilt tends to hang around for a long time. Go back to the story of the Prodigal Son in Luke 15. It was the sinner-son who came limping home carrying a load of guilt. It was the father who was ready to throw a party, extend a lot of grace, and make things new again. It's the same with us. We tend to insist on carrying a load of guilt. But if God is willing to forgive and forget, who are we to do any less? Some of you have carried a load of guilt around for a very long time. Maybe today you need to hear God saying, "It's time to put it down." It's not easy. In fact, guilt will try to hang around the shadows of your life for many years. But it's not the life God has in mind for you. So confess your sins and pray for forgiveness. Then sit in God's presence for a while and let God's grace wash over your life and set you free.

Prayer
Father, may we know this day, the freedom that is found in your forgiveness. May your grace become more powerful than our guilt. Amen.

Day 564 — Psalm 86: Maintaining Reverent Distance

> "Bend down, O Lord, and hear my prayer; answer me, for I need your help." Psalm 86:1 (NLT)

Observation
This psalm is the only psalm in Book 3 of the Psalms that is attributed to David. It is a psalm of lament in which David expresses his concern about his lowly state, asking God to hear his prayer and come to his aid. In our focus verse, David expresses the distance between himself and God as he asks God to "bend down" to hear his prayer. David acknowledges that God is in a place of grandeur on high while David has a humble place on earth. David describes himself as a servant of God who will find his ultimate joy in serving the Lord. The psalm also describes the way in which ancient nations often tied their identity to the pagan gods they worshipped. When their gods proved to be false, they would be forced to acknowledge that the Lord alone is God. Even those pagan nations will one day glorify the Lord.

Application
There are people who, because of their authority and position, command respect. For example, I don't presume that I will ever have an audience with the Pope, but if I do, you can bet that I will have on my best suit and polished Sunday shoes. My appreciation for the position he holds will garner my respect. It's the same with an important politician like a state governor. I wouldn't presume to barge into that office and start a conversation. Out of respect, I would set up an appointment, wait my turn, and prepare myself for the interaction. In my role here at Belmont University, on occasion, I meet with the university president. I treat those meetings with a sense of importance because of his position with the university.

At least in this psalm, David seems to have a very healthy respect for the sovereignty and majesty of God. He humbly asks for God to "bend down" to hear his prayer. He makes no demands, but humbly requests the intervention of God in his life. I am forced to consider our interactions with God… do we treat God respectfully, honor God's position, value God's time? I am fearful that we sometimes fail to maintain a reverent distance. Sometimes, we get a little too comfortable, a little too friendly, maybe a little too indifferent to being in God's presence. Yes, God is always accessible and attentive to our prayers, longing to hear from us. But God is not equal with us. God is sovereign, the supreme authority in the universe. Who are we to call God, "The Big Man Upstairs," or to throw God's name around in our crude speech as though that is not offensive? We are God's servants and the sheep of God's pasture. Let's treat our interactions with God with reverence, respect, and importance.

Prayer
Father, may we be ever mindful of your authority and lordship. Amen.

Day 565 — Psalm 87: Sacred Soil

> "The Lord loves the gates of Zion more than all the other dwelling places of Jacob." Psalm 87:1 (NASB)

Observation
This psalm has been described as a psalm of Zion because it declares, forcefully, the glories of Jerusalem, the city of God. (This psalm does seem to anticipate the New Testament mission to present the Gospel to the entire world. All nations are drawn to Jerusalem and by implication; all peoples are included within the scope of the Gospel.) God has established Jerusalem as the center of true worship. God ordained Solomon to build a Temple for his dwelling among the Israelites. The city is a holy spot because God has declared it to be so. In fact, according to Revelation 21, the future reign of the Great King will be in Jerusalem. God speaks in this psalm. He calls out to the residents of Egypt, Babylon, Philistia, Tyre, and Ethiopia declaring their kinship with those who are born in Jerusalem. And, by the late period of King Hezekiah's reign, foreigners were worshipping in the Temple alongside of the Jews. Verse 6 indicates that God will register all the people of the earth who worship God.

Application
Although all the earth is the Lord's and although God can be found in any place, there are still some places, at least in our minds, that seem to be more holy than others. We all have the memory of some place where God's presence felt especially strong and where we experienced God's closeness and counsel in unique ways. For me, Ridgecrest, North Carolina, is one of those places. When I was a child, I attended conferences there with my parents. When I was a teenager, our youth group attended Youth Camp in that setting. I once worked there for a summer as a college student. As a pastor, I took numerous groups there to experience the mountains and perhaps a special word from God. And so for me, it's sacred soil. I have found God present in that place on many occasions.

When I was a pastor, from time to time, people came to our church in the middle of an ordinary day to ask if they could go into our Sanctuary to pray over some important need in their lives. There was something about being in a space set aside for worship that brought them a sense of God's presence. I hope that you have a place where you feel the presence of God in a unique way. I hope you have some sacred soil. And if you do, I hope you make a pilgrimage to that place from time to time. No, it's certainly not the only place where you can encounter God, but the pilgrimage is important. The moments spent in that place can refresh your soul, clear your mind, and strengthen your resolve.

Prayer
Father, thank you for those special, holy places where we allow ourselves to be found. Amen.

Day 566 — Psalm 88: Praise from the Grave

> "Are your wonderful deeds of any use to the dead? Do the dead rise up and praise you?" Psalm 88:10 (NLT)

Observation

Psalm 88 is a very unusual psalm. It is a prayer in which the psalmist pleads with God to be delivered from death. But unlike other "psalms of lament," this psalm contains no typical resolve at the conclusion in which the psalmist would write of God's provision and mercy. It begins and ends with a very desperate cry for God's intervention. The subscription of the psalm indicates that it is written by Heman the Ezrahite. He is mentioned in 1 Kings 4:31 as being a gifted and wise man. Apparently, some calamity or illness has overtaken his life. In fact, he suggests that this song be sung to the tune of "Mahalath Leannoth," which means, "Dance of Affliction." He offers the language of desperate weeping. In the first verse he mentions that he has "cried out" to the Lord. This phrase is literally translated as "loud scream." So, Heman has been screaming at God about his condition. He feels so near to death that he claims he is "adrift with the dead." Adding to his dismay is the belief that his troubles have been brought on by God. He feels isolated, alone, and separated from his friends. He reminds God that if he dies, he can no longer use his voice to praise God in the Temple. As one of the Sons of Korah, it has been his life-long commission to lead the people in worship. The psalm ends with no resolve or word of hope from Heman.

Application

In our focus verse, Heman asks rhetorically, "Do the dead rise up and praise you?" He, of course, is pleading for God to restore his health and life. He tries to convince God that if he dies, his voice will no longer be heard. I hate to question the wisdom of Heman the Ezrahite this morning, but I would insist that the dead can, in fact, rise up and offer their praises. I'm not talking about the great resurrection day when the dead in Christ will rise and join the saints of all the ages in offering praise of our Savior Jesus. Certainly, that moment will come, but more specifically this morning, I want to lean into the thought of the ways we can praise God even from the grave. It's called legacy living. If we choose, while still living, to honor the Lord in our relationships, our finances, our commitments, and with our passions, we will leave behind "echoing choruses of praise" that reverberate long after we are gone. Maybe through careful planning we leave behind a monetary gift to a faith institution that insures the continuing work of the Kingdom. Maybe we invest "relational equity" into the lives of the younger generation so that they learn and live the Christian faith. Maybe we leave behind a trail of involvements in which the poor are served, the grieving find comfort, and the lonely find friendship.

Prayer

Father, may we see beyond the living of these days so that we honor you always. Amen.

Day 567 — Psalm 89: The Tough Love of Discipline

> "But if his descendants forsake my instructions and fail to obey my regulations, if they do not obey my decrees and fail to keep my commands, then I will punish their sin with the rod, and their disobedience with beating. But I will never stop loving him nor fail to keep my promise to him." Psalm 89:30-33 (NLT)

Observation
Psalm 89 is written by Ethan the Ezrahite. It is a celebration of God's covenant with David. The psalm begins on a bright note as it describes, with a joyful tone, the covenant once extended to David. It contained three key provisions: an eternal dynasty, an eternal kingdom, and an eternal throne. David's line of descendants would rule and reign. And yet the psalm ends on a note of lament as the psalmist describes the failure of David's descendants to remain faithful. God had certainly promised that God's loyal love would always rest on David's sons, but it seemed, given the circumstances under which the psalm was written, that God had forsaken his people. And yet God is praised in this psalm as the great deliverer who is without comparison. Reading the psalm from a much later perspective than that of the psalmist, we affirm that despite errors, rebellion, sin, and apostacies, that God would indeed fulfill God's covenant. The psalmist obviously writes in a time of great despondency and disillusionment and such sentiment is reflected in his words. (This is the final psalm in Book 3.)

Application
You may have heard the old phrase when you needed to be disciplined by your father when you were young, "This is going to hurt me more than it's going to hurt you." Raise your hand if you ever believed that… no? I didn't believe it either. But when you become a parent, whether you say such words or not, the sentiment surely echoes in your mind. It is a painful thing to discipline a child. It is painful because a child has misbehaved. It is painful because you have to impose punishment on someone you love. I think that's the message of this psalm. Notice in our focus verses that God clearly states that God has to punish the descendants of David because of their failure to obey and honor God. But also notice that God also affirms an everlasting love that will never change. Discipline is for the sake of correction, not abuse. It does not represent a loss of love. Even as an earthly father may grieve at the necessary punishment of his child, the love of that father never wanes, never weakens, and never ends. It's the same with God. There are times that we certainly disobey God and fail to live up to God's expectations for our lives. And, because of our poor choices, we may have to suffer the consequences of our sins. And even though we may feel the chastisement of God, we are never loved any less, nor cared about with less resolve.

Prayer
Father, punish us as we need it, but love us despite our mistakes. Amen.

Day 568 — Psalm 90: Borrowed Time

> "Seventy years are given to us! Some even live to eighty. But even the best years are filled with pain and trouble; soon they disappear, and we fly away. Who can comprehend the power of your anger? Your wrath is as awesome as the fear you deserve. Teach us to realize the brevity of life, so that we may grow in wisdom." Psalm 90:10-12 (NLT)

Observation

Psalm 90 is the first in Book 4 of the Psalms. It is well placed because it reflects the main theme of the entire Book 4, describing God's fatherly correction of Israel. It is the only psalm written by Moses, although he did write two additional poems, both found in the Pentateuch (Exodus 15, Deuteronomy 32). Moses was, of course, the great leader of Israel who led the nation out of captivity. In these words, Moses pleads for God's continual interaction with God's people. He prays for a renewal of relationship so that the Israelites will know prosperity and success. More to the point, this psalm also speaks of the brevity of life. Moses contrasts God's eternal existence with man's brief lifespan… "For you, a thousand years are as a passing day, as brief as a few night hours" (90:4). Moses prays that men would gain a sense a wisdom in the light of that brief existence to focus on eternal things. Our focus verses declare that man might live 70 or even 80 years. The point is not that God has set an absolute maximum in the number of years we will live, but rather, that we would learn to value our days and use them wisely.

Application

My grandfather Roebuck talked about "borrowed time." He reasoned that most of us are given a lifespan of 80 years. Anything beyond that number was in his description, "borrowed time." He borrowed a few extra years, as did my grandmother who lived to be 96. My own parents are now nearly a decade into that same rarified existence. They are living on "borrowed time." Maybe we all are to some degree, in that none of us have been promised or guaranteed any certain number of days or years to live. Experts indicate the children born in this new century will most likely live to see 100 or even a few years more because of improvements in healthcare, disease control, and nutrition. But even if we live 100 years, it's still a brief stint on the planet. Time really does pass very quickly. As parents, we sit back and watch our kids grow and wonder how the years slip away so quickly. So, listen well to what Moses is suggesting. Considering the brevity of life, invest your days in the things that matter. The ripple effect of your life will only last a few generations at best. So rather than mindlessly focusing on the stuff that you can't take with you, focus on the things you can, like grace, forgiveness, faith-sharing, role-modeling, and salvation.

Prayer

Father, teach us to value our days that we might present to you a heart of wisdom. Amen.

Day 569 — Psalm 91: Guardian God

> "For He will give His angels charge concerning you, To guard you in all your ways. They will bear you up in their hands, That you do not strike your foot against a stone." Psalm 91:11-12 (NASB)

Observation

Psalm 91 has no author identified. It is a very positively worded psalm that describes the safety found when abiding in God's presence. There are only five psalms in which God speaks, and this is one of them. (The others are Psalms 12, 60, 75, and 87.) The words are filled with powerful images. The opening phrase describes the shelter that is God, viewed as a mighty mountain. Safeguarded are those who live in the shadow of God's presence. Another common image is that of God as a mother bird who gathers her chicks under the shelter of her wings. The psalmist describes the fact that God protects the faithful from any assault, while giving punishment to the unrighteous. Verse 14 indicates that God has known the name of the psalmist, which indicates a very close, intimate relationship. Our focus verses may sound familiar. These are the words quoted by Satan when he tempted Jesus in the wilderness. The words themselves, however, are spoken by the psalmist indicating that God will provide deliverance and protection, even through the use of God's angels or messengers.

Application

Let's be honest... We worry about safety issues. We buy cars that have a good crash rating. We insist on living in homes that are well-built. We make our kids put on a seatbelt every time they get in the car. We put deadbolt locks on our doors and fences around our property. Even with our electronics, we worry about safety. We password protect our computers. We buy products to protect from malware. We put cases on our phones. We do all that we can to keep the enemies at arm's length.

The psalmist is writing about physical danger. He speaks of terror at night, arrows in the day, pestilence, and wicked soldiers who long to do battle. And yet he has found security and peace of mind in a relationship with God. Listen again to the focus verse, "He will give His angels charge concerning you, to guard you in all your ways." I don't know about you, but that verse gives me a lot of comfort. Whether or not you choose to believe in actual winged creatures who float in the sky watching over your steps, you should take comfort in the promise of scripture that God will watch over you and protect you in all your ways. Armed with an all-seeing God, a loving Savior, and an all-powerful, indwelling Spirit, we should walk into each new day with a sense of God's protection. God is real and God provides for our safety.

Prayer

Father, thank you for watching over each of us this day. Keep us safe. Amen.

Day 570 — Psalm 92: Chalk One Up for the Old Guys

> "The righteous man will flourish like the palm tree, He will grow like a cedar in Lebanon. Planted in the house of the Lord, They will flourish in the courts of our God. They will still yield fruit in old age; They shall be full of sap and very green" Psalm 92:12-14 (NASB)

Observation

Psalm 92 is subtitled: "A song for the Sabbath Day." It is a psalm that celebrates the person and work of God in an exuberant way. The psalmist declares in the opening verses that it is good to give thanks to God and to praise God's name. The imagery of the Hebrew text is of giving thanks and praise to God verbally in a public setting. It's like standing on the street corner and joyfully singing songs of praise. (Give that a try and let me know how it works out for you...) The central theme of the psalm is expressed in verse 8 where God is described as "On high forever more." The eternal nature of God is contrasted with the brevity of God's enemies. The psalmist also hints at the coming of the Messiah as he describes his anointing with fresh oil (v. 10). The final section is interesting. He compares the righteous man to a flourishing palm tree that grows straight and tall like the cedars of Lebanon. Planted well into the soil of God's goodness, the tree (righteous man) will still yield fruit in old age.

Application

Remember the mid-to-late 1970s when we all had to own a powerful radio receiver so that we could rattle the house with our music? I had a Pioneer SX-880 that would kick out about 65 watts per channel. I played Lynyrd Skynyrd in the den of our home like I was at a concert! I connected a turntable to it along with a cassette player. Surely, I was the envy of all. I used that old receiver for several years before I finally tucked it into the back of a closet at home. Just recently, I thought about the old Pioneer SX-880. I dug it out, brought it to my office, and plugged it in for the first time in at least two decades. I connected my iPhone to it with a cable. And voila! Perfect, crisp, stereo sound. There is still a little life left in the old receiver.

The psalmist insists that the faithful person, even in old age, can still produce fruit for the Kingdom of God. In fact, as we age, we can flourish if our lives remain firmly planted in scripture and in our spiritual disciplines. We simply never retire from the Christian faith nor from our responsibilities to influence future generations. Because God's Spirit continually indwells our lives, there is a fire in our bones, a hope in our hearts, and a desire in our minds until the day we die. So, if you are feeling the effect of age this morning—feeling like your best days are behind you and not in front of you—you might want to rethink everything. God is not finished with you yet. You have fruit to give, hope to share, and a place to serve.

Prayer

Father, may we continue to play the music of the Kingdom for as long as we live. Amen.

Day 571 — Psalm 93: The God Who Defies Description

> "Your throne, O Lord, has stood from time immemorial. You yourself are from the everlasting past." Psalm 93:2 (NLT)

Observation
Psalm 93 is a royal psalm. It focuses on the eternal reign of God over the earth. Some of the language used in the psalm, author unknown, makes use of language sometimes found in the Canaanite worship of Baal, which was popular at that time in history. Baal was believed to be the god of the storm. For example, if a farmer needed rain for his crops, he might pray to Baal to bring rain. Remember Elijah's experience on Mount Carmel with the 450 prophets of Baal (1 Kings 18). Each attempted to call down fire (lightning) from heaven. Baal was also believed to control the waters of the sea. Notice in this psalm that the psalmist counteracts such a belief proclaiming that the waters themselves have lifted their voice in praise of God. The psalm goes on to proclaim the incomparable nature of God. There is no rival, no equal, and no power on earth or in the universe that can seize control away from God's hand. Our focus verse centers on the eternal nature of God. With an interesting insight, the psalmist proclaims that God has always existed, even from the "everlasting past."

Application
Because we are human, we all struggle a little with the concept of eternity. It's hard for us as "finite" human beings to wrap our minds around that which is infinite. It's hard for us to process the concept of time and space, not bound to any future ending point. And perhaps, equally hard to grasp, is the concept introduced in this psalm of the "everlasting past." It is hard for us to consider an everlasting past that predates the creation of our world and even our universe. So, when we say that God has always existed, we must step out in faith, proclaiming that which we can't fully understand or explain. We just have to rest in the mysterious knowledge that God has always been and will always be. The concept of God's eternal nature is not the only aspect of God that defies description. Consider for a moment that Old Testament name of God, "Elohim," introduced in Genesis 1:1. It's a plural noun. The name literally translates as, "Gods," as in a "plural of majesty." It speaks to the limitless qualities of God. It is certainly difficult to attempt a descriptive name for God that encapsulates all that God is. For example, God is love, God is Savior, God is King, God is provider, God is sustainer… The name Elohim attempts to simply say the "God of many attributes… the God who is all things." If we could fully define God with our descriptive words or thoughts, He would cease to be the eternal and almighty. How great therefore, is our God who defies our limited attempts at definition.

Prayer
Father, you are great, and you are good. And that is enough. Amen.

Day 572 — Psalm 94: Stemming the Tide of Anxiety

> "When my anxious thoughts multiply within me, Your consolations delight my soul." Psalm 94:19 (NASB)

Observation

Just like the preceding psalm, Psalm 94 is a royal psalm because of the language used in verse 2, with God is described as "The Judge of the Earth." The psalm itself is a call for the divine judge to punish the evil that exists in the world. The psalmist acknowledges that God clearly decides when to exercise God's wrath and judgment. Yet, the psalmist has a concern over the timing of God's wrath. How long are the wicked allowed to defy God? Through their evil speech, the wicked brazenly disregard the laws of God, specifically noted are the laws that pertain to the treatment of widows, orphans, and strangers in the land. God is not deaf nor is God blind to such sins, according to the psalmist. Evil cannot be tolerated by a holy God. Final judgment will surely come to the wicked.

Application

We have all had them... those restless nights when we are robbed of sleep and our minds begin to race in a thousand different directions. As the psalmist writes in our focus verse, our "anxious thoughts multiply within us." Surely you have felt that cascading torrent of one worry that leads to another, and then to another. Maybe you have awakened worried over the brokenness of a relationship, or over something at work, or over something that needs fixing at the house. Soon, your mind starts to race in a thousand different directions and the worry makes it all but impossible to sleep. Recently, I had one of those nights. When I first awoke, I found myself worried about a tree sapling that was growing too close to the house... will its roots damage the foundation? Will a backhoe be needed to one day uproot it? Crazy, right? And that led to worry about the gutters, which led to worry about the age of the shingles on the roof. One worry led to another and then to another and then to another. They multiplied within me.

In Philippians 4:6, Paul says to replace worry and the anxiety it causes with faithful, life-sustaining, mind-clearing prayer. It's odd to me that when we have one of those sleepless nights, the anxiety seems to dissipate with the morning. But why wait until the dawn's early light? How can you and I cast out our fear in the middle of the night? This may seem a bit radical, but give this a try. Keep a notepad and a pencil in your nightstand. The next time anxiety takes away your peaceful slumber, sit up and write down all the fears, frustrations, and worries you have floating around in your mind. And then take the time to specifically pray about each one and then leave the matter at the throne of God's grace. God is bigger than our fears. Always.

Prayer

Father, relieve our anxious worries and teach us a humble dependency upon you. Amen.

Day 573 — Psalm 95: Fall On Your Knees...

> "Come, let us worship and bow down, Let us kneel before the Lord our Maker." Psalm 95:6 (NASB)

Observation
Psalm 95 represents yet another royal psalm because it acknowledges God as the "Great King above all gods" (v. 3). Yet it is also considered as a worshipping psalm because of its particular emphasis on the act of worship. It calls the hearer to celebration, contemplation, and obedience. Notice the positive and exciting tone of celebration recorded in the opening verse, "O come let us sing for joy to the Lord, let us shout joyfully to the Rock of our Salvation" (NASB). The unnamed psalmist continues, calling for the worshipper to literally bow down before the Lord both reflectively and humbly. The psalm closes with a reminder of the importance of obedience. God's judgment on God's own people was evident at the rebellion of Meribah (Exodus 17:7) when the people did not take God seriously and even doubted God's provision for their journey.

Application
As I read this psalm, I am reminded about the importance of attitude as we stand in the presence of God. Words like, "bow down," and "kneel before the Lord" are used. Clearly, we are to stand in God's presence with a sense of humility, deep respect, reverence, and awe. It is not a casual conversation when we speak to the King of Kings and it is not a simple thing to stand in God presence. I think there are times when we fail to offer the reverence and respect needed when we spend moments in prayer. Sometimes it's a lack of focus. We pray without really concentrating on our words or the petitions. Sometimes we pray without acknowledging the authority of God. We jump into prayer with an attitude that God owes us something. We make our demands and submit our requests without first acknowledging what a joy it is to be loved by God and invited to speak with God. Sometimes it is even about posture. Why does the psalmist remind us to kneel and bow down? It says something about lordship. Kneeling in the presence of God teaches us that we are not God's equal. There is a sense of honor and respect that is due. Don't misunderstand. I am not suggesting that there is a formula or position or methodology that should always be employed each time we pray. We can certainly offer many kinds of prayers in many different ways. My point is to remind us all to value the importance of praying and to always acknowledge and honor God.

Prayer
Father, we thank you this morning for the privilege have to communicate with you each and every moment. May we never treat our prayers with a sense of flippancy, but rather, with a great sense of importance and reverence. Amen.

Day 574 — Psalm 96: Sunday Clothes

> "Worship the Lord in holy attire; Tremble before Him, all the earth."
> Psalm 96:9 (NASB)

Observation

Psalm 96 is also considered to be a royal psalm because of its positive, powerful, and upbeat message of God's glory and God's worthiness to be praised. Verse 4 indicates that "The Lord is great and greatly to be praised." The psalmist, again unnamed, encourages and commands all people to sing praises to God. Three times in the first two verses the reader is told to "sing unto the Lord." He goes on to say that God's glory is to be told among all the nations. The so-called gods of the surrounding nations are not gods at all, he writes. They are merely idols. (The Hebrew word literally means "that which is worthless.") His words were particularly poignant in the cultural context of the day. There was a belief among pagan nations that gods could rise and fall in terms of their power. In contrast to that, the Almighty God of Israel is the "living God" who remains in authority for all of eternity.

Application

I never know what to wear to worship anymore. Times have changed and a lot of the traditional practices around worship have gone through various transitions. I get that. I recognize that more and more churches are moving away from traditional styles of worship to adopt a more "user-friendly," contemporary style. And with the change of format and style, attire has changed as well. I grew up as a "coat and tie" kind-of-guy on Sunday mornings. In fact, throughout my entire pastoral ministry, I have always gone to the pulpit wearing my best suit. But now, I don't know what to wear anymore. If I go to church all suited up with a coat and tie, I standout like a stranger. But if I go in just jeans and a polo it seems a little too casual and awkward. My wife usually offers the best advice. She says, "It's always better to be overdressed for worship than underdressed."

So take a look at our focus verse. The psalmist, in calling for a sense of awe, reverence, and respect for God, states that we should worship the Lord with "holy attire." I am reminded of my younger days when Sunday clothes meant a suit and tie and polished shoes. I have always felt that it was important to dress for worship. We should offer God our best. Something about the day should be distinct and different. Yet I also recognize that "holy attire" might not have anything to do with the clothes we wear. Surely it also applies to the attitudes we carry into worship and the status of the sins we have committed. We need to recognize the importance of that sacred moment each week. We need to present our best... physically, emotionally, and spiritually. God is indeed worthy to be praised. As you head for church this weekend, make sure that you are ready. Be dressed in holy attire.

Prayer

Father, may we treat worship as the sacred hour you intend for it to be. Amen.

Day 575 — Psalm 97: The Choices Christians Must Make

> "Hate evil, you who love the Lord, Who preserves the souls of His godly ones; He delivers them from the hand of the wicked." Psalm 97:10 (NASB)

Observation

Another in the collection of royal psalms (93-99), Psalm 97 has a particularly apocalyptic tone in that it describes God's final judgment on the wicked before God's great Kingdom is established. The psalmist expresses the thought that the Lord reigns. This expression is one of the key elements in the royal psalms. He goes on to say that the all the earth and even the islands of the sea will rejoice. The imagery suggests that all the earth and even the smallest parts (islands) will join in praise of God. As the psalmist describes the clouds and thick darkness, he is pointing towards God's final judgment and God's power. God is as a "fire" (v. 3) offering a final, searing judgment of God's enemies. Verse 11 offers a unique and interesting image. God will "sow light" like seeds of righteousness on the earth. God's goodness will emerge from every corner of the earth until God's light overtakes and eradicates all evil.

Application

We sometimes think of hate and love as emotions… strong feelings we have towards others. Yet in the context of our focus verse, these ideas are not emotions but willful choices to make. The psalmist is reminding us to express our love for God by hating evil. It is a choice to love God… intentional, willful, active. It is also a choice to hate that which is evil. Most of us grew up being taught that it was wrong to hate. And it is. We are never given the right or the authority to hate anyone. Ours is a Gospel of love. What we are directed to hate are those very things that God hates… the evil and demonic forces of our world. Demonic forces are those things that tend to dehumanize the lives of those with whom we share the planet. Prejudice, abuse, racism, misogyny, envy, greed, and the like are the soil in which evil grows. God says for us to hate those things. But here's my point, our hatred has to be active. It is one thing, as it is said, "to curse the darkness… it is quite another to light a candle." It is not enough for us to simply decry and condemn the evil around us. We must be proactive in our assault on the strongholds. When we see racism, we must confront it. When we observe abuse, we must report it. When we discover a destructive anger, we must speak peace into its combatants. When we see the destructive power of shame, we must offer grace. You get the point. We will not change the world by our idleness, nor by our private devotions. It is our will, our passion, and our involvement that will sow light like seeds of righteousness. There are choices to be made… this very day. Prove your love for God by your hatred of evil.

Prayer

Father, may we give practical expression to the deep desires of our hearts. Amen.

Day 576 — Psalm 98: Ongoing Inspiration

> "O sing to the Lord a new song, For He has done wonderful things, His right hand and His holy arm have gained the victory for Him."
> Psalm 98:1 (NASB)

Observation
Psalm 98 is a royal psalm of exuberant praise. It is very joyful in tone. Although the author is unknown, early Jewish tradition attributes it to David. The psalmist declares that God has done "marvelous things." That short phrase, "marvelous things," is reserved in scripture to describe only the works of God. No other person or nation has done "marvelous things." As the psalm continues, the writer reminds the reader that God's salvation of Israel is revealed and remembered by all nations. God's strong and mighty hand testify to God's power. In the Canaanite culture of the day, the seas were thought to be under the control of the pagan deity Baal. But in this psalm, the hearer is reminded that God completely controls all the earth. The seas will roar, and the rivers will clap their hands all in praise of God. The psalm closes with a reminder that God is the great judge who is coming to judge the world. The righteous will rejoice in God's coming because God will establish a Kingdom on the earth.

Application
When I read this psalm, I was struck with the phrase, "new song." For me, the idea means something that is fresh, engaging, and exciting. In other words, don't get so caught up in the repetitious singing of an old song to the extent that it loses its meaning and power. Think about what you want to say to the Lord in song. Consider all of God's mighty works and let your song give expression to those thoughts. Sing a new song. But before you label me as a proponent of contemporary worship where it seems each Sunday brings an onslaught of new songs that no one seems able to really sing, let me offer a little more insight. I love the old hymns. I grew up with them. They have great meaning and depth for me and each time I sing those hymns I am drawn into the Lord's presence. I think a lot of contemporary worship services miss the blessing of singing those well-worn affirmations of faith. But… having said that, the old hymns can certainly lose their meaning. We can recite the words without even a thought about their meaning. My point is for us to really think about worship and how the songs we sing offer our praises to God. Understand that not all the great hymns were written years ago. I believe that God is continually in the process of inspiring men and women to write new songs. Some of the "modern" choruses we sing have great power and depth. So, hopefully, there is room for all. We need both the old and the new. We need to sing whatever song we can to bring honor, glory, and praise to God each week.

Prayer
Father, even this day, may we sing to you a new song from the depths of our hearts. Amen.

Day 577   Psalm 99: Praise from the Footstool

> "Exalt the Lord our God And worship at His footstool; Holy is He."
> Psalm 99:5 (NASB)

Observation
This is the last of the section of the royal psalms. This psalm praises God as King. The psalmist declares that the Lord reigns and that the earth shakes. The ability to shake the foundations of the earth is a testimony to God's almighty power. The cherubim, mentioned in verse 1, are a reference to the two angels most closely related to the glory of God that graced the mercy seat atop the Ark of the Covenant. He goes on to mention that God is "great in Zion." This is a reference to the holy Temple in Jerusalem where the presence of God was uniquely felt. Three times in the psalm, the writer uses the phrase "Holy is He." To be holy was to be distinct and different. The word translated "holy" is the primary word used in Hebrew (*qadosh*) to describe the transcendence of God. The psalmist also makes mention of the "footstool" of God. Though this sometimes refers to the city of Jerusalem, here it specifically refers to the Temple. While we normally don't give much thought or honor to an ordinary footstool, here the meaning is elevated. The image is that of the people of God worshipping at the foot of their creator. As the psalm winds down, it makes a reference to Moses, Aaron, and Samuel. (This psalm is the only one to mention Samuel by name.) Just as God answered the prayers of the ancestors, God will continue to hear the prayers of God's people.

Application
I'm a little intrigued by this image of a footstool. I've never given much thought to having one in my house. My mother-in-law has a small one that makes its way around her den. It's been part of the family furniture for years. And… it does help to rest your feet on it at times. A few years back, I built an Adirondack chair for my back porch. I had some leftover wood and so I added a small footstool. It works well and seems to make a difference when you sit in the chair.

Would you ever think of a footstool as a place to worship? Of course not. It's where you place your feet. It's a humble little piece of furniture. Maybe that's the psalmist's point. Who are we that we would dare to worship God with anything but humility? Maybe the image of worshipping at God's footstool reminds us of both place and perspective. We should truly bow at God's feet. We should be humbled in God's presence and reliant upon God for all things. I don't know about you, but every once in a while, I need a gentle reminder to be humbled before the Lord. I need to acknowledge God's authority, wisdom, and control over my life. I need to be reminded that God is God, and I am not.

Prayer
God, may we know a healthy humility in our lives that acknowledges your lordship. Amen.

Day 578 — Psalm 100: A Different Kind of Worship

> "Worship the Lord with gladness. Come before him, singing with joy."
> Psalm 100:2 (NLT)

Observation
Psalm 100 is well-known to many. It is a psalm of thanksgiving that demands a public acknowledgement of God's glory and work. It is well-placed in the collection of psalms, following the set of royal psalms. Anonymously authored, it is certainly written from the heart of one who has experienced the joy of the Lord. The psalm is one of joyful praise in which the reader is invited to join in the worship of God. It speaks of the shepherding love of God and of God's lovingkindness that extends to all generations. The reader is also reminded that we are like sheep in God's pasture. We are protected, encouraged, and loved. We are to offer our glad worship and joyful songs because of God's goodness. God's mercy and truth are enduring to all generations.

Application
I want you to notice the attitude with which we are to enter God's presence, according to our focus verse. Worship with "gladness." We are to come before God "singing with joy." I wonder if such an attitude is clearly reflected in us each time that we enter our sanctuaries for a time of worship. Do we worship with gladness? Do we long to sing with joy? To be honest, many enter church without a lot of forethought concerning the experience. We come and sit and critique… the temperature is too warm, the organ is too loud, the praise team is too expressive, the songs are too long, the sermon is too boring, and the teenagers' dresses are too short. We base our experience of worship on how good the "performance of the day" turned out to be. We base our evaluation on the effectiveness of worship by the results at the invitation. If someone joined the church, it was a good day. If no one walked the aisle, it was all a waste of time. Is that really the experience of worship that we ought to have? Go back and read this psalm carefully. It speaks of gladness, joy, and celebration. True worship is not about musical volume, effective preaching, nor clothing style worn. It is about entering into the presence of God and asking God to melt our hearts, change our thoughts, and inspire our living. It is about connecting with God who loves us and who watches over us like a shepherd. I challenge you to let your day of worship be different. As you enter your church next Sunday, do so with an expectant heart, a humble spirit, and a joyful attitude. Unburden. Meditate. Praise. Laugh. Cry. Rejoice. Ponder. Give thanks. Worship with gladness and come before God singing with joy. It will be an altogether different experience.

Prayer
Father, thank you for the experience of worship that is ours to claim each week. May we go joyfully into your presence as we rub shoulders with the Saints of God. Amen.

Day 579 — Psalm 101: Faith Into Action

> "I will be careful to live a blameless life—when will you come to help me? I will lead a life of integrity in my own home." Psalm 101:2 (NLT)

Observation
Psalm 101 is a royal psalm, written by David while he serves the Lord as king over Israel. In the psalm, David asks for God's help in maintaining righteousness in the land. He promises to be faithful to God and hold the nation to a high standard. In verse 2, he declares that "he will be careful to live a blameless life." As proof of his pledge, he promises not to look at anything "vile or vulgar." He will have nothing to do with those who "deal crookedly." He will reject perverse ideas. He will search for faithful people as companions. And in the closing verse he also insists that his daily task will be that of ferreting out the wicked from the city of the Lord so that they cannot gain a grip on the city. In essence, David will hate all that God hates and love all that God loves.

Application
When I became pastor of my former church, I made a promise to the congregation the day they welcomed me as their leader. I promised that I would never enter the pulpit unprepared. I promised that I would always do the hard work and essential discipline needed to bring a fresh word from the Lord every single Sunday. For more than 17 years, I honored that promise. It was not always easy. Every week had its challenges and interruptions. There were always distractions that sought to force me to break my pledge. But keeping the promise was important and I dedicated myself to the task of preaching.

It's one thing to make a commitment… it's another to honor it. King David knew that it would take specific steps in his rule and reign to honor his commitment to live a blameless life. He knew there were guidelines to follow, rules to obey, and core values not to betray. For us, living a life that honors God takes constant vigilance. There are many distractions, many temptations, and many disruptions. We need to cling to our own set of core values and life commitments and dedicate ourselves each day to being the person God has willed for us to be. Maintaining our core beliefs takes discipline, reflection, and constant monitoring. Inattention to the things that matter will surely cause an erosion of our character and of our reputation. So, in the words of King David, be careful to live a blameless life. In your home and in your work and in your daily routines, be committed to honoring God in all that you do. Remember each day to acknowledge to whom you belong and pledge fidelity to the commitments that you have made.

Prayer
Father, as each of us make commitments to live in a way that pleases you, may we have the courage and the conviction needed to live out those commitments. Amen.

Day 580   Psalm 102: Future Praise

> "For the Lord has built up Zion; He has appeared in His glory. He has regarded the prayer of the destitute and has not despised their prayer. This will be written for the generation to come, that a people yet to be created may praise the Lord." Psalm 102:16-18 (NASB)

Observation
Psalm 102 is distinguished by a very unusual inscription. It states, "A prayer of the afflicted, when he is overwhelmed and pours out his complaint before the Lord." Though this psalm is written by an unnamed individual, it is most apparent that the writer is in great distress. The words of the psalm reflect both lament and penitence. The writer pleads for God to hear his prayer and his cry for help. He will speak about the fragility of life as he states that "his days are consumed in smoke" (v. 3). The psalmist also refers to three different kinds of birds… a pelican, an owl, and a sparrow. All three are known to live in distant, lonely places. This reference reflects the isolation and vulnerability of his own life, emotions intensified by the mocking of his enemies. But as the psalm progresses, the writer expresses hope that God will deliver him from his plight. He anticipates a time when God will reign over all the nations. The psalmist's joy is so intense over his deliverance that he wants future generations to learn of what God has done.

Application
Because we are all created with a lifespan, and because we daily feel the effects of aging, we have difficulty, at times, in thinking about the future that will extend on earth long after we are gone. I am blessed to have raised children and now even more abundantly blessed to have grandchildren. It is mind-boggling to think about how the story of God's redemption and grace through Christ is already being spoken into their lives. If I live long enough, I may even have great-grandchildren! But beyond that generation, it is hard to even imagine the generations yet to come. The psalmist pleads for the stories of God to be written so that "a people yet to be created may praise the Lord." I'm taken by that thought. First, I am taken with the idea that there are generations yet to be called into existence that will one day praise the Lord. I am fascinated by the idea that the praise of God each of us feels led to express, will be felt in the hearts of those born hundreds and perhaps thousands of years from now. Second, I am taken with the thought that you and I have a responsibility to write the God's stories so that those who come after us will know of God's faithfulness. Each of us has a story to tell. Each of us has experienced the mysterious movement of God in our lives at some point. There has been an answered prayer or the miraculous resolve of a troubling situation. Write the story down. Others will need to hear.

Prayer
Father, thank you for the role we play in telling your story to those yet to be created. Amen.

Day 581 — Psalm 103: Oxy Clean

> "As far as the east is from the west, So far has He removed our transgressions from us. Just as a father has compassion on his children, So the Lord has compassion on those who fear Him."
> Psalm 103:12-13 (NASB)

Observation

Psalm 103, written by David, is one of the most positive, uplifting, and hopeful of all the psalms. It is a psalm of praise that praises God for all of God's mercies. It begins with a singular voice as David pours out his thoughts but ends with a plural voice as both people and angels offer their praises to God. The psalm begins and ends with a call to "bless" the Lord. To bless the Lord is to remind ourselves that God is the source of all our blessings. The Hebrew word is "*barak*," which literally means, "to kneel." We are to kneel before God in joyful acknowledgment of all God's extended mercy. David declares that God heals us of all our diseases. Every healing event, mental, physical, or emotional, is the result of God's active grace in our lives. David also declares that God "satisfies our years with good things" (v. 5). As God's children, we experience the on-going, continual blessings of God. Even the oppressed find strength and celebration according to David. The theme of God's mercy is clearly stated in verse 10, "He has not dealt with us according to our sins, nor rewarded us according to our iniquities." Indeed, the call to bless the Lord is right and good.

Application

Most of us labor under a lot of guilt and shame. As we remember our transgressions, we continue to diminish our self-esteem and lower our self-image. We regret the things we have done and we continually "beat ourselves up" over our mistakes. It's just human nature to do so. But not so with God. In fact, the Bible consistently reminds us that God is merciful, loving, and even forgetful, when it comes to our sins. God chooses to remember them no more. I love the image of our focus verse, which reminds us that "as far as the east is from the west, so far has He removed our transgressions from us." Go stand on a hillside on some clear day. Look as far as you can to the east and then as far as you can to the west. In most cases, the distance from one horizon to the other is about 100 miles. That's a long way. It just illustrates the truth that God's desire to separate us from our sins, even the guilt and shame of our sins, is expansive. Because God has compassion on us, like a father has for his children, God's love erases even the memory of our sin. God carefully and swiftly spans the relational distance that our sins once created. Hebrews 8:12 reminds us that "He remembers our sins no more." So, when you are struggling with self-forgiveness, remember that God is not having the same struggle. So, bless the Lord… today and every day.

Prayer

Father, thank you for your compassion that bridges the gap our sins once created. Amen.

Day 582 — Psalm 104: Boundaries

> "You set a boundary that they may not pass over, So that they will not return to cover the earth." Psalm 104:9 (NASB)

Observation

Psalm 104 is referred to by some as both a wisdom psalm and a creation psalm. It certainly celebrates the creation of the world by God in poetic fashion. It is a joyful retelling of God's creative acts. If the reader were to "overlay" Genesis 1 on top of this psalm, he/she would quickly see the similarities as the psalmist describes the various moments of creation. Verse 2, for example, describes light as being the garment with which God is covered. Certainly the creation of light was a foundational work of creation. The psalmist describes the "beam of God's upper chambers," in reference to the heavenly dwelling place of God which goes beyond human comprehension. With descriptive language, the psalmist states that God "makes the clouds His chariot and rides the winds" (v. 3). God's power is displayed as God lays the foundations of the earth, separating the dry land from the watery abyss. Verses 14 and 15 describe the plants and animals God created to provide for the needs of humankind. The message is clear… all of creation depends upon God for birth, life, and sustenance.

Application

Every year I take on the same battle. It's the classic struggle with the crabgrass in my yard. There are clearly established boundaries where I want the grass to grow and where I don't want it to grow. Grass belongs in the yard, not on the sidewalk and not on my driveway. So, part of my weekly routine in the summer months, is that of using my "weed-eater" to trim the grass away from the places it doesn't belong. It's a continual battle.

Our focus verse speaks about the boundaries created by God when in separating the sea from the dry ground. The land belongs in one region, the waters in another. That's not the only boundary that God established. The 10 Commandments are a set of boundaries intended to govern relationships, emotions, and desires. God knew that all of us would need guardrails to control our lives. It has never been God's intention to limit our lives or lessen the joy of living. Just the opposite. God has given us boundaries to protect us, encourage us, and define us, so that we would experience the best life possible. Let's be honest. We need the boundaries. We need someone to establish the guidelines and the rules lest we allow our uncontrolled desires, passions, and thoughts overtake our best judgement. And just like the crabgrass that always attempts to overtake the boundaries, we have to be vigilant to carefully guard our lives to make sure we have not "crept" into those areas that lead to trouble. Don't be afraid of little self-reflection. Pay attention to the boundaries and live well.

Prayer

Father, thank you for the guidelines you have established for our successful living. Amen.

Day 583 — Psalm 105: The Importance of Our Promises

> "He has remembered His covenant forever, The word which He commanded to a thousand generations." Psalm 105:8 (NASB)

Observation
This is a psalm of praise in which the psalmist focuses on the positive experiences of Israel during her early history. The point is not to celebrate the faithfulness of the nation, for certainly there were difficult moments of rebellion, but the point was to celebrate the faithfulness of God. "Remembering" is the key theme to this psalm. The people needed to be reminded of God's continual faithfulness. There is speculation that this psalm was written as the people returned from the Babylonian exile to encourage them as they returned to the land. In the psalm, much of the history of the Egyptian captivity, exodus, and wilderness experience is told. The story of the plagues is recounted. The provision in the desert of quail, manna, and water is also remembered. Over and over again, the writer points to God's faithfulness towards God's chosen people. It is a reminder that God has been and will be faithful to promises made.

Application
Many of you were fans of the television comedy series, *The Office*. Michael Scott, the manager of the Dunder-Mifflin paper company, is a terrible leader who creates many awkward and cringe-worthy moments. By common consent, the worst of his mistakes is told in an episode called, "Scott's Tots," where he fails to make good on a promise given to a group of high school students to pay their college tuition.

Let's face it… there is nothing worse than a broken promise. When commitments are made, agreements established, and covenants begun, the expectation is that those promises will be kept. When we take out a loan at a bank, the expectation is that we will repay. When we recite our wedding vows, the expectation is that we will honor those commitments. When we give our word and shake hands on a deal, the expectation is that we will keep our word. Our integrity, character, and morality are all on the line with each promise that we make, whether great or small. When we break our promises or betray our vows, lack of trustworthiness and deception become our reputation. Do we keep our word? Can people count on the things that we say? The psalmist points to God's reliability. God stands by God's covenant, keeping promises to a thousand generations. We count on that. Our hope and assurance are nailed to the belief that God will do exactly as God says. We count on God's forgiveness, acceptance of us, and preparation of our place in eternity. So let's walk in God's footsteps today and honor all the commitments that we make.

Prayer
Father, may our words have intentionality and integrity. May we be trustworthy. Amen.

Day 584 — Psalm 106: The Deep Well of Praise

> "Who can list the glorious miracles of the Lord? Who can ever praise him enough?" Psalm 106:2 (NLT)

Observation

This psalm celebrates Israel's joy in finding forgiveness for her sins. It is a wisdom psalm, and recalls the history of Israel from the time of the exodus through the time of the conquest. The psalmist calls for praise despite the short memory of the people. They were forgetting the mercies of God and needed to be reminded. It appears that Psalms 105 and 106 are companion poems and are probably written by the same writer. This psalm includes a word of confession on the part of the contemporary community of Israelites. It speaks of the way they committed iniquity and behaved wickedly as their fathers had done. The story of the golden calf, recorded in Exodus 32, is recalled. The psalm also recalls God's judgment for Israel's refusal to drive out all the people of Canaan, which resulted in corrupt worship practices for generations to come. The psalmist is also careful to remind the reader of God's faithfulness to God's covenant even though the people did not always act obediently. The final call to "Praise the Lord!" (v. 48) is the concluding verse of Book 4 of the Psalms.

Application

There was an old hymn that was often sung in my home church back in the day when congregations drew strength from the singing of the great hymns of faith. Written by Johnson Oatman (1897), it was titled, "Count Your Blessings." The refrain went like this… "Count your many blessings name them one by one, count your many blessings see what God has done. Count your blessings. Name then one by one. Count your many blessings see what God has done." Like the words of our focus verse, that hymn was a call for all believers to take a moment to recall and even count all the bountiful blessings of God poured out on every life. The psalmist asks, "Who can list the glorious miracles of the Lord? Who can ever praise Him enough?" It is true that our blessings come in such abundance and with such consistency that we are amiss at times to praise the God who has sent them our way. They really are too numerous to count. Each day adds to the list. Though we might occasionally praise the Lord for some great and mighty answer to prayer, we often neglect to thank God for the simple blessings of each day… like life, health, food, shelter, friendship, etc. There should be a deep well of praise from within us. Words of gratitude should continually flow from our lips.

Let me give you a challenge today. I'm not going to ask you to name all your blessings, but to name the first five that come to your mind. Scribble them down a scrap of paper, then take a moment to express your praise to the Father.

Prayer

Father, teach us to have thankful hearts and consistent words of praise. Amen.

Day 585 — Psalm 107: The Lost Art of Faith Sharing

> "Has the Lord redeemed you? Then speak out! Tell others he has redeemed you from your enemies." Psalm 107:2 (NLT)

Observation
Psalm 107 marks the beginning of Book 5 of the Psalms. This is the final section in the collection (Psalms 107-150). It is a wisdom psalm that reviews God's actions in the experiences of God's people. Much of the experiences described are not mentioned in the Torah narrative. The key theme is to illustrate the ways in which God's mercy endures forever. God is seen as always being willing to reach out to those who call out. Among other experiences described in the psalm, the writer talks about those caught in a wilderness experience and those who sit in dark prison cells. The wilderness experience may be a reference the Sinai experience or it may refer to some other generic experience when people were separated from the familiar surroundings of their home. The dark prison experience may describe those who are in distress because of their own rebellion. In both situations, God brings deliverance. The psalm also teaches that because of sinfulness, God may, at times, bring a curse on the land or afflict the people to bring them back into a proper, obedient relationship.

Application
What a powerful and important reminder is given to us as readers in our focus verse. "Has the Lord redeemed you? Then speak out!" The word redemption literally means, "to buy back," or "to reclaim through the means of a payment." Has the Lord redeemed you? Redemption is central to our understanding of the Christian faith. Our sins and mistakes have distanced us from God. We are separated from God with no hope of bridging the divide. But through the sacrificial death of Christ, our sins have been paid and we have been reconciled to God. We are redeemed... bought back. Most of us as Christians understand that thought. What we fail to do however, is to "speak out" about it. We rarely tell the story of our redemption because we rarely seek opportunities for doing so. And yet, the greatest single task left to us by Christ is that of preaching and teaching the Gospel to the entire world so that we can create disciples.

Here's the problem with the 21st century church here in America. We have drifted towards a "faith in action" mentality almost to the exclusion of faith sharing. Don't misunderstand. Humanitarian relief efforts, social justice concerns, housing the homeless and giving food to the hungry are all vitally important concerns that the church must address, but so is the need for faith sharing. We cannot fail to speak out and proclaim our redemption. Even in our noble efforts, we must proclaim the reasons for those efforts.

Prayer
Father, may we never lose sight of our calling to share the Gospel as our priority. Amen.

Day 586   Psalm 108: Finding Power

> "With God's help we will do mighty things, for he will trample down our foes." Psalm 108:13 (NLT)

Observation
Psalm 108 is a psalm of David in which he expresses his assurance of God-led victories over his enemies. He speaks of the trust that all of God's people can experience as they make God the Lord of their lives. To the reader, some of the verses may sound familiar. The verses are a medley of two earlier psalms of David. Verses 1-5 are taken from Psalm 57:7-11, and verses 6-13 are taken from Psalm 60:5-12. Even though these words are written by David, it is possible that an anonymous editor arranged them in this order to be used in Temple worship. David's zeal to praise the Lord is contagious. In verse 2 David declares, "I will awaken the dawn with my songs." He wants to sing the Lord's praises even before the sun arises. Verse 7 is interesting. The verse states, "I will rejoice." These words are not spoken by David, but by God. The Lord has pleasure in defending God's people and giving them victory.

Application
Are you familiar with a piece of heavy equipment called a "Bobcat?" It's like a small bulldozer used to haul dirt, scoop-up gravel, and dig trenches. Years ago, I had a couple of big yard projects to undertake. I needed to move a lot of stone from one end of the yard to the other. I needed to tear out some bushes and build a dirt embankment. Using only hand tools would have taken forever. But a friend offered to drop off his Bobcat for the day so that I could get my work done. It was great. I felt like a kid with a brand-new toy. I was moving gravel, pushing over small trees, and digging my way to China. A project that could have taken days, was completed in only a few hours. The difference? A powerful piece of equipment. With that power, I could do mighty things. David reminds us that with the strength of the Lord undergirding our lives, passions, and vision, that we can do mighty things. Tasks that seem impossible, obstacles that seem insurmountable, and barriers that seem unscalable can all be destroyed by the power of God at work within us. Think about the way in which the Lord accomplishes tasks. God plants a vision into the heart of one of God's children, then equips that person with talents, abilities, and passion. God arranges the circumstances… the people, place, and moment, so that what God needs to accomplish will be accomplished. With God's help we do mighty things. Sometimes our doubts overrule our passion. Sometimes our sense of meager resources thwarts our plans. It is in such moments that we must remember the power of God that longs to work through us.

Prayer
Father, this day… couple your vision with your power in each of us. Amen.

Day 587   Psalm 109: The Nasty Business of Revenge

> "Let his years be few; let someone else take his position. May his children become fatherless, and his wife a widow. May his children wander as beggars and be driven from their ruined homes." Psalm 109:8-10 (NLT)

Observation
Psalm 109 is a psalm of David in which he pleads for God to bring judgment upon those who have accused him falsely. Some categorize this psalm as a "precatory" psalm. (A precatory prayer is one in which the person praying asks for God to bring judgment upon enemies.) David calls upon God to no longer keep silent about his enemies. He declares his innocence and insists that his enemies have rewarded his good intentions towards them with evil responses. He vents his anger with words and not action. He asks God to make his enemies suffer in the ways they have suggested that David suffer. He, in essence, throws their curses back on them. They had prayed that his wife would become a widow and that his children would become beggars. He now prays for his enemies to know such suffering. He is clearly lashing out in the midst of his suffering. There is a redemptive note at the end of the psalm. David wants his enemies to see the name of God proclaimed and honored. David closes the psalm by praising God for deliverance.

Application
Revenge is a nasty business. It escalates conflict. It explodes into further violence. It is open-ended. And… it is not the way of our Lord. Let me illustrate it with this simple scenario. A child is chasing a soccer ball during a pee-wee league soccer game. An opponent steps in front of him at the last second to steal the ball, but in so doing, the first child is bumped out of the way. Believing that he has been wronged, he retaliates by pushing the other player. The other player then pushes back. Within seconds the two are scuffling on the ground. Coaches come out onto the field to break it up, but words are exchanged. Soon, parents in the stands get into the name-calling fray as well. Things are about to get out of hand.

Let's admit this… revenge is a part of our human nature. When we are wronged, it is only natural to want to respond, push back, get even. There might be a momentary satisfaction with such action, but the tension is still present, and any potential relationship is still very broken. When speaking about the topic of revenge, Jesus said to "turn the other cheek." His ethic demands a very different response to injury. Rather than revenge, his ethic demands a de-escalation of conflict. Jesus demands that we do whatever is necessary not to fan the flame of further angry action. Jesus knew that no seeds of peace, harmony, or relationship are ever sown in the soil of angry revenge. It's a choice… war or peace. Which will you choose this day?

Prayer
Father, may we demonstrate the grace and forgiveness of Jesus in all things. Amen.

Day 588 — Psalm 110: Finding Refreshment

> "But he himself will be refreshed from brooks along the way.
> He will be victorious." Psalm 110:7 (NLT)

Observation

Psalm 110, written by David, is a royal psalm, and is the most directly messianic psalm of them all. It is cited nine times in the New Testament with exclusive reference to the Messiah. Jesus himself identified David as the writer and asserted that David was speaking of someone greater than himself. Since no ordinary son of David could be greater than the king, "the Lord" of verse 1 refers to the coming Messiah. Hence, this psalm describes a conversation between God the Father and Christ the Son in which the Father grants the Son royal and priestly honors. To sit at the right hand of the Father is the place of highest honor given to Christ upon his resurrection and ascension. As he writes, David envisions God appointing the coming Messiah as the great high priest for all of time. He is a priest by divine proclamation and not by human descent.

Application

In describing the conquering of nations, David describes the sense of refreshment that the Messiah will find along the way. Notice his words, "but he himself will be refreshed from brooks along the way." Catch that image. David is describing the ways in which God will provide for the Messiah's needs, quite literally in some cases, by providing him with fresh water to quench his thirst. The psalm also speaks of God's continual provision and watchcare over our lives. So where do you find refreshment in your life? What sustains you and keeps you going? We all need a little help. Many need the morning jolt of coffee to get their day started. Some are refreshed by a long walk or maybe even by a run late in the day. Some are refreshed by reading a great novel or taking a warm shower. Barney Fife used to require "a little sugar pick-me-up" late in the afternoon! All those things and more can certainly refresh us from time to time, but the kind of refreshment that the Bible offers goes much deeper. Rather than a refreshment of the body, it's a refreshment of the soul. Connecting with God and learning to rest in God's provision for our lives gives to each of us a constant renewal. Our trust in God gives us assurance each day, grace for every moment, strength for every task, and hope for every situation. We are impoverished without such help. We need God's refreshment each day in our lives. Today, I challenge you to do more than merely satisfy the need for physical refreshment. Work on satisfying the need for spiritual refreshment. Pray. Meditate. Seek. Read. Confess. Ask. Question. Rest. God waits to keep you refreshed along the way. Trust God today to lead you beside a brook of refreshment.

Prayer

Father, thank you for your sustaining presence that longs to nourish and sustain us. Amen.

Day 589 — Psalm 111: The Power of the Crowd

> "Praise the Lord! I will thank the Lord with all my heart as I meet with his godly people." Psalm 111:1 (NLT)

Observation
Psalm 111 is both a psalm of wisdom and praise. It is linked to Psalm 112. Together the lines are written as an acrostic of the Hebrew alphabet with 22 lines. The distinct purpose of the psalm is to praise the Lord. God's creation is obligated to give God worship. According to our focus verse, this worship is to be given with all one's heart. Further, worship is not just a private activity, but should include an experience with others who are collectively joined in praise. The psalmist recognizes that food and all the other provisions of God are gifts from God. The closing verse should be familiar to most readers. "The fear of the Lord is the beginning of wisdom" (v. 10). Fear means to come into the presence of God with a sense of wonder and awe. Obedient response demonstrates our appreciation of who God is. The wiser we become, the more we value the importance of obeying God's commands.

Application
There is something to be said for corporate worship. Although we can certainly worship God in any place and at any time, there is a special and unique moment created when God's people praise the Lord together. There is something about the experience of being surrounded by others who lend their voices in praise, which allows each of us to "thank the Lord with all our hearts." There is an energy. An excitement. A euphoric feeling. Being with others allows us to lose our inhibitions and our self-consciousness so that we can openly and verbally express our praise. Think about it… are you more likely to sing with fervor and zeal when all alone in a room, or when you are surrounded by hundreds of others doing the same thing?

One of my favorite memories of attending The Southern Baptist Theological Seminary in the mid 1980s was singing the great hymns of faith during chapel services. The room would be filled with eager, young ministers, caught up in the joy of their calling and their preparation for service. The hymns, accompanied by both organ and piano, were powerful, forceful, and encouraging. There was a strength provided. There was camaraderie of spirit that filled the room. We were doing as the psalmist suggested… we were thanking the Lord with all our hearts and with godly people. Even now, separated by decades of time and distance, I can still remember those special moments.

Such moments are awaiting you this coming Lord's day. When you raise your voice with others in joyful, exuberant praise, your spirit is lifted, and the Lord is pleased. So, when you go to church this week, don't hold back. Sing out with all your heart.

Prayer
Father, may we offer you an exciting song of praise as we worship this week. Amen.

Day 590 — Psalm 112: Ability to See Beyond the Present

> "Light shines in the darkness for the godly. They are generous, compassionate, and righteous." Psalm 112:4 (NLT)

Observation

Psalm 112 is a wisdom psalm and, again, is very closely related to Psalm 111. Together they are a matched pair of acrostic poems. Some scholars attribute them to David, yet his name is not connected with either poem. Both psalms begin with the words, "Praise the Lord!" The Hebrew word for that expression is the word, "Hallelujah." Throughout the collection of psalms, the destiny of the righteous and the wicked are sharply contrasted. This psalm pays special attention to the elevated joy and security of those who remain obedient to God. According to the psalm, the righteous person will have prominence and a lasting sense of worth. Verse 8 declares that the righteous will face their foes triumphantly.

Application

There are a few basic tools that should be a part of every household. Everyone needs a hammer, a good set of screw drivers, a pair of pliers, an adjustable wrench, maybe a tape measure, and a good set of end wrenches. I'm not suggesting that just those tools can solve any household need, but they would certainly be helpful in most situations. Add to that list, a good, sturdy, and bright flashlight. There are times when the ability to shine a little additional light into a dark room, or even into a dark corner can make all the difference.

The psalmist reminds us that the righteous person can shine light into the darkness of culture and situation because of abiding relationship with God. In fact, the righteous person can see beyond the present. The righteous person can look well beyond the difficulties of the present moment and know that God is at work. Because the righteous can see the movement, protection, and grace of God in every moment, they are able to be generous, compassionate, and righteous. They have an appreciation for the big picture of God that allows them to see and offer perspective well beyond the present moment.

All of us need to have in our lives those righteous people who can shine a light in a present darkness. That light could be a word of encouragement, or a voice of reason, a promise of scripture, or a shoulder on which to cry. We need people to remind us of the goodness of God so that we will know that "the sufferings of the present time are not worthy to be compared to the glory that will be revealed in us" (Romans 8:18 NASB). I hope you have such persons in your life. And... I hope that as a person of faith, you can be that "light" in the dark moment of someone else's life. Light shines in the darkness for the godly. We see beyond the present moment. We know of a greater Kingdom. We live with a hope that is inextinguishable.

Prayer

Father, give us your light of wisdom, and use us as your light of guidance. Amen.

Day 591 — Psalm 113: Balancing Act

> "He lifts the poor from the dust and the needy from the garbage dump. He sets them among princes, even the princes of his own people!"
> Psalm 113:7-8 (NLT)

Observation

This psalm begins and ends with the word, "Hallelujah!" It is obviously a psalm of praise in which the majesty of God is described. Psalms 113 and 114 are recited as a part of the Passover Seder celebration, spoken before the serving of dinner. Psalms 115-118 are also a part of the Seder experience but are recited following the meal. When the psalmist declares that the "Name of the Lord" is to be praised, he refers to the whole person of God. The reader is challenged to center his/her thoughts on the character of God. From "east to west," in every place, the name and nature of God is to be praised. God is sovereign over all, not limited to a tribe or territory like the pagan deities. The psalmist goes on to declare that God's glory cannot be contained in the universe. It is beyond the capacity of human language to describe. A common theme in the psalms, one especially highlighted in this psalm, is God's care for the poor and needy. This psalm tells of God's redemption and salvation on their behalf, raising them to the status of full citizens in God's Kingdom.

Application

I recently received a very unusual and precious gift from a friend in Gatlinburg, Tennessee. She and her husband owned and operated a wonderful local restaurant in that town for several years called The Mountain Lodge. Unfortunately, the devastating fires that attacked that region a few years back burned the small restaurant to the ground. As they sifted through the debris, my friend found several pieces of pottery that survived the fire that once sat on the tables in the restaurant. She gave me one of those pieces because of the friendship that our two families have shared for the past 25 years.

It's interesting how pieces of great worth and value can be claimed from the remnants of a fire, or even, as the psalmist declares, from "a garbage dump." Only he is not describing pottery, but persons. Notice the balancing act of God. God takes the lowly, the abused, the forgotten, the marginalized, and sets them among princes. He balances the poor condition of their plight with a joyful eternity. What joy there is in knowing that God lifts the poor, both in possession and spirit, and sets them in a place of prominence in the Kingdom. And if our God is so concerned about lifting the poor from the plight they suffer, shouldn't it be part of our daily work? We must be reminded that in the eyes of God, each of us, even the poorest of among us, is of great worth. As believers, we must set the standards for how the underprivileged among us are treated. Dignity, respect, and grace should set the agenda.

Prayer

Father, may we continually lift the downtrodden and celebrate their humanity. Amen.

Day 592 — Psalm 114: The Power of Our God

> "The Red Sea saw them coming and hurried out of their way! The water of the Jordan River turned away. The mountains skipped like rams, the hills like lambs!" Psalm 114:3-4 (NLT)

Observation
This psalm offers praise to the Lord for deliverance at the time of the Exodus. It has a light, lively tone that balances the heavier tone and theology of the first psalm of deliverance, which is recorded in Exodus 15. Remember that this psalm was read along with Psalm 113 at Passover before the Seder meal was served. In some translations, the opening verse speaks of the deliverance of Israel "from a people of a strange language," in reference to Egypt. Such a statement is an affirmation that the worth and value of the Israelites is not bound up in the splendor of Egypt… her power or riches. This psalm also offers the image of God that cannot be contained in a simple sanctuary made by human hands. The psalmist also describes the way in which the seas, hills, and mountains all shake as a frightened animal before the presence of an all-powerful God. The water references are obvious. The shaking of the mountains refers to Sinai "quaking" when Moses received the 10 Commandments.

Application
I know someone who has a taser… the kind like the police use to subdue a perpetrator. Don't ask me why this person has a taser, or if he is supposed to have a taser… just know that I have seen it and have heard it when he turns it on. It makes the most awful, electrical, static discharge kind of noise. Think bug zapper on steroids! The sound is so scary, that you think, "Man, I don't ever want to be zapped by one of those." It doesn't take much to realize that a great amount of power is contained in that small device.

Now consider the power of God. Of course, there is no comparison. But if a small electrical device can instill fear, just imagine the power of God that can make the waters of the sea flee in terror and cause the mountains to skip like a ram. How great, how powerful, how frightening, how majestic is such a force. This psalm is a reminder that we serve an all-powerful God. This is God's world, God's universe, God's dominion to control. And just think… God wields that power in a way that brings security, safety, and hope to our lives. Paul asks rhetorically, "Who will separate us from the love of Christ?" (Romans 8:35 NASB). Just think, the power that holds the universe together… the power that moves mountains and calms seas… the power that lights the morning sky… the power that calls all things into being… that same power is the force that holds us close to the heart of God. In God's arms we are safe and secure. By God's grace, we will be held until the end of the age. Nothing can challenge or change that.

Prayer
Father, we stand amazed in your presence. Thank you. Amen.

Day 593 — Psalm 115: Idol Worship

> "Their idols are merely things of silver and gold, shaped by human hands. They have mouths but cannot speak, and eyes but cannot see. They have ears but cannot hear, and noses but cannot smell. They have hands but cannot feel, and feet but cannot walk, and throats but cannot make a sound." Psalm 115:4-7 (NLT)

Observation

This is a community psalm of praise that focuses on the glory of God and God's superiority over all the created idols of men. In the opening verse, the psalmist is careful to direct praise in the direction where it should be placed. "Not to us, not to us, O Lord, but to Thy name be glory given." God is always and only the object of our praise. Praise and glory should never be offered to ourselves nor the idols we create. God is supreme. Unlike the idols of men's creation, God is not bound by place or the incantations of men. The psalmist speaks of the inability of idols to provide any comfort, answer any prayer, or display any power. Idols are simply "things" created by the hands of men. They cannot speak, see, hear, smell, feel, walk, or utter a sound. They are inert, lifeless, spiritless objects. How foolish to worship that which is not alive.

Application

It's a lesson some 3,000 years in the making… this teaching of false idols and their inability to do a single thing for our lives except turn our focus from God. Remember the days of the wilderness experience when the Israelites were encamped at the foot of Sinai? During Moses' long delay on the mountain top, the people grew restless and fashioned an idol of gold in the form of a calf. They bowed down, offered prayers, danced lively, and sang their songs of worship. When Moses returned, they suffered the wrath of God as a result of their disobedience. Three-thousand men were put to death because of their heinous actions.

Such a narrative would never describe us, or so we think. We are enlightened. We would never chase after false gods… idols made of human hands. Or would we? Truthfully, we chase after a lot of man-made stuff, lifting such things to places of importance in our lives. Think about it… how much time and energy do you spend each day with your smart phone and the social media apps that are installed on it? How berserk do you go when the cable goes out and you can't watch television? How much pride do you put in your car or house? If we are not careful, we can make almost anything into an idol that draws both our focus and our time. It's all about priorities. What is of greatest importance to you? What gets the focus of your life? Where do you invest your time? Where your treasure is, there shall your heart be also. Take a moment this morning to consider what or whom you really worship.

Prayer

Father, forgive us when we make our "things" the focus of our lives. Amen.

Day 594 — Psalm 116: We Pray Because God Listens

> "I love the Lord because he hears my voice and my prayer for mercy. Because he bends down to listen, I will pray as long as I have breath!"
> Psalm 116:1-2 (NLT)

Observation

This is one of the Passover psalms, recited as a part of the celebration of the Seder meal. Because it was a part of the meal, it was most likely recited by Jesus on the night of his arrest, which occurred just after his celebration of Passover with his disciples. Read through the lens of Christ's sacrifice, there are several messianic components and thoughts in this psalm. The psalm itself reflects a deep sense of excitement and emotion. Like Psalm 40, this psalm describes God's bending down to hear and meet the needs of God's children. The writer has obviously experienced some moment of suffering through which he has found the salvation of God. He has been saved from his sufferings. In the latter part of the psalm, the writer declares that he will praise God with an audible voice in the public arena. He closes by promising to fulfill his vow of offering praise. One other important detail is to know that this psalm was recited just after the third cup of wine was passed during the Passover celebration. This was the "Cup of Salvation/Redemption." This connection again has many implications for the role of Christ on this night as he cries out to God in the garden.

Application

Let me be transparent this morning about my personal prayer life. I am careful to keep a rather extensive prayer list. It contains the names of more than 100 people. I pray for the people on this list every day without fail. It is interesting in my prayer discipline that some of the names emerge with a greater need than others from time to time. And though I am careful to recite the whole list, there are some for whom I make special petition as the need arises. To be honest, there are moments when the discipline gets a little tedious and maybe a little mundane. It is a challenge at times, not to just quickly read through the list and offer a bunch of phrases like, "God bless this person," but to truly make meaningful petition. And so, I try to pray in different ways with different strategies in the hope that I don't get caught in the trap of meaningless repetition. But again, my goal is to remember each person on the list, each day.

And here's why I do it day after day. I do it because of the truth contained in our focus verse. God hears my voice when I pray. God "bends down" to listen. That's why all of us should pray… because God listens. Our inner selves listen, too. We pray because God listens, and we pray because we also need to be reminded each day of our utter dependency upon God. Each prayer is a reminder to self that we don't have the answers, the power, nor the wisdom to solve the problems of each day.

Prayer

Father, may we be faithful to practice our discipline of prayer because you listen. Amen.

Day 595   Psalm 117: All Inclusive

> "Praise the Lord, all nations; Laud Him, all peoples! For His lovingkindness is great toward us, And the truth of the Lord is everlasting. Praise the Lord!"
> Psalm 117 (NASB)

Observation

Psalm 117 is the shortest of all the psalms. (The entire psalm is quoted above.) It is a psalm of praise calling on all the nations to praise the Lord. It is also one of the hallel psalms (113-118). These psalms, used in conjunction with Passover worship, all end with the phrase, "Praise the Lord!" or in the Hebrew, "Hallelujah." Most likely, this was one of the praise songs sung by participants who had just finished consuming the Seder meal at Passover. Notice the use of the word, "Laud" in the opening verse. The Hebrew word is *"shabach,"* and literally means, "to speak well of." Thus the psalmist is directing all nations to speak well of the God of Israel. The reason for doing so is because of God's faithfulness in fulfilling promises to Israel. Part of God's promise was that all the nations of earth would be blessed by the descendants of Abraham. In the fulfillment of God's redemptive plan, Christ would come as a Savior to all who would accept him in faith. Thus, all the nations of the earth are called to bless the Lord because all the nations of the earth are included in the redemptive purposes of God.

Application

Whenever we think of the term "all-inclusive," we generally think in terms of a vacation deal or resort offer, where everything is included in the vacation package price… all the lodging, travel, food, etc. Nothing is left out. All travelers have to worry about is having a good time. I have a friend who recently took one of those exciting European riverboat tours that offered an all-inclusive package. He said it was amazing and one of the most relaxing trips he had taken. He added however, that the cost for the all-inclusive plan was a little daunting.

Let's move away from vacation packages or riverboat cruises and talk about God's redemptive plan. From the very beginning of time, God has always had an answer for humanity's sinfulness. It has always been God's plan that all the nations, all tribes, and all people could find solace for their sin-wounded lives. John's Gospel opens with the words, "In the beginning was the Word and the Word was with God and the Word was God." The Greek word in that verse translated as "Word," is the word *"logos."* In the beginning was the *logos*… One of the possible translations in Greek of the word *logos*, is "answer." Try plugging that into the same verse… "In the beginning was the answer." Amazing, right? That from the start, God, through the redemptive work of Christ, has been providing an answer for the sins of the world. It's an all-inclusive offer that even reaches to each of us. Praise the Lord! God has THE answer for us.

Prayer

Father, we thank you this day for the forgiveness and salvation we have through Jesus. Amen.

Day 596 — Psalm 118: The Gift of Each Day

> "This is the day the Lord has made. We will rejoice and be glad in it."
> Psalm 118:24 (NLT)

Observation
Psalm 118 is a psalm of praise and is the last of the Passover or hallel psalms used in worship during the Passover Celebration. The first four verses contain an antiphonal response. The people were to declare in response, "His love endures forever!" In praising God for mercy, the psalmist also declares God's triumph even in impossible circumstances. He boldly declares, "The Lord is on my side" (v. 6). Though surrounded by his enemies, he knows that God will help him to gain victory. He summons the people to join him in his praises. He mentions the "strong right hand of the Lord" (v. 15), a direct quote from the psalm of Moses in Exodus 15:6. He further extols the limitless strength of God to save. One notable verse is verse 22, which describes the stone that the builders rejected becoming the chief cornerstone. This verse, of course, is quoted three times in the Gospels as it describes both the rejection and exultation of Jesus. In verse 25, the psalmist cries out to God saying, "Save now, I pray O Lord." The words "save now" are the most common translation of the Hebrew word, "hosanna." Remember that on the day of Jesus' triumphant entry, he declared that if his followers had failed to offer such a word of praise that even the rocks would have cried out with celebration (Luke 19:40).

Application
Our focus verse is among the more familiar verses of this psalm. It's quoted in song and often found in the places where people want to be reminded of God's daily presence in their lives. It is a careful reminder that this day and every day are days created by God. And if so, there is reason to rejoice and be glad. Let's unpack that for a moment. All of us have lived long enough to know that not every day is a day in which we feel like rejoicing. We've all had those bad days when we feel scared, alone, confused, and maybe abandoned. And yet we are told to rejoice and be glad for the gift of each day. Through the lens of faith we need to see the value and worth of each day because of what God is doing in our world and in our time. Every day is a moment for God's glory to be displayed, God's truth to be revealed, and God's work to be accomplished. Each day moves the needle a bit further towards God's redemptive plan and the coming Kingdom. And even though certain days may not be "good days" for us, we need to consider that each day is the deliberate creative act of God who will use that day for God's purpose. It may well be that, even on our worst days, God will work through our experience to bring others into the Kingdom. So rejoice today. God is at work.

Prayer
Father, we thank you for this very day. May you be glorified through us. Amen.

Day 597 — Psalm 119: God Said It, That Settles It

"Forever, O Lord, Your word is settled in heaven." Psalm 119:89 (NASB)

Observation
Psalm 119 is the longest of all the psalms. In fact, at 176 verses, it is by far the longest chapter in the entire Bible. Even a casual reading of the text will take the average reader about 11.5 minutes. It is uniquely and beautifully structured. There are 22 letters in the Hebrew alphabet. The psalm is broken into 22 sections of eight verses each. In each section, all eight verses begin with the particular letter for that section. For example, the first eight verses begin with the Hebrew letter "aleph." The entire psalm is a song of praise dedicated to the celebration of God's word to the people. The psalmist gives nearly an exhaustive affirmation of the ways in which God's law gives direction and guidance to the people of Israel. ("Law" here means more than the five books of the Torah. The psalmist is referring to all of God's instruction.) The law was not given as a means to find salvation, but so that the people of God would learn to live as God's holy and distinct people. There is some question of authorship. Some argue that this is a psalm of David, used by David to teach the Hebrew alphabet to his son Solomon. Others argue that Ezra is the author. Ezra was the "great law giver," second only to Moses, whose task it was to re-establish a fervor and dedication to the Law in the hearts of the people of God following the time of the exile.

(In reading the text, you will discover several well-known and recognizable verses. I personally have found it helpful to underline key verses that seem to "jump off the page" as you navigate your way through this long passage. Nearly all the 22 sections will leave you with verses to ponder. Some of my favorite verses include: 9, 10, 11, 46, 103, 105, 133, and 164, in addition to our focus verse 89.)

Application
We live in a culture and age where opinions, thoughts, and guidelines seem to be in a constant state of flux. Values change. Morals relax. Boundaries get moved. Standards are rewritten. Unfortunately we often set our opinions of what is right and wrong by the ever-changing winds of culture. In contrast to such ebb and flow, the psalmist reminds us that God's Word is settled in heaven. It has been established from day one. God doesn't change guidelines to adjust to our slippery slope of morality. The goal should not be our attempt to make God's Word conform to our thinking, but to make our thinking conform to God's unchanging Word. "Thy Word is a lamp unto my feet, and a light unto my path" (v. 105 KJV).

Prayer
Father, we praise you for your strong and powerful Word. Make us obedient. Amen.

Day 598 — Psalm 120: Changing Your Culture

> "I am tired of living among people who hate peace." Psalm 120:6 (NLT)

Observation

Psalm 120 is the first of a collection of psalms known as the psalms of ascent (Psalms 120-134). Most likely, these psalms were sung by pilgrims making their way to Jerusalem and to the Temple to worship the Lord during one of the three annual national Jewish festivals (Passover, Pentecost, and Tabernacles). These songs may have been sung along the way as encouragement during the midst of long and sometimes arduous travel. The term "ascent" is quite literal. Jerusalem was built on a high hill and the Temple was built on the highest spot within the city. The Temple could be seen for miles by those coming from the surrounding areas. Pilgrims literally "ascended" to the city and to the Temple. This psalm pays particular attention to the lies told by the wicked that sometimes affect the attitudes and thoughts of the righteous. The wicked speak with "lying lips" (v. 2). The pilgrim knew however, that once in Jerusalem, they would join with the people of God and would hear the truth of God.

Application

The psalmist expresses great lament over being forced to live among people who were hostile to his faith and to his God. He became weary of living among those who hated peace. Apparently, he lived amidst persecution, hostility, and alienation. He lived among people who had little regard for his expression of faith. Ever feel that way? Ever grow weary of the crowd that surrounds you, especially those whose life-focus is all about greed, selfishness, meanness, and corruption? Sometimes, in our attempt to live out the claims of the Gospel, we will find ourselves caught up in a culture that scoffs at our morality and ridicules our passion for God. What to do in such a setting? One choice is to flee. Flee your circumstances. Move to a better city. Find a safer job. Surround yourself with people who think just like you do. The other choice is a bit more difficult. It is that of deciding to be the change-agent within your circle of influence. Let me remind you that the world is not impressed with your private devotions. Our culture is not changed behind the cloistered walls of your pious spirituality. It gets changed when dedicated Christians choose to live out their faith with intensity, authenticity, and consistency. Rather than throw up our hands and declare that all is lost, we need to throw up our prayers and declare that the things that are lost must be reclaimed. I challenge you this morning to pray for the culture in which you live and then to recommit yourself to living distinctively within that culture. Evil will always triumph when the godly remain silent. If you are tired of living in a godless culture, become as Christ within that culture and let your lived-out Gospel transform others.

Prayer

Father, may we live boldly, courageously, and consistently as your people. Amen.

Day 599 — Psalm 121: Safe & Secure

> "I will lift up my eyes to the mountains; From where shall my help come?
> My help comes from the Lord, Who made heaven and earth."
> Psalm 121:1-2 (NASB)

Observation
Psalm 121 is a very familiar song of trust and is the second in the songs of ascent recorded in the pages of scripture. It has been referred to as, "a song for the road." It sets the stage for pilgrims who are literally ascending their way up to Jerusalem. The psalmist states, "I will lift up my eyes to the mountains…" It is the image of a traveler approaching the city from below. He asks as he travels, "from where shall my help come?" A bold affirmation is given… "My help comes from the Lord." This phrase may have been an antiphonal response as pilgrims sang this song along their journey. For many, the pilgrimage journey was long and arduous. Many would have stopped along the way to find shelter, to rest, or to sleep. They would be comforted by this song that insisted that they were always in the care of God, who never slumbers nor sleeps. They trusted in a living God who provides constant watch care over God's children. The mention of the sun and the moon indicate that there is never a moment when God is not protecting God's people.

Application
As I read this psalm, I am reminded of hiking to the top of Mount LeConte, located near Gatlinburg in the Great Smoky Mountain National Park. Mount LeConte is 6,594 feet in elevation. There are five trails that get to the top. The steepest, but also the shortest, is the Alum Cave Trail, which is 5½ miles long. A hiker in good shape can make the trek to the top in four to five hours. Once on the top, the hiker is rewarded with amazing views of the mountains and some good home cooked food at the Mt. LeConte Lodge. (If interested, you will need reservations to stay or eat at the Lodge through the National Park Service. The Lodge is rustic and there is no electricity.) As you make your way up the Alum Cave Trail, there are several places as the trail winds back and forth, where you can see spots along the trail that are farther ahead and much higher in elevation. The traveler is reminded that there is still a long way to hike but encouraged to know that the summit awaits.

Many have compared human life to a journey with many twists, turns, and struggles. At times, it's hard to put one foot in front of the other as you attempt to move ahead. At other times life is easier and the journey becomes more of a stroll than a difficult hike. But regardless of where your steps take you this day on your personal journey of life, whether they be difficult or smooth, don't be afraid to lift your eyes upward and ask where you will find strength. Your strength, as always, will come from the Lord, who will guard your steps.

Prayer
Father, thank you for your vigilant and constant protection over our lives. Amen.

Day 600 — Psalm 122: Prayers for Your City

> "Pray for the peace of Jerusalem: 'May they prosper who love you. 'May peace be within your walls, And prosperity within your palaces.'"
> Psalm 122:6-7 (NASB)

Observation

Psalm 122 is the third song of ascent and the first of four written by David. Though most often remembered for its opening verse—"I was glad when they said unto me, let us go into the house of the Lord"—it primarily focuses on a prayer for the city of Jerusalem. It begins with the joyful expression of a pilgrim who had made his way to the city to worship. "I was glad," literally means, "I was filled with laughter and delight." It is the attitude of someone who understands and appreciates where he is standing... in the very epicenter of worship. There is no other place on the planet like it. Obviously, as David writes this psalm, he is overwhelmed by both the beauty of the city and the collective worship of God that takes place in that spot. Verse 4 mentions that this is where the tribes of Israel go to give thanks, or to make a public declaration of praise to God. David closes with a prayer for the city. He instructs others to pray for the peace and prosperity of Jerusalem. In the mind of David, there is a "trickle down" effect. When God pours out blessings on the city, peace and prosperity trickle down to all those who live within its walls.

Application

I've had the opportunity to live and work in some great cities and towns. I was born in Atlanta and grew up in Rome, Georgia. Then I was educated in the Magic City (Birmingham) and now I work in the Music City (Nashville.) I live in historic Franklin and vacation in my former town of Gatlinburg. I even lived in Mililani Town, Hawaii for a while. Not a bad group of cities, right? But I must confess that as much as I enjoyed living in all those places, I'm not sure I took the counsel of King David who reminds me this morning to pray for the city... for its peace and prosperity. As you may know, I keep a pretty thorough prayer list. I pray for a lot of people each day... I feel called to do so. It's part of my discipline of faith. But can I confess that I never think to pray for the city in which I live, or the city in which I work? And maybe I should. What if I prayed for the city of Nashville, that the people here would know peace and prosperity? And what if thousands of others prayed the same prayer each morning? Would our prayers move the heart of God in such a way that blessings would come new and fresh each morning? I think it would make a huge difference, at least in the way we view our city and build compassion for all its residents. Here's today's challenge for you. Stop right now and pray for your city. Pray for peace and prosperity so that those who live around you will know the blessings of God. As always, your prayers will make a difference.

Prayer

Father, would you grant peace and prosperity to this town. Amen.

Day 601 — Psalm 123: Binge Watching

> "To You I lift up my eyes, O You who are enthroned in the heavens! Behold, as the eyes of servants look to the hand of their master, As the eyes of a maid to the hand of her mistress, So our eyes look to the Lord our God, Until He is gracious to us." Psalm 123:1-2 (NASB)

Observation

Psalm 123 is the fourth psalm of ascent. It is a brief song in which the psalmist seeks the Lord's help in overcoming the scorn and contempt of arrogant people who pay no attention to the things of God. In verse 1, he describes God as being "enthroned in heaven." Although the Temple was the "dwelling place of God," the Israelites knew that the God who created the heavens and the earth did not live in structures made by human hands. The dominate image in this psalm is wrapped around the steady gaze of slaves and servants who look continually and carefully at their masters. The focus of their attention is on the one in authority so that, as servants, they would be careful to respond to any need or desire. In like fashion, we would do well to offer God our constant gaze and attention so that we would not become distracted by the affairs of everyday life. The closing two verses focus on the psalmist's prayer for the mercy of God for all those who were suffering scorn and contempt from their neighbors, perhaps at a time when the prayers of the faithful seemed to go unanswered.

Application

Most, if not all of you, are familiar with the phrase "binge watching." That phrase refers to the act of watching a television series, originally aired over months, in just a few days. For example, my wife and I just finished bingeing our way through the Netflix original show, *Stranger Things*. We didn't watch it when it first aired during the past two years, but instead we watched all the episodes in about two weeks… maybe two episodes a night. This idea of binge watching is a little all-encompassing. As a viewer, it sort of takes over your life and you can't seem to do much else until you have "powered your way through" some series. (We enjoyed *Stranger Things*, by the way. But beware if you have children in your home. There is strong language in places.)

There is a need for all of us as believers, to do a little binge watching in terms of our relationship with God. He needs to draw our constant and deliberate focus. There are way too many competing voices and distractions that swirl around us each day. We need to "fix our gaze on the author and perfecter of our faith" (Hebrews 12:2 NASB). We must carefully pay attention to the things of the Lord, being careful to respond to even the smallest command or direction God offers. Where is your focus today? What are you watching?

Prayer

Father, keep our eyes set on you so that we might be faithfully obedient. Amen.

Day 602 — Psalm 124: What If?

> "What if the Lord had not been on our side? Let all Israel repeat: What if the Lord had not been on our side when people attacked us? They would have swallowed us alive in their burning anger. The waters would have engulfed us; a torrent would have overwhelmed us. Yes, the raging waters of their fury would have overwhelmed our very lives." Psalm 124:105 (NLT)

Observation
Psalm 124 is the second song of ascent attributed to David. It was most likely written to be read aloud as an antiphonal response. Within the text, the people are encouraged to repeat the opening phrase. The psalm itself is a call for God's people to celebrate and confess God's continual deliverance in their lives. In asking what their plight would have been apart from God, the original Hebrew rendering is interesting. It literally reads, "The Lord was for us." So the people are asked to ponder how desperate, hopeless, and defeating life would be without God's protection. Two images of their enemies are offered. One is a ravenous beast that longs to tear them apart and the other is that of raging waters that long to overcome them. The final verse (8) acknowledges that help is found always and only in the name of the Lord, the maker of heaven and earth.

Application
"What if...?" Sometimes we use that phrase as we wonder about the timing of certain events in our lives. For example, several years ago on a mission trip to the Dominican Republic, I stepped into the director's office late one night to confirm some details about the next day's work. The director's young daughter was playing in the next room. As I was about to walk out of the office, I glanced in her direction only to discover that she was about two seconds away from sticking a screwdriver into an electric outlet. I yelled at her. My voice startled her, and she dropped the screwdriver. What if I hadn't been there? What if...?

We use the phrase a lot. "What if the fire extinguisher hadn't been close by? What if my doctor was not already on call? What if I hadn't missed the train? What if I had not answered my phone?" In such moments we think in terms of luck or coincidence. What if things had just not happened the way they did? But maybe, rather than having our lives governed and directed by karma, fate, or luck, what if every facet of our lives was governed by the mysterious providence of God? What if every special moment was arranged by God's watch care? What if every moment of protection was the result of God's hand? What if God arranges people, place, and circumstance to God's glory and purpose? "What if the Lord had not been on our side?" The great news to consider this morning is that God is, in fact, on our side. Always has been. So as you go through this day, be reminded that the Lord is watching over your life.

Prayer
Father, we praise you for your continual involvement in our lives each day. Amen.

Day 603 — Psalm 125: A Safe Place

> "Just as the mountains surround Jerusalem, so the Lord surrounds his people, both now and forever." Psalm 125:2 (NLT)

Observation
Psalm 125 is the sixth song of ascent. It is a song of trust and assurance in the protection of God. In the Jewish mindset, there was a very strong sense of the invincibility of Jerusalem because God had chosen it. (This was one of the reasons that the destruction of the city in 587 B.C. by the Babylonians was so devasting.) The city itself was built on one of seven mountain peaks in the region. Jerusalem was 2,400 feet above sea level and rested in the Coastal Highlands, which is a range of hills and low mountains that run from the North to the South in central Israel. The city is nestled among these mountains and thus the image described by the psalmist as he writes about the "surrounding" protection of God's people. For an invading army to attack the city, they would have to march over treacherous mountain paths to gain access. The psalmist also declares that the "wicked will not rule the land of the godly" (verse 3). The Hebrew phrasing states, "the scepter of the wicked shall not rest on the land." The psalm closes with the phrase, "May Israel have peace!" This phrase, which is also found at the end of Psalm 128, may be a shortened version of the priestly benediction found in Numbers 6:24.

Application
To be surrounded is to feel safe, secure, and protected. Most of us, in fact, look for ways to surround our lives. We enjoy the comfort, encouragement, and protection that we experience when we are surrounded by a group of close friends. Such a gathering helps us to feel somewhat insulated from the onslaught of life's difficult moments. We also appreciate what it is to be surrounded by a safe home, both physically and relationally. Physically we find comfort in having four strong walls around us to give shelter, warmth, and protection from the weather. Relationally, we find great peace and assurance in being surrounded with family members who love us and who always seek to nurture and protect us. Even when purchasing a car, we look for safety, right? Are we protected when we drive this car? Will it shelter us in an accident? Even something as simple as purchasing a new coat makes us long for protection. Will it hold up? Is it thick enough? Will it keep the cold winds at bay? We long to feel protected, surrounded, and encompassed by those who have our best interests in mind. And so, the words of Psalm 125 serve as a reminder this morning of God's protection and watch care over our lives. Like the mountains that surround Jerusalem, we are surrounded by God's presence, grace, and power. Assurance and comfort are ours knowing that every step is watched, every moment is seen, every hurt is healed, and every prayer is heard.

Prayer
Father, may we work, rest, and play this day in the safe confines of your shelter. Amen.

Day 604 — Psalm 126: The Joy of Restoration

> "When the Lord brought back his exiles to Jerusalem, it was like a dream! We were filled with laughter, and we sang for joy. And the other nations said, "What amazing things the Lord has done for them." Yes, the Lord has done amazing things for us! What joy!" Psalm 126:1-3 (NLT)

Observation

Psalm 126 is the seventh song of ascent. It is unique in that it is tied to a specific period in Jewish history, describing the euphoria and sweet joy after the very dark and lonely period of the Babylonian exile. (The Babylonian Exile lasted approximately 70 years. After defeating the Israelites and destroying the Temple in 587 B.C., the Babylonians forced the Jewish population to live in Babylon where they felt estranged from their land, heritage, and in some ways, even their God. See Psalm 137 to read a description of the Jewish mindset during their time in Babylon.) According to this psalm, as the Jews returned to Israel the joy was uncontainable and the praise was unstoppable. The mood was upbeat and positive, with much laughter and joyful singing. Verse 4 pleads for God to "restore," or "bring back," the fortunes of Israel. The psalmist is asking God to complete the restoration of God's people. Many of the people had yet to return. The process would be somewhat gradual and would take years to fully complete. As the final verse states, the people had gone to Babylon in tears yet returned with great rejoicing because God had rescued them from captivity.

Application

One of the highlights of growing up in First Baptist Church of Rome, Georgia, was the annual Christmas Eve service. It was always a wonderful night of music, candles, and praise. One year, Derwood Powell, a deacon and member of the choir, played a beautiful rendition of "Silent Night" on his vintage Martin guitar, a guitar given to him by his father. He played that night from the baptistry behind the choir loft. The baptistry was made of polished granite and reflected the sound in a beautiful way. After playing, Derwood quietly stepped out of the baptistry in the darkness. He stumbled and fell on top of his priceless guitar! His knee shattered the back of the instrument. He was all but inconsolable, as were all his friends who knew both the monetary and sentimental value of the instrument. With a hope and prayer he sent it away to the Martin Guitar company who kept it for nearly a year. The day came, however, when it was returned, completely restored. He wept tears of joy. Not kidding.

Restoration of the broken, lost, or separated always brings great joy. How gladdened our hearts should be at even the hope of restoration with God. Though broken, disobedient, and rebellious, God's love never changes. Restoration happens each day.

Prayer

Father, even this day, may we feel the joy of a restored relationship with you. Amen.

Day 605   Psalm 127: Futile Effort

> "Unless the Lord builds a house, the work of the builders is wasted. Unless the Lord protects a city, guarding it with sentries will do no good."
> Psalm 127:1 (NLT)

Observation
Psalm 127 is the eighth song of ascent and is one of only two psalms attributed to Solomon. (The other is Psalm 72.) One lens through which to read this psalm is the construction of the Temple, the "house" of the Lord. Remember that Solomon had been given the responsibility to build the Temple and did so with a splendor that was unparalleled. This psalm could surely speak to God's direct involvement in that process. On the other hand, the psalm certainly has much broader application. It speaks of the vanity of doing life without the Lord's help. The suggestion is that life lived apart from God is not worth living. Solomon points to three examples of futility when persons seek to live their lives without God's guidance. It is vain to build a house, vain to keep watch over a city, and vain to work day and night unless the Lord has initiated and guided the process. God gives rest and provides for the needs those who seek God's guidance. The second half of the psalm seems to take on a slightly different theme. Solomon speaks of the value of many children. He affirms that children are God's gifts. They are a symbol of strength. This is particularly true in an agricultural economy where many children would add to the productivity of the farm. Many children would also provide strength and encouragement to the family name when falsely accused.

Application
Years ago, I led a team of volunteers to the city of Brasilia, Brazil, to build a church. It was a simple, brick and mortar type of construction project. When we arrived on the scene, the foundation had been poured, so we began the work of laying brick. At the end of a long and tiring day, the construction foreman/missionary called our team together and asked us to look at the wall that I and my partner had spent the day building. I thought that he was going to use it as an illustration of a job well done. Instead, it was just the opposite. He pointed out several key mistakes we had made and then said, "This wall has to be torn out tomorrow and reconstructed." I was devastated at the thought of all my wasted effort. What was the problem? We built in vain because we did not use the right mix of mortar. The wall simply would not stand for very long. Using the right materials is essential to the success of any endeavor.

Our lives will gain success or know failure based on the materials that we use to construct them. The key, according to Solomon, is to involve the Lord with each project. We should build at God's initiative and proceed with God's guidance. To do otherwise is foolishness.

Prayer
Father, teach us to seek your involvement in every phase of our lives. Amen.

Day 606   Psalm 128: Successful Living

> "How joyful are those who fear the Lord—all who follow his ways! You will enjoy the fruit of your labor. How joyful and prosperous you will be!"
> Psalm 128:1-2 (NLT)

Observation
Psalm 128 is the ninth song of ascent. Like the preceding psalm, it addresses God's blessing in the home and family. The festivals of ancient Israel were always family affairs. Families traveled to Jerusalem to celebrate and share in the experience. On these treks, they would often join with other families. The festivals provided opportunity for new conversations and relationships as well as renewing old friendships. Together, the people of faith celebrated the goodness of God. Imagine the joy of collecting old friends along the way to the city to spend days together in exciting celebration. This psalm drives home the theme of trusting in God and doing God's will. The psalmist writes that the person who does so will be blessed, or made happy. There is certainly a quality of life that is experienced by those who respect, revere, and wonder in amazement at God's work. The psalmist promises the fruit of one's labor… the reward and satisfaction that comes from good, honest labor. The psalmist also reminds readers of the promise of longevity to those who place their trust in the Lord… "May you live to enjoy your grandchildren" (v. 6).

Application
My wife and I have family friends who spend their summer in an unusual way. They are "hosts" for a campground just outside of Gatlinburg. What that means is that they are the "go to" people during the evening hours when the main office is closed. They take care of emergency needs, or help people set up who arrive late, or just keep a vigilant watch over things going on in the campground. There's a pavilion near their RV. Some nights there are worship services, or Bible studies, or sing-a-longs, or parties. They enjoy meeting new folks and seeing old friends who pop in to stay on their yearly vacations. It's a good life. But if you knew my friends well, you would know that the good life they enjoy is not found in their campground setting, or in their fancy RV, or in their daily, "laid-back" routine. No. It's found in their faith. They are faithful followers of Christ and allow that relationship to define all the other relationships in their lives. Their prosperity and success are not found in their possessions, but in their respect, reverence, and wonder in the amazing work of God.

The psalmist reminds us all of what it takes to prosper and have a successful life. It's in our love for God and in our willingness to walk in God's ways. The psalmist writes that we will know joy… a joy not found in what we have, but in the security of the relationship that we have with the Almighty. Success will come through our faithful obedience.

Prayer
Father, may we know the joy of a prosperous life that is the result of our faith. Amen.

Day 607 — Psalm 129: Wounded, But Not Defeated

> "From my earliest youth my enemies have persecuted me, but they have never defeated me." Psalm 129:2 (NLT)

Observation
Psalm 129 is the tenth psalm of ascent, repeatedly sung by pilgrims making their way to Jerusalem to celebrate the great festivals of their faith. Like several others, this psalm has an antiphonal quality. The leader asks the people of Israel to repeat the phrase, "From my earliest youth my enemies have persecuted me." The antecedent of the pronoun "me," is actually the nation of Israel. The psalmist is asking the people to be mindful of the constant assault that Israel has suffered at the hands of her enemies, but the point to be made is that, even in the midst of the assaults, God has been faithful… the enemies have not prevailed. There are two very vivid images that are drawn from an agrarian setting. The first describes the suffering that Israel has endured. The sufferings are like someone with a wounded back that is covered with cuts, as if a farmer had plowed long furrows (v. 3). The second is an image of "withering" enemies. Sod was often placed on the rooftops of homes to provide insulation. When the spring rains came, this grass would often spring to life only to soon wither when the hot sun scorched the rooftops. The psalmist indicates that the enemies of Israel are like "rooftop grass" that quickly withers (vv. 6-7).

Application
From time to time, if you read the accounts of battles in the sky from World War II, you will occasionally come across the stories of planes like the B-17 Flying Fortress, or the P-51 Mustang, which took on a lot of enemy flak during their missions but kept flying. There are pictures of planes with holes in the wings or part of the tail section completely shot away. It is a testimony to the pilots who were able to keep these planes in the air and limp them back to their home bases.

Let's admit that as we go through our life journeys, that we too, take on a lot of enemy flak. There are abusive and devastating words, difficult moments, and devastating losses that can certainly cripple even the best of us. But as this psalm reminds us, even when we are assaulted by life-draining moments, our God is always with us. God's presence cannot be removed from our lives, nor God's watch care averted. Though we may be wounded, we are never defeated if our hope in God remains steadfast. The Apostle Paul wrote, "We are pressed on every side by troubles, but we are not crushed. We are perplexed, but not driven to despair. We are hunted down, but never abandoned by God. We get knocked down, but we are not destroyed" (2 Cor. 4:8-9 NLT). Your enemies will not defeat you today… God guarantees it.

Prayer
Father, today we pray for your protection and strength in the midst of whatever comes. Amen.

Day 608 — Psalm 130: Living in the Hope of Grace

> "Lord, if you kept a record of our sins, who, O Lord, could ever survive?"
> Psalm 130:2 (NLT)

Observation

Psalm 130 is the eleventh song of ascent. The theme is of repentance before God. This psalm turns the topic of suffering more inward. The psalmist considers that some of his sufferings are a result of personally-committed sins. According to verse 1, he shouts from the depth of his despair. It was his own sins that were eating away his soul. He recognized, however, that God does not keep a record of our sins. Through the sacrificial system and now, through the ultimate provision of Christ, our sins are removed and the record is destroyed. There is a great image in verse 6, "I long for the Lord more than sentries long for the dawn, yes, more than sentries long for the dawn." Just as a watchman anticipates the calm and safety of the coming morn, the psalmist lives with the anticipation of the Lord's forgiveness.

Application

Quite a question, right? "If you kept a record of our sins, who, O Lord, could ever survive?" He's right, you know. If we were punished for every sin, every errant thought, every misspoken word, or every act of disobedience, who among us could survive? Who could bear such judgment? No one. We all live in the hope of grace. We all survive by trusting in the promise that God, through Christ, forgives our iniquities and separates us from our sins as far as the east is from the west. Sometimes we are challenged by preachers or teachers or even by a hymn, to "Count our many blessings." We spin off into the discussion of how great and many are the blessings that come our way each day and how grateful we should be for those gifts. But what if we were challenged to keep track of our sins? What if we had to record each transgression in a journal? Could the world contain the books? Would we even be aware of all the ways we fail to live according to God's intention for our lives? The sins come too quickly. The listing would be too overwhelming. But if we did attempt such a feat, even to list a single day's sins, we would be reminded again of the overwhelming grace of God. Greater than our sins is God's desire to offer forgiveness. Understand that God doesn't take our sins lightly. Every sin can disrupt our relationship with God. Let us not think for a moment that God simply "looks the other way." Instead, God looks to the cross of Christ where his son died an agonizing death to pay the price of our sins. So don't be flippant about your sins. They still break God's heart. But in grace, God chooses to forgive. This day, seek to live well. Let your desires be those of Christ. Let your thoughts be those that honor God.

Prayer

Father, thank you for forgiving our sins and for forgetting our mistakes. Amen.

Day 609 — Psalm 131: The Calming Effect of Trust

> "Instead, I have calmed and quieted myself, like a weaned child who no longer cries for its mother's milk. Yes, like a weaned child is my soul within me." Psalm 131:2 (NLT)

Observation
Psalm 131 is the twelfth song of ascent and is one of the four attributed to King David. Though very short with only three verses, it celebrates David's trust in God out of a sense of genuine humility. This psalm certainly highlights the qualifications of David "as a man after His (God's) own heart" (1 Sam. 13:14 NASB). He confesses a humble status before the Lord. He claims that there are matters that are far beyond his wisdom or ability to control. He states that he will not concern himself with such things. The "great matters" are only under God's control and authority and David clearly understands that God is great and that he is only God's servant. The psalm utilizes the image of a child who finds comfort in the arms of his compassionate mother. A child that could be distraught or unsettled is quickly calmed in the presence of his mother. So too, David, though at times distraught or fearful, finds a calm and quiet soul when he trusts fully in the Lord.

Application
How many times have you seen the calming effect that a loving mother has on a distraught child? For example, have you ever witnessed a child fall on the playground, then run to her mother with tears streaming down her face? Within seconds, the mother can soothe the pain and quiet the tears. Or what about a child who is cranky and tired after a long day, weepy when the mother comes to pick him up. Again, within moments, the child is calmed and a smile returns to his face. You've seen those scenarios played out a thousand times in situations where a loving mother gently cares for her child. Transpose that image to an image of our relationship with God. When we choose to trust fully in God's care, a lot of things can happen. Fears dissipate. Worries calm. Anxiety lessens. Hope grows strong. Assurances increase. Joy returns. Life has a way of chipping away at our strong resolve, our resilient faith, and our glad hope. Sometimes situations just get to us. We lose our perspective. We let anxiety rob us of another night's rest. We let the agenda for the day overwhelm us. We allow our fears to overtake us. We become like frightened children who have temporarily lost the loving hand of our mothers. In this psalm, David offers a comforting word. He reminds us that in the presence of God, our fears are calmed and our souls are quieted. I don't know what fears, pressures, or worries are running through your mind this morning. But I do know who is watching over your life. This very day, God, who loves You more than you will ever know, longs to hold you close. May you find peace in God's presence.

Prayer
Father, may we find a gentle calm amid of our restless worries. Amen.

Day 610 — Psalm 132: No Place Like Home

> "For the Lord has chosen Jerusalem; he has desired it for his home. 'This is my resting place forever,' he said. 'I will live here, for this is the home I desired. I will bless this city and make it prosperous; I will satisfy its poor with food. I will clothe its priests with godliness; its faithful servants will sing for joy.'" Psalm 132:13-16 (NLT)

Observation

Psalm 132 is the thirteenth song of ascent and holds the distinction of being the longest of these songs. Like Psalm 89, it reflects on God's covenant with David (2 Samuel 7) in which God makes the promise of a royal household that would stand forever. This psalm was possibly written late in Israel's history after the time of the exile to Babylon. Students of Biblical history may recall that this 400-year post-exilic period was a very confusing time for the people. They waited for God to act on their behalf and to re-establish the throne of David (which would be accomplished with the coming of the ultimate King and Savior—Jesus.) So, if in fact, this psalm was written during this period of waiting, the calling upon God to renew the covenant with David makes sense. Those traveling to Jerusalem to celebrate the various festivals would have found encouragement as they called upon God to fully restore God's Kingdom. Notice that this psalm not only highlights the Davidic line, but also Jerusalem as God's dwelling place. Verse 7 refers to the Temple as the "footstool" of God. His true dwelling place is in the heavens.

Application

The older I get, the more I become intrigued with the idea of owning an RV (Recreational Vehicle) or travel trailer. I envision the golden days of retirement when my wife and I jump in the RV and motor our way across the country. We could visit the grandkids, drop in on old friends, or visit the National Parks, all in the comfort of our spacious home on wheels. We could sell the house and hit the road. I bet it would be a lot of fun… at least for the first year or so, or maybe for the first month or so, or maybe for the first week or so. Who knows… we might get three or four days into the adventure and decide to sell the thing. Even though people often say, "Home is where you lay your head," I kind of think that there is more to it than that. Home is where you belong. It's where things are familiar and the people know you. It's where you feel settled. It's the place to which you always return when you are ready to rest and find a little calm. It's the place from which you can never fully escape, and never really want to fully escape. I grew up in the small town of Rome, Georgia. And though I haven't lived there in 40 years, and don't get back very often, it still feels like home in a lot of ways. According to the psalmist, God claimed Jerusalem. I get it. We all need a place to belong. I pray you feel "at home," in the place where you live.

Prayer

Father, may we find joy this day in our thoughts of home. Amen.

Day 611 — Psalm 133: The Blessing of Oneness

> "How wonderful and pleasant it is when brothers live together in harmony! For harmony is as precious as the anointing oil that was poured over Aaron's head, that ran down his beard and onto the border of his robe. Harmony is as refreshing as the dew from Mount Hermon that falls on the mountains of Zion. And there the Lord has pronounced his blessing, even life everlasting." Psalm 133 (NLT)

Observation

Psalm 133 is the fourth song of ascent attributed to King David. The emphasis of the song is on the unity of God's people. It speaks of the beauty and blessing that come when God's people are united. Perhaps this was an important reminder when sung by pilgrims making their way to Jerusalem from various corners of the world. All ethnic, geographic, and language divisions were to be erased as the people joined together to worship. David writes that it is "wonderful and pleasant" when brothers live in harmony. It is the image of a peaceful, calm, and serene experience. He mentions the anointing oil once poured on Aaron's head. A fragrant, distinctive, and expensive oil was used to anoint the priests of Israel as a way of symbolizing the Lord's blessing on their holy office (Ex. 20:22-33). Mentioning that the oil ran down his head, onto his beard, and even onto his robe, signifies that a large amount was used. This abundance of oil illustrates the overflowing blessings of God on the people. To further symbolize abundance, David mentions Mount Hermon. Mount Hermon was in the northern part of Israel and is the tallest mountain in the nation. It is also snowcapped year-round. It received a large amount of rainfall and moisture each year and was seemingly the source of water for the nation as the runoff found its way into rivers and streams like the Jordan. Again, the image is that of an abundant flow of water symbolizing an abundant flow of God's blessings. The psalm ends with the promise that God longs to bless the people, not only in the here and now, but in the life that is to come.

Application

According to John 17:21, as Jesus prayed for his disciples in the upper room, he prayed "that they may all be one" (NASB). Notice that Jesus didn't pray that they would be the "same." It was not his desire that all his followers look the same, talk the same, or think the same thoughts. His prayer was that they would be one... unified, living in harmony and peace with each other so that the collective witness of God's people would go forth boldly. There are many divisive issues that seek to tear apart the harmony of the Christian voice in our world. Though we may disagree on the fine points of doctrine, church polity, or even worship style, let us, as people of faith, pledge that our love for each other will usurp any divisive interruption.

Prayer

Father, make us one so that through our witness the world will know you. Amen.

Day 612 — Psalm 134: Turn Out the Lights, the Party's Over

> "Oh, praise the Lord, all you servants of the Lord, you who serve at night in the house of the Lord. Lift up holy hands in prayer, and praise the Lord. May the Lord, who made heaven and earth, bless you from Jerusalem."
> Psalm 134 (NLT)

Observation

Psalm 134 is the last of the songs of ascent. It was likely read as a responsive song of praise like several of the other songs of ascent. It conveys a two-way flow of blessing. First, the people offer a blessing for the priests and their work. Second, the priests offer a blessing to the people who will make their way back to their homes and villages after their celebrations of worship. To "bless" is to recognize that God is the source of all blessings. To ask the Lord to bless both priests and people is to ask that God's favor fall on them all. The priests, described in this psalm, continued the ministry of the Temple all hours of the day and night. There were those who literally worked through the night, making preparation for the following day and those who kept the eternal flame burning throughout the night. They are being praised for their on-going efforts. In like fashion, the priests offered a word of blessing on the departing pilgrims.

Application

There is a world of dependency that makes our daily routines possible, though we rarely consider how networked and connected we are to each other. For example, when I stop on my way to work to grab a drink or fill my car with gas, I typically don't consider all the people who work behind the scenes to make that moment possible. There are vendors, delivery truck drivers, stock people, and gasoline producers. I just sort of take for granted the fact that there will be gas and food and snacks. When I get to work, I make other assumptions. I assume the lights will work, the room will be the correct temperature, and that someone, somewhere will make my lunch possible by providing goods and services. Here's my point… there are a lot of people that work behind the scenes to make our lives go smoothly. We are connected and blessed by the work of others on a continual basis.

The same thing happens at church. Someone unlocks the doors and turns on the lights. Another person brews the Sunday school coffee. Someone else prints the bulletins. Another person cleans the children's area. We depend on such people doing their tasks, consistently and quietly behind the scenes. But let me also say a word in praise of pastors. All throughout the week, they are praying, reading, and writing a sermon so that they can share truth with you each coming weekend. Don't take that for granted and don't belittle the gift they bring to you each week. Why not offer a word of blessing the next time you see them? It matters.

Prayer

Father, we ask that you bless those who help to make our world spin. Amen.

Day 613   Psalm 135: Where God Lives

> "The Lord be praised from Zion, for he lives here in Jerusalem. Praise the Lord!" Psalm 135:21 (NLT)

Observation
Psalm 135 is a psalm of praise. It begins and ends with the declarative phrase, "Praise the Lord!" There are several themes that thread their way through the verses. One is of praising God for God's wondrous works. The psalmist mentions the Exodus experience and the defeat of the kings the Israelites faced on their way to the land of promise. A second theme is challenging the priests and those who serve within the Temple to praise God continually. A third theme is warning about the vanity of serving false idols. God alone can create and control. The pagan idols of the various nations have no power at all. Our focus verse speaks of praising God from Zion. Zion, of course, is another name for Jerusalem. The Temple is the focal point of the city. It is where the Spirit of God inhabited a place of worship among the people of God.

Application
Some of our theology concerning the Spirit of God has certainly changed between the days of the Old Testament and now. In the Old Testament, the Spirit of God came upon certain people, at certain moments, to empower them to accomplish certain tasks. An example would be the great prophets of God who were empowered to proclaim the works and deeds of God. The Spirit tended to visit a person, for a time, to accomplish what God needed done. New Testament belief about the Spirit is different. Beginning with the Day of Pentecost, the belief is that the Spirit of God now indwells individuals at the time of their conversion. The Spirit, therefore, abides in each believer, serving as a constant source of strength, correction, and encouragement. During the days of the Old Testament, when Temple worship was at its height, the Temple became the dwelling place of God's Spirit. The presence of the Lord was continually in that spot. (One of the dramatic events at the crucifixion of Jesus was the tearing of the Temple veil indicating that God's presence was no longer bound to that place but was to be found in the hearts of all believers.) In our focus verse, the psalmist mentions that God "lives in Jerusalem." My question is… "Where does He live now?" God is not bound to structures of brick and mortar, but instead lives within human hearts. Thus God lives wherever we choose to allow God to dwell. Though God is present over all the earth, God only dwells in those hearts that welcome God in. I pray that God is living in you… in your house, in the life of your family, in the places where you live and work. God stands at the door of your life, knocking, waiting to be welcomed in. Trust God. Love God. Welcome God.

Prayer
Father, thank you for indwelling our hearts and being present with us always. Amen.

Day 614 — Psalm 136: Delicate Deliverance

> "He acted with a strong hand and powerful arm. His faithful love endures forever." Psalm 136:12 (NLT)

Observation

It is apparent that this psalm was used in worship. It is a descriptive psalm of praise in which a priest or worship leader read the first line of each stanza, with the people responding in unison, "For His mercy endures forever." This repeated line occurs more than any other repetitious line in any Biblical passage. The "mercy" of God refers to God's "loyal love." This is the most significant term in the psalms to describe God's character. God's loyal love is part of that eternal character. This worship psalm tells the story of both the creative acts of God and the continual deliverance of God's people. When called to give thanks by the psalmist, the people offer public acknowledgement of God. Our focus verse offers two important images of God's work. One is the strong hand of God. This is reminiscent of the work of creation. The powerful, outstretched arm is reminiscent of the powerful deliverance that only God can offer.

Application

Like his father before him, my dad has strong, powerful, large hands. I have noticed through the years how easily he could hold a Bible while preaching, or palm a basketball, or grasp a tool while working on a car. I also remember the day that my father held my baby son for the first time. Just after Andy was born, my parents came to see our new addition. I remember watching my dad cradle little Andy in those big hands of his. Something so powerful and large, holding something so delicate and tiny… quite a juxtaposition. That image comes to mind as I consider the phrase, "the strong hand and the powerful arm." When I think of the delicate intricacies of creation, I am amazed at God's ability to create with such detail and dexterity. Even the smallest of things are carefully crafted by God's hands. And then I consider the powerful deliverance that God has always offered God's people… deliverance from both the enemies of earth and the enemies of the heavens. How can we not praise God for both delicate detail and powerful deliverance? As you go through this day, you need to be reminded of God's ability to move in both the great and small. God continues to move the arc of history in a redemptive direction. God is slowly, but powerfully transforming the world into the Kingdom through the love of Jesus Christ. The Kingdom will come on earth as it is in heaven. And yet, even amid world-wide concerns, God is also working in the lives of each of God's children. That includes all of us. God knows the details, concerns, and pressures of your life. Big hands… delicate work.

Prayer

Father, we thank you for your redemptive, transforming work in our lives. Amen.

Day 615 — Psalm 137: The Darkness of Revenge

> "For our captors demanded a song from us. Our tormentors insisted on a joyful hymn: 'Sing us one of those songs of Jerusalem!' But how can we sing the songs of the Lord while in a pagan land?" Psalm 137:3-4 (NLT)

Observation
One of the most unusual and distinctive of all the psalms, Psalm 137 expresses both tremendous grief and the longing for revenge. The psalm is written during the Babylonian exile. The Babylonians conquered and destroyed Jerusalem in 587 B.C., taking most of the captives away into exile to live in Babylon. It is during this involuntary exile that the writer offers his words. He longs for Jerusalem. In his grief, he prays an impassioned "imprecatory" prayer meaning that he prays for revenge and punishment to befall Israel's enemies. He speaks of weeping over the loss of the city. It is hard to overstate how important Jerusalem was to the Jewish mindset. It was, of course, a beautiful city, but more importantly, it was the center of their faith experience. The Temple stood in that place... the presence of God dwelt in the city. And so, with painful remorse and sorrow, the Jews refused to listen to the taunts of their captors and would not play the joyful songs about Jerusalem that they once played. In verses 7-9, the dark side of their revengeful thoughts emerges as they pray for the destruction of Babylon and even the slaughter of the Babylonian babies.

Application
The desire for revenge displays the dark side of our human nature. And because it is woven into our DNA as human beings, it is a difficult emotion to overcome. We've all felt the emotion in both small and large doses. For example, someone may cut us off in traffic and we secretly desire that the police would give them a ticket. No big deal. But other revenge-desiring circumstances are much harder to ignore. Someone betrays you... someone steals something valuable from you... someone harms the people you love... and suddenly the darker side of your psyche begins to emerge. Like the psalmist, we can think of terrible, destructive revengeful acts that we long to commit. We want to inflict pain. We want to cause harm. We want our pound of flesh, because we think that when we have acted in revenge that we will find peace and rest and solace for our pain and injury. But revenge never makes us better. It only makes us less and less like Jesus. Remember his solution for revenge? "Turn the other cheek... walk the second mile... forgive up to 70 x 7." Jesus longs to transform us from our human nature to the nature of the Spirit abiding within us. The Spirit offers peace, joy, love, and self-control, among other things. Which wins out in your life? The Spirit or human nature?

Prayer
God, with your help, may the Spirit within us defeat the power of human nature. Amen.

Day 616 — Psalm 138: Completed Plans

> "The Lord will work out his plans for my life—for your faithful love, O Lord, endures forever. Don't abandon me, for you made me."
> Psalm 138:8 (NLT)

Observation

Psalm 138, a song of praise written by David, reflects a very positive and upbeat theme. In this song, David longs to praise God with his whole being (heart). He pledges to sing God's praises even in the presence of foreign and pagan nations. One interesting aspect of this psalm is contained in verse 2, as David declares that he will "bow before the Holy Temple as he worships." The problem is that the Temple has not yet been constructed. Is it possible that David is not the author? Most scholars tend to think that David is using more of a generic term when he mentions the Temple. Perhaps David is referring to any building or space that is used as a place to worship God. The psalm also has a forward-looking aspect. David writes about the coming day when all the kings of the earth will praise God. As the psalm draws to a close, David confesses his trust in God while living in the present context when he is "walking in the midst of trouble." He is confident of God's continual blessing.

Application

This past summer marked a proud moment for Belmont University when a new residence hall was dedicated. It's called Tall Hall because it rises 11 stories into the Nashville skyline. It's a beautifully constructed building that is home to more than 600 residents. It's been interesting to watch the process from ground-breaking to final completion. There were plans, sketches, blueprints, and hundreds of construction workers. The plans became reality with a lot of hard work and many dedicated people.

Notice what David writes in our focus verse… "the Lord will work out His plans for my life." David lived with the confidence that: a) God had a plan for his life, and b) that God would bring those plans to completion. We should live with the same confidence. God doesn't randomly call us into being without forethought or vision. Just the opposite. We are purposefully created with an entire set of plans laid out for our lives. "For I know the plans I have for you, declares the Lord" (Jeremiah 29:11 NASB). To be sure, at times, we may not see all the careful plans and details of what God longs to do with our lives. Like a contractor following a detailed blueprint, God is carefully at work in our lives. There is purpose, direction, and planning. God will bring those plans to completion. He doesn't call us into being only to set us adrift and hope for the best. All the days are known. We will live even this day within the framework of God's greater plan.

Prayer

Father God, may we live in the bright confidence that you have a plan for our lives. Amen.

Day 617   Psalm 139: 24/7

> "O Lord, you have examined my heart and know everything about me. You know when I sit down or stand up. You know my thoughts even when I'm far away. You see me when I travel and when I rest at home. You know everything I do. You know what I am going to say even before I say it, Lord." Psalm 139:1-4 (NLT)

Observation

If a student of God's Word wanted to spend some time mining the gems to be found in a particular portion of scripture, Psalm 139 would be a good place to dig for a while. The psalm, written by David, contains several rich images and powerful thoughts. It is a psalm of wisdom that describes God's perfect, complete, and intimate knowledge of humankind. It illustrates how full is God's knowledge of our lives. God knows our motives, our desires, our words, and even our thoughts. And according to the language of the fifth verse, God's knowledge is not to condemn or judge, but to offer help and protection. David affirms that there is no place in all of creation where the presence of God is separated from us. Even in the darkness of death, God is present. There is no realm in heaven or on earth where God is not found. David also writes that God's work in our lives extends back to our development in the womb where God skillfully has woven us together. And, in a display of God's infinite knowledge, before a single day of our lives are lived, they are all written in scripture… all the days, all the struggles, and all the victories. How amazing is God's knowledge in our lives!

Application

If you are the parent of a newborn, you know the constant vigilance required to safeguard your child. As a responsible adult, you watch over every moment in the life of your son or daughter. You know when they rest and when they wake. You know when they cry and when they laugh. You know when they are hungry and when they are content. You give constant, moment by moment attention to every facet of their lives. Nothing escapes your notice because the responsibility is that important.

Just as all of us have felt the constant, loving nurture of our parents, so much more have all of us felt the nurturing presence of the Lord. Imagine a being that knows everything there is to know about us… every thought, every action, every word. And how much more amazing to think that even with such knowledge, God continues to love us so powerfully. Like a loving parent, God watches over us, not to limit our lives or scrutinize our actions hoping to observe some guilty, wayward step, but to encourage, nurture, protect, and defend us. How reassuring it is to know that we can never out distance God's reach, live beyond God's mercy, escape God's grace, or disrupt God's love.

Prayer

Father God, thank you for your loving and constant vigil over our lives. Amen.

Day 618

Psalm 140: Caustic Words

> "Their tongues sting like a snake; the venom of a viper drips from their lips." Psalm 140:3 (NLT)

Observation

This is another psalm of David in which he prays to God for protection from evil people. He longs for God's judgement to fall upon the wicked. He describes such people as "violent" men. The term violent means those who are harsh and ruthless and who plan destruction of the righteous. The opening words set a tone for the rest of the psalm... "Rescue me, O Lord, from evil men." Knowing that his salvation and rescue are in God alone, he affirms in verse 6 that "You are my God." In verse 10, David prays that God would allow "burning coals to fall upon them." This image recalls the fire and brimstone that fell on Sodom and Gomorrah (Genesis 19:12-29). David wants his enemies to experience the same judgment. In our focus verse, David describes the words of evil men that sting like that of a serpent's bite.

Application

Most of us, at some point in our lives, have been on the stinging end of caustic comments. Whether it was a childhood taunt, a teenage insult, or a recent remark at work, most of us know what it feels like for others to speak evil of us. The words sting. The comments leave us undone. The callous insult leaves us wounded. And so, you would think... having felt such pain, that we would be the last to offer a critical, insulting word to others... but we are not. It's tough for us to tame the tongue. Remember the words of James? "But no one can tame the tongue; it is a restless evil and full of deadly poison. With it we bless our Lord and Father, and with it we curse men who have been made in the likeness of God; from the same mouth come forth both blessing and cursing. My brethren, these things ought not to be this way" (James 3:8-10 NASB). I would go so far as to say that our words are a real measure of the maturity of our faith. If we use our words to praise God in one breath and curse men with the next, how Christ-like have we really become? Our words are important. What we say to others and how we say it, is always significant. We can heal or hurt, encourage or belittle, buildup or tear down. So, pay attention to your words today... the comments, the under-your-breath remarks, the little stinging insults that might leap out. Your words reflect your relationship with Christ. You honor him or dishonor him by what you choose to say. So, speak well. "Let the words of your mouth be acceptable in His sight." Jesus himself reminds us through the words of Matthew's Gospel, "But I tell you that everyone will have to give account on the day of judgment for every empty word they have spoken" (12:36 NIV). Choose yours well.

Prayer

Father God, may we be accountable unto you for the words we use this day. Amen.

Day 619 — Psalm 141: Strong Medicine

> "Let the godly strike me! It will be a kindness! If they correct me, it is soothing medicine. Don't let me refuse it." Psalm 141:5 (NLT)

Observation
This psalm of David echoes many of the same themes expressed in early songs of David. He prays for safekeeping. He prays that his enemies would receive judgment. Though David prays this psalm during an obvious time of distress, we don't know the particular event. It does contain a beautiful image of prayer (v. 2). David depicts his prayers as though they were sweet incense floating up to the heavens. It is his hope that the sweet aroma would be compelling to the Lord. He even describes his prayers as an "offering" before the Lord. (Would that our words would be so eloquently crafted that we would consider them an offering before the Lord.) David also prays that God would take control of his mouth. He longs to have the correct words, good words, meaningful words… nothing that would be offensive before God. In our focus verse, David also states that he is willing to accept the corrections of the righteous. The words of the righteous will be like a soothing medicine that will heal his heart and soul.

Application
Okay… reach way back in time. Do you remember Vicks 44 Cough Medicine that we had to take when we were kids? It was absolutely awful! I don't think a group of gifted chemists could have conspired together to make a worst tasting liquid. Even to this day, I have a visceral reaction just thinking about it. But of course, who ever said that medicine should taste good? In fact, maybe it's better when it doesn't. The poor taste might just motivate us to get well sooner so that we don't have to take that nasty stuff!

Dive into David's thoughts for a moment. He is willing to take the sometimes-bitter medicine of the righteous for it to correct and soothe any wayward step in his life. He longed for the healing, correction, and guidance that the righteous could offer. Good for David. I wonder how well we receive the correction of the righteous whenever we have stumbled along the way. When we need correcting, are we willing to listen and learn from those who share insight with us? Criticism can sting a little. Correction can cut deeply. We don't always welcome the messenger or the message. But discipline is important. It keeps our pathway clear and our journey straight… especially the correction that we receive through the work of the Spirit. It might be a word from the pages of scripture. It might be an inspired sermon. It might be the advice of a godly friend. The wise among us will recognize the need for correction and heed the counsel that is offered our way. It might be a little bitter, but we need to hear it.

Prayer
Father God, make us and mold us after your will and not ours. Amen.

Day 620 — Psalm 142: Right Side, Strong Side

> "Look to the right and see; For there is no one who regards me; There is no escape for me; No one cares for my soul." Psalm 142:4 (NASB)

Observation

Psalm 142 is a psalm of David that is tied directly to an experience as he hides in a cave. There are actually two such moments in David's life from which this reference could be drawn. Both occur as David flees from King Saul. One reference is an incident when David is hiding in a cave in En Gedi (1 Samuel 24). The other reference is drawn from the moment David hides in a cave in Adullam (1 Samuel 22). This second reference is probably the correct one. In that narrative, David felt very alone and frightened. He begins to doubt God's support and presence in his life. Yet, even during his dark moment, David turns to God in prayer to find encouragement and peace. With a loud voice he cries out to the Lord. In his prayer he juxtaposes his own defenselessness with God's power and presence. He knows that there is no one to protect him in this moment, but God alone.

Application

There is an image embedded within this psalm that I don't want you to miss. In our focus verse, David says, "Look to the right and see; for there is no one who regards me..." In the world of ancient warfare, battle lines were drawn with soldiers standing shoulder to shoulder. In their right hands, soldiers held a spear with which to attack. In their left hands, they held a shield with which to offer defense. So as they stood side-by-side, the shield of the soldier on one's right side, actually defended the vulnerable arm which held the spear. Protection came in the form of unity as the armies advanced.

Who is defending your life? Who's got your right side? Who is protecting your heart from danger? Of course, there is a good "church" answer to offer. It is God who protects us and defends us in the midst of all our battles. But move away from that easy answer for a moment to consider a different question. Who around you is protecting your life? Who defends your honor? Who keeps you safe? Who battles the enemy on your behalf? If you are married, you carry the responsibility of protecting your spouse. You are called to defend, protect, nurture, and safeguard their lives, their hearts, their emotions, and their journeys. If you are a parent, you carry the responsibility of protecting your children. God has placed them in your charge for a reason. You are called to get them safely to adulthood. And so you pray and watch and protect with constant vigilance. If you are a friend to others, you are called to defend, shield, and guide those in your circle. Life is tough. We need to protect others and to be protected by them. Set your mind to that task.

Prayer

Father God, may we be courageous defenders of our family and friends. Amen.

Day 621 — Psalm 143: Hot Lava

> "Let me hear of your unfailing love each morning, for I am trusting you. Show me where to walk, for I give myself to you." Psalm 143:8 (NLT)

Observation
David writes this psalm out of a sense of great peril and distress. He cries out to God for deliverance. He asks for God's mercy, not because of his own innocence, but because of God's nature. In fact, in verse 2, he observes that everyone is sinful. In describing the depth of his despair and fear, David insists that he is walking in darkness like those who inhabit the grave. To bring comfort, he lets his mind recall better days... more hopeful days... when he rejoiced at moments of Temple worship. In our focus verse, David speaks of hearing from God "each morning." That phraseology of hearing from God each morning reflects a popular theme in the psalms that God's power and direction is revealed with the coming of the new day... in the glow of the morning light. He closes his prayer, appealing to God's "namesake." Prayers were often tied to the various characteristics and traits of God. By praying that God would respond "for the glory of His name's sake," David was relying on the authority of God's name and the character that it represented.

Application
"Show me where to walk, for I give myself to you." Recently I came home to discover the floor of our bonus room covered with strategically placed blankets that led from one Cinderella castle to the other. (Yes, we have two castles in our bonus room.) My wife had spent the day entertaining two of our granddaughters. The portion of the carpet, not covered with blankets, was "hot lava." If you stepped on it, you would burn your feet. So, to get from one castle to the other, it was important to stay on the blankets. My granddaughter, Lydia, kept saying in her best 18-month-old voice, "Hot Lava! Hot Lava!"

Most of us are not going to struggle today with walking on hot lava. We don't need blankets on the floor to keep us from burning our feet. Instead, what we will struggle with is safeguarding our steps, so that we don't get off the path that God intends for us to walk. There are many types of distraction that seek to pull us away from walking with God. We can be diverted by human nature, by temptation, by the lure of things, or by greed. If we are not careful with our steps, we may drift well off the path outlined by God for living our best lives. To be off course, even by one degree, can move us very far from our intended destination. David asks for God to show him where to walk. He willingly offers to "give himself" to God's direction. Our prayer this morning should be the same. We should seek to align our steps with the direction that God's Spirit provides, lest we step into "hot lava."

Prayer
Father God, direct our paths and give us wisdom for this day. Amen.

Day 622 — Psalm 144: Building a Strong Wall

> "May there be no enemy breaking through our walls, no going into captivity, no cries of alarm in our town squares." Psalm 144:14 (NLT)

Observation
Psalm 144 is a song of praise written by David. As he often does, he petitions God to rescue him from danger. Like Psalm 18, this psalm describes the salvific work of God in terms of great heavenly phenomena. He describes the thunderbolts that crash out of the sky as a sign of God's deliverance and power. Verse 3 is a direct quote drawn from Psalm 8:4… "What is man that Thou art mindful of him?" David speaks of the frailty of man and man's continual need for God's help. He describes man as a mere breath of air or a passing shadow. Another interesting aspect of this psalm is David's mention of his own name in verse 10. He also mentions the continual lies of the enemy that are cast in his direction, the principle lie being that God could not save God's people. David refuses to hear such a deceptive word. The song ends with a prayer for blessing and prosperity.

Application
Imagine the terror of being awakened in the middle of the night from the sound of someone shouting in the street that the walls of the city had been breached by an enemy. Think of the fear, the upheaval, and the hysteria that such a moment would bring as you scrambled to protect your family from the invading enemy. Fortunately, for most of us, such an event is unlikely. We live with the protection of the constant vigilance of military and police protection. Warning sirens and text alerts also announce the coming of potential danger so that we can prepare. What we hope to never face, however, is the presence of an enemy at our door.

Let's think more in terms of spiritual warfare and the work of evil that is present in our world. How can we build strong walls of protection? How can we keep from being drawn into the captivity of addiction, abuse, greed, or lust? We protect ourselves by building the strength of our faith. We must awaken each day with the awareness that the devil prowls around like a roaring lion, waiting for someone to devour. We must build a wall of protection based on the assurances of God and the practice of our spiritual disciplines. We fortify our lives with prayer, with scripture reading, and with the fellowship of godly persons. To ignore the building of our faith is to leave the gate that should protect our hearts wide open to danger. On our own, there is no wall tall enough, or wide enough, that we can construct that will keep the enemy out. But with the strength of God we shall be more than conquerors. Take the time this day to add a little more protection. Spend time in scripture and with God.

Prayer
Father, this day, deliver us yet again, from evil. May we know your protection. Amen.

Day 623 — Psalm 145: Shouldering the Load

> "The Lord helps the fallen and lifts those bent beneath their loads."
> Psalm 145:14 (NLT)

Observation

Psalm 145 is a praise song written by David. Like several of the other psalms, it is an acrostic. There is a verse for each letter of the Hebrew alphabet. When David writes, "Great is the Lord," he is offering an expression of God's grandeur and perspective. David acknowledges that God is great and we (humankind) are small in God's presence, but of absolute importance and value in God's eyes. In verse 4, David challenges each generation to tell its children of God's mighty acts. The story of God must be conveyed to every generation. In verse 8, David uses God's own words found in Exodus 34:6-7 to describe the Almighty… "the Lord is gracious and full of compassion." When David suggests in verse 14 that God promises to help the fallen, he reminds us that there is no limit to God's power, love, or concern.

Application

I was struck by the words of our focus verse. Ever feel that way? The truth is that most of us all but succumb to the weight the world places on our shoulders. The pains, pressures, and headaches of life become a weight too heavy to bear. I think of the senior adult who watches his wife die a slow and agonizing death to cancer. I think of a single mom who desperately tries to raise her teenage son. I think of a delusional college student who desperately tries to make sense of his world. I think of a low-income wage-earner who can barely keep food on his table. I think of the determined wife who struggles to live with an abusive husband. Look around. There are many living within our communities who are "bent beneath their loads." Where is their hope? How can they find respite in the midst of their struggle? The Gospel has a promise to share. Jesus said, "Come to Me, all who are weary and heavy-laden, and I will give you rest. Take My yoke upon you and learn from Me, for I am gentle and humble in heart; and you shall find rest for your souls. For My yoke is easy, and My load is light" (Matthew 11:28-30 NASB). Here's the key to surviving the problem of a heavy load. It's called trust. You drop the load that is heavy in order to pick up one that is light. Christ promises to give rest to those who are heavy-laden. He offers to take the load from our shoulders and shift it to his. Easier said than done, right? How do we unburden our lives? Acknowledge the load that you bear. Admit to the stress and the strain. Then ask God to give you renewed strength and energy… enough for even one day. And then trust God to do as promised. Trust God to walk with you, strengthen you, and give you rest. Life can be pretty heavy at times. But God helps the fallen and lifts those bent beneath their loads.

Prayer

Father, this day, give us enough strength to carry today's load. Amen.

Day 624 — Psalm 146: In It for the Long Haul

> "I will praise the Lord as long as I live. I will sing praises to my God with my dying breath." Psalm 146:2 (NLT)

Observation
The final five psalms have been described as the "grand pinnacle of praise." All offer exuberant praise for God and all begin and end with the Hebrew word, "Hallelujah," which is translated, "Praise the Lord!" The psalmist (unnamed) expresses his pledge to praise God with his entire being. He vows to praise God for the rest of his life. He goes on to exalt the love and mercy of God. He reminds his listeners not to put their trust in princes, for even though they may be the best of men, they are still woefully inadequate to address the stress and anguish present in the lives of people. Ultimate help can only be found in the transcendent God. He alone consistently comes to the aid of the righteous. Verses 7-9 speak of the special attention given by God to the impaired, helpless, lonely, and needy. The psalm closes with a reminder of the present and eternal reign of God.

Application
From time to time, we make "life promises." We vow to owe allegiance, or love, or fidelity, or loyalty to something or to someone for as a long as we live. And then something changes and our promises fade. For example, when I was a young pastor, I once said, "I will always be a Southern Baptist." But then the definition of Baptist polity changed and what it meant to believe in traditional Baptist doctrine got swept away by a fundamentalist takeover including a dangerous wedding to the political right. So, I no longer feel the same way about the denomination in which I was raised. Don't get me wrong... I still love Baptist theology and the emphasis on both the priesthood of the believer and the autonomy of the local church, I just don't love the judgmental politics that are often found in our churches. Separation of church and state is still a really good thing to acknowledge.

How many couples stand before the preacher and promise to love and to cherish each other, till death alone breaks the commitment, only to fall prey to the relentless temptation and pressure to break the marriage vow? I even know folks who have changed their college football loyalties somewhere along the way... who can do that!? But look at the promise of the psalmist who says that he will praise God till his dying breath. I hope that all of us can make the same vow... and we just might, because even though our loves and loyalties and priorities might change along the way, God doesn't. God's love for us is unfailing, uncompromising, and never ending. It will be God's attachment to us that will keep us from ever breaking our attachment to God. Even today you are held with strong arms.

Prayer
Father, may we love you and praise you till our last breath. Amen.

Day 625 — Psalm 147: Mind Boggling

> "He counts the stars and calls them all by name. How great is our Lord! His power is absolute! His understanding is beyond comprehension!"
> Psalm 147:4-5 (NLT)

Observation

This is a psalm of praise that contains a strong emphasis on creation. It was likely written by someone following the return of the Jewish people from the Babylonian exile. The psalmist affirms that it is good to sing praises to God, who is worthy of such adoration. In verse 2, the psalmist describes the way God is rebuilding Jerusalem, which gives hope to the people who are struggling as they return. But in addition to rebuilding the city, according to verse 3, God is also rebuilding the hearts of the people, a much more significant work. God's ability to count the stars (v. 4) reveals God's infinite knowledge. But God's main concern is not for the stars, but for the people God has created. Verse 8 contains the common theme of God's provision of rain, which displays tender mercy for the world that God created. The final section of the psalm declares that words of praise are needed for God's particular care for Jerusalem. According to the last verse, God has done more for Jerusalem and for Israel than for other nations.

Application

A few years ago, our church raised money for a church outside New Orleans that had been devastated by hurricane Katrina. We wanted to have some kind of fund-raising event in which everyone in the church could participate, from the youngest to the oldest. We decided to collect pennies. We wanted to raise a "Million for Metarie." A million pennies would equal a $10,000 donation. And so for six weeks, we collected pennies in a huge, plexiglass container. It was exciting and a lot of fun. The day finally came for us to count all the pennies in order to send them to the bank. We fell short of our goal, but still collected more than 850,000 pennies. Counting those coins was difficult. We used scores of volunteers, some funnels, and PVC pipe to aid in the process. It took hours and hours to complete the task.

Imagine having the ability to count, not just a bunch of pennies, but billions of stars. Such a task can only be completed by an infinite, all-knowing God—the same God who is able to hear your prayers, know your fears, and protect your steps. Hard to believe, right? That inability of ours to even comprehend the majesty of God should humble each of us to offer words of exuberant praise… today and every day. Certainly God is worthy of our mindful and deliberate offerings of praise. Why not express your sense of awe and wonder this day?

Prayer

Father God, may we praise you with all that we are. Amen.

Day 626 — Psalm 148: Our Reason for Being

> "Let every created thing give praise to the Lord, for he issued his command, and they came into being." Psalm 148:5 (NLT)

Observation

For those who like to classify the psalms into various categories, this psalm is a bit challenging. It could be classified as a psalm of wisdom, or a psalm of creation, or even a psalm of jubilant praise. Without question, it is highly charged with energy and praise. It declares that all of creation should praise the Lord, from the highest heavens to the human heart. The phrase, "Praise the Lord!" is repeated throughout the psalm. The words follow a progression. The first six verses describe the heavens and the universe. Verses 7-12 describe the earth and the creatures of the earth. Mountains, hills, cattle, and creeping things are all intended to offer their praise. The final two verses describe the people of the earth and their need to praise God.

Application

As I read this psalm, I am reminded of the words of the Doxology, which were forever seared into my consciousness as it was sung weekly in my home church in Rome, Georgia. "Praise God from Whom all blessings flow, praise Him all creatures here below, praise Him above Ye heavenly hosts, praise Father, Son, and Holy Ghost" (Thomas Ken, 1674). Sometimes we wonder about our existence. We wonder why we were created and why we are on the planet. This psalm erases all the mystery behind such questions. We were created, purposefully, by God to bring God glory and praise. We are here to honor God with our words, our actions, and our lives. Simply put, we are here to praise God, to reflect God's glory, to exalt God's name.

Years ago, I led the youth ministry for Eastern Hills Baptist Church in Montgomery. A member of our youth group was a gifted athlete and received a scholarship to play football at the University of Alabama. Coach Bryant had come to his house to recruit him. He kept in touch with me while he was in college. He told me about the first game he ever played on the freshman team at Bama. All the players were getting dressed for the game in the locker room. The team trainer walked up to each player and gave them their gameday jersey. My friend said that when he put on that crimson jersey for the first time, that he just started shaking as he realized what it meant to represent his school.

You and I have been dressed in the robe of human flesh by God, who called us into creation. We exist at God's will for God's purpose. Perhaps we should shake in the sheer awe of knowing that we are wonderfully made and that we are made for a purpose. Let us this day join the chorus of the angels, the birds, the roaring seas, and the kings of the earth in praising our God.

Prayer

Father, may we live out our God-given purpose this very day. Amen.

Day 627 — Psalm 149: Dancing Shoes

> "Praise his name with dancing, accompanied by tambourine and harp."
> Psalm 149:3 (NLT)

Observation
This psalm was used not only by those in worship, but also by the armies of Israel as they trained for battle. For the fourth time in the collection of Psalms, the psalmist calls for the people to "sing a new song." (The others are 33, 40, and 144.) The call for a new song is a call to praise God with a sense of freshness and integrity. Worship is too important to become stale or routine. A new song would imply a conscious and thoughtful act of worship. The psalmist also insists that God should be praised in "the assembly of saints." Worship and praise are unifying factors. The psalmist knew that unity would be the result of their corporate worship. In our focus verse, the psalmist even suggests sacred dance as an important part of worship. In verse 5, he also suggests that the people should praise God "on their beds." This refers to the moment when the faithful were celebrating the festivals of their faith as they "reclined" at the feast table. The act of reclining was symbolic of contentment and enjoyment as they considered the work of God in their lives. In addition to moments of worship, this psalm was also used by the army of Israel. A strong component of their training was learning to properly praise and worship God, who would lead them in battle.

Application
My grandchildren have introduced me to the song, "It's Raining Tacos." I can't explain the song, nor can I explain the effect that it has on my grandkids. Whenever it starts to play, they become "slaves to the rhythm." They stand to their feet and start dancing around like a spirit has a hold on them. They laugh and sing and dance with reckless abandon. There is so much joy.

Most of our faith traditions don't do much with dancing in worship. We leave such things to the charismatics or to the practices of some far away group of people. I'm afraid that we might be missing out on something really exciting. What if we got so caught up in our worship of God that our feet started to dance and our hands started to clap? Now, I know that there is much to be said for reverence and self-control in worship. But there is also something to be said for staying out of the ruts and routines that stifle our expression of praise. You may or may not want to dance a little jig this coming Sunday, but you might want to think in terms of a fresh expression of your own personal worship of God. Can you bring an excitement, a joy, or maybe a contagious spirit with you when you step into God's presence? Let's sing new songs of worship… let's be thoughtful and fresh as we encounter our Lord.

Prayer
Father, give us dancing shoes with which to worship you. Amen.

Day 628 — Psalm 150: Daily Praise

> "Let everything that breathes sing praises to the Lord! Praise the Lord!"
> Psalm 150:6 (NLT)

Observation

Psalm 150 is simply titled, "A Psalm of Praise." Maybe that's an understatement. Though the psalm is only six verses long, the word "praise" is used 13 times! And in most cases, it is in the form of an imperative—something that you should do or must do! The psalmist challenges the reader to praise God both in the sanctuary and in the mighty heavens. The idea is for God's people to continually offer words of praise. In fact, everything that has breath is to praise the Lord... remembering that it was God who first breathed life into all of us. So from our first breath to our last, we must offer God the glad praises of our hearts.

Application

According to Genesis 2, God formed man from the dust of the earth and breathed into him the breath of life and he became a "living being." Breath is what defines our existence. We are said to be alive at the moment we take our "first breath." Life continues until the day we draw our last one. This "wind" or "breath" of God is what sustains our lives. I like the image of breath as a metaphor for the presence of God in our lives. Each time that we breathe in, we ought to be reminded that God's Spirit indwells our lives. Just as breath fills our lungs, the presence of God fills us completely and consistently.

Do this... take a long, deep breath. As you feel the air fill your lungs, be reminded that God's presence is in you, filling you completely. Now back to the focus verse, "Let everything that breathes sing praises to the Lord!" As long as you are alive, you are challenged to sing the praises of God. Praise is a deliberate act that is never dependent upon our prosperity nor situation in life. It is something that we do simply because we have been created by God to do so, and because we are loved beyond measure. In other words, praise is not simply something we offer to God whenever we happen to have a really good day... "I'm happy so I will praise God." No. It's deeper and more deliberate than that. Praise is to acknowledge God's presence in both the joyful and challenging moments of our lives. I can't know your life situation this morning. Maybe you are cheerful or maybe the weight of the world rests on your shoulders. But I do know this... if you have breath in your body, your purpose this day is to offer praise to God. Take a moment just now to acknowledge God—who loves you, watches over you, and is present with you. Praise the Lord. That's not just a suggestion. It is imperative.

Prayer

Father, with the breath you give us this day, may we sing your praises. Amen.

Day 629 — Proverbs 1: Trickle Down Wisdom

> "My child, listen when your father corrects you. Don't neglect your mother's instruction. What you learn from them will crown you with grace and be a chain of honor around your neck." Proverbs 1:8-9 (NLT)

Observation
The opening verse of the book of Proverbs identifies King Solomon of Israel as the author of these wise sayings. The next six verses clearly explain the purpose of the book. According to verse 2, these wise sayings are given to… "teach people wisdom and discipline, to help them understand the insights of the wise." Wisdom is more than the attainment of knowledge… it is the ability to apply such knowledge to daily living. Thus, Solomon is giving wise instruction in the hope that those who are young and inexperienced will apply wisdom, so that behavior will be altered and minds will be renewed. The words are written to the young with the belief that those who are inexperienced will avoid making some tragic mistakes. A very familiar verse sets the stage for what will follow… "The fear of the Lord is the beginning of wisdom" (v. 7). Fearing the Lord is to understand God's authority and superior insight and to therefore, be submissive to God's will. To refuse to know God is to reject that wisdom. Beginning in verse 8 and continuing through chapter 9:18, the words reflect the lessons of a parent to a child. There are clearly life and death ramifications about seeking and following wisdom. Solomon warns prudence so as not to be caught in the snares of the wicked that lead to destruction.

Application
Parents give their kids a lot of advice. In fact, the process of giving advice is a lifetime endeavor. It only makes sense that it should be that way. Those who have lived more days on the planet are better positioned in nearly every way to give better advice. And understand… it is a process, not a "one and done" kind of moment. We hear and share words of wisdom over a long period of time. Over the course of my lifetime, my mom and dad have given me lots of words of wisdom and advice. They still do. And I am the better for listening to their words. And part of what is important, is that I trust the ones offering the advice. I know, and have always known, that my parents speak to me out of love and out of a desire to help me have the greatest, most rewarding life possible. Because I am confident of their unwavering commitment to me, I trust the words they offer. It's how we should treat the wisdom given to us by God. Because we live each moment wrapped in the embrace of God's unfailing love, tender mercy, and overwhelming grace, we trust the instruction that God offers. God's wisdom is perfect, complete, and protective. You can trust what God says.

Prayer
Holy Father, give us wisdom for the living of this day and every day. Amen.

Day 630 — Proverbs 2: If You Want to Know Something...

> "Cry out for insight, and ask for understanding. Search for them as you would for silver; seek them like hidden treasures." Proverbs 2:2-3 (NLT)

Observation

Chapter 2 represents the second "My Son" passage, which continues the theme of the first chapter as a wise father imparts wisdom to his son. It develops the protective benefits of wisdom. The "son" is advised to stay on the path of wisdom and find successful living. The son is reminded that wisdom is always available and accessible, but not always embraced. This chapter contrasts the ways of justice with the ways of darkness. This idea is a key theme in the book of Proverbs, that of having a choice to make between two roads... a narrow road on which one finds righteousness, justice, and equity, and a broad road on which one finds easy answers, many distractions, and life-threatening temptations. Jesus perhaps had this passage in mind as he said, "You can enter God's Kingdom only through the narrow gate. The highway to hell is broad, and its gate is wide for the many who choose that way. But the gateway to life is very narrow and the road is difficult, and only a few ever find it" (Matthew 7:13-14 NLT). The message is consistent: those who choose wisdom gain success, while those who choose perversion will find disruption and deception.

Application

It was one of those weird days that just sort of sticks in your mind. I was in high school. One afternoon, a group of us piled into the new Wendy's restaurant that had just opened in my hometown. A stranger sat near the entrance. He clearly looked out of place. He had a long beard, his clothes were ragged and dirty, and his face was tanned and grimy. He looked straight at me and said, "Young man, if you want to know something, ask somebody who knows." That was it. We exchanged no other words. At the time I thought, "Well how stupid... of course, if you want to know something, you need to ask somebody who knows." It was only later that I began to see the wisdom contained in the simple words. For reasons of pride, selfishness, and ego, we sometimes are hesitant to ask the advice and counsel of others. We don't want to appear ignorant or ill-informed and so we struggle our way through an issue or problem, when there are many around us who could help. At least now we have the power of Google and we can research an answer on our smart phones. But even such a search on the internet doesn't always work. We can find information, but can we apply such knowledge to our needs? The scriptures consistently remind us that the answers we need to the really big, important, life issues that we face can be found in the heart of God, who longs to be revealed to us. All we have to do is ask. Want to know something? Ask someone who knows.

Prayer

Father, forgive our foolish insolence. Teach us to seek the wisdom you provide. Amen.

Day 631 — Proverbs 3: Lean on Me

> "Trust in the Lord with all your heart and do not lean on your own understanding. In all your ways acknowledge Him, And He will make your paths straight." Proverbs 3:5-6 (NASB)

Observation
Proverbs 3 continues the theme of giving guidance to the young. In fact, it begins with the repeating phrase found in the first two proverbs, "my son." The admonition of this chapter is to not forget the advice and teaching that the father longs to instill in the life of his son. He speaks of the importance of loyalty and kindness, suggesting that the son tie such life qualities around his neck like a necklace. Our focus verses are perhaps the best-known verses of this chapter. King Solomon teaches a trust in the Lord and a continual dependency upon the Lord's wisdom. He suggests that individuals not lean on their own understanding, but instead, lean on the directions and laws of the Lord. Like "leaning on a tree for support," leaning on God will provide stability and strength. Verse 28, offers a word of counsel concerning one's neighbor: If you are in a position to help, then do it. don't put your neighbor off or hold them at arm's length.

Application
I grew up with the Bill Withers hit song, "Lean on Me," resonating in my mind and drifting across the radio waves of the nation. First released in 1972, the song offered the following lines. "Lean on me, when you're not strong, I'll be your friend, I'll help you carry on, for… it won't be long, till I'm going to need, somebody to lean on." Obviously, his words spoke about the need of having the strong voices, hearts, and words of trusted people in our lives on which we could lean in times of trouble. And certainly experience has proven that to be true. All of us have needed the advice, the strength, and the support of another person at a critical moment. And hopefully, we have been that voice of reason, counsel, and comfort to someone else. But notice that King Solomon suggests that we lean on God for support. Our own understanding and counsel will surely fail us. We need the strong voice, the proper direction, the solid counsel of God if we are going to succeed. Our problem comes with our unwillingness to "acknowledge Him in all our ways." To acknowledge God is to observe God, know God, and seek God continually. If we want to choose the right path… make the right decision… have the wisdom to make good choices, then we must deliberately, continuously, and obediently seek God's direction. We acknowledge that God's wisdom is superior, God's strength is mightier, God's love more perfect, and God's knowledge is far broader than that of our own. We lean on God. We cling to God like a mighty oak when the storms of adversity blow in our direction. So, where have you anchored your life this day?

Prayer
Father, may we be smart enough to lean against your beating heart of love. Amen.

Day 632 — Proverbs 4: The Compass

> "Guard your heart above all else, for it determines the course of your life."
> Proverbs 4:23 (NLT)

Observation

Chapter 4 continues the pattern of a father sharing words of instruction with his son. It has a very warm and affectionate tone, yet also speaks clearly about the discipline needed to seek and hold wisdom. There are a couple of interesting differences about this chapter. First, the recipient of the father's instruction is now plural. He no longer addresses his son, but his sons. Second, there is a generational aspect to the instruction. In verse 3, Solomon mentions that he is passing along the instructions and counsel once given to him by his father. And so, some of what Solomon shares with his sons are the words of wisdom that come from David's generation. There is a nod to the idea that each generation must teach their children well, just as described in Deuteronomy 6:7. Verses 5-9 offer a strong plea to obtain wisdom at whatever cost. It is that important. Solomon restates this theme repeatedly. Wisdom, in his eyes, is viewed as a "crown of glory" (v. 9). The latter verses of the chapter emphasize honesty in speech and steadfastness in gaze.

Application

I'm a pilot. Although I don't get to fly as often as I would like, I faithfully carry my license in my wallet and dream of flying each day, if time and money would allow. Back when I was learning to fly, things were different. That was long before the days of GPS use. We had to plot a course with a compass and rely on a map. But now, pilots use the latest tools like autopilot and GPS. The skies are safer and pilots have better tools at their disposal. The GPS unit is vital. It keeps the plane on course even in the darkest night or fiercest storm. A GPS unit is accurate within three feet of any location on the planet. Obviously, we don't have a GPS implanted within us. No mechanical device sets the direction of our lives. Solomon rightly declares that one's heart (passion, desire, strength) will determine the course of one's life. The wise person will guard it above all else. We guard our hearts in a number of ways. First, we must monitor the intake. We should only allow that which is good, sacred, and pure to dwell within it. When the darker emotions of greed, lust, jealousy, and the like, squeeze their way in, we must be careful to swiftly remove them before they take root. Second, we must give care to the other hearts we are willing to connect to ours. Other people and their passions can have an effect on our hearts. If we align our lives with those who are angry, pessimistic, or filled with hatred, such emotions may climb over into our lives. If it is indeed the center of our being and compass of our lives, we must guard our hearts with all that we possess.

Prayer

Father, may we understand the importance of guarding our hearts to honor you. Amen.

Day 633   Proverbs 5: Scrutiny

> "For the Lord sees clearly what a man does, examining every path he takes. An evil man is held captive by his own sins; they are ropes that catch and hold him." Proverbs 5:21-22 (NLT)

Observation
Proverbs 5 speaks specifically to the peril of adultery and to the blessings of marital fidelity. A lot of instruction is given to the topic of why someone should avoid an immoral woman. Again, Solomon begins by offering instructions to his "son." The descriptions of the immoral woman are vivid… "her lips are as sweet as honey, her mouth smoother than oil." Yet he cautions that those lips drip with deadly poison. They are as dangerous as a two-edged sword. To follow the steps of a promiscuous woman is to step onto a slippery slope that leads to death. Such a temptation is to be avoided at all costs. In verse 8, the words are strong… "Stay away from her!" To enter into a relationship with an immoral woman will bring dishonor and will consume all who fall victim to such a temptation. Public disgrace will be the result. On the other hand, the "wife of your youth" is to be treated as a prized treasure, a relationship to be carefully nurtured and cared for at all costs. Solomon teaches his son to "drink from his own well," in reference to an exclusive sexual relationship with his wife.

Application
We hear a lot these days about identity theft and on-line piracy. We are warned to carefully guard our accounts and change our passwords often. Such advice could save us a lot of trouble and keep us protected. I try to be vigilant with my banking accounts. I check the balances on-line each morning and once a month when the written statement comes, I scrutinize every charge just to make sure that there is no fraudulent activity going on with my account. Maybe there is a fine line between paranoia and prudence, but still I'm willing to go the extra mile to make sure that my money is safe. Notice what King Solomon states in our focus verse. He declares that the Lord clearly sees everything we do and examines every path we take. I find that to be a little troubling, don't you? All of us have a few thoughts and maybe even actions that we don't really want anyone to know. We long to keep our thoughts hidden and our poor actions covered. And though we might hide them well from all those around us, our thoughts and actions are never hidden from God. God sees the secrets, knows the hidden thoughts in our minds. We only kid ourselves when we think that as long as sins are hidden that they are of no consequence. It is my belief that hidden sins are always problematic. As Solomon writes, they are the ropes that capture us and destroy our relationship with God. Let's be honest with ourselves and confessional with God. Let clear the air and cleanse the heart.

Prayer
Father, remind us of both your scrutiny and grace. Amen.

Day 634 — Proverbs 6: What the Lord Hates

> "There are six things the Lord hates—no, seven things he detests: haughty eyes, a lying tongue, hands that kill the innocent, a heart that plots evil, feet that race to do wrong, a false witness who pours out lies, a person who sows discord in a family." Proverbs 6:16-19 (NLT)

Observation

Proverbs 6 addresses a number of themes. Most prominently, it speaks warnings against foolish people. Three types of foolish people are listed. In verses 1-5, Solomon speaks about those who foolishly join themselves to a monetary loan obligation. It's an "if, then" conversation. If you have obligated yourself to someone else's loan as a cosigner or guarantor, then free yourself of that obligation as soon as possible. Remove yourself from a foolish entanglement. In verses 6-11, Solomon warns against being lazy. Using the illustration of an ant, he suggests diligence, prudence, and hard work. "Get up and get productive" is his advice. Verses 12-19 speak of the dangers of associating with worthless persons. Such persons agitate against all that is good. They speak with a perverse mouth, they are sinister in their intentions, and perverse in their hearts. This chapter also gives a list of seven things that God hates… seven qualities… seven habits. Obviously, there is wisdom in avoiding such people. The chapter ends with a warning against any association with adulterous women. The reader is advised to carry the teaching of wisdom continually… tied around one's neck to provide needed restraint.

Application

Notice in his list of things that the Lord hates (see our focus verse above), that there is no mention of people that God hates. It is never people that are the objects of disdain, but rather, the qualities in those people that God detests. That's a really good word for all of us. You've heard the old expression… "God hates the sin, but loves the sinner." It's true. God loves us, but hates the distance, the brokenness, the lack of obedience, the selfish leanings of our hearts. God longs to forgive and seeks to extend mercy because of unalterable love for each of us. Think about your darkest sins and deepest transgressions. We could all recall a moment, an act, a poorly made decision that brings both guilt and shame to our lives. Such choices make us hate ourselves. How much more should such things bring on the condemnation of God? And yet, it doesn't. God condemns our sins, but not our hearts. We are too important to simply be abandoned because of our wayward acts. Though we may cause God grief at times, we never leave God's thoughts, nor surrender our relationship. We must pray that our sins become as detestable to us as they are to God… not to add guilt, but to bring correction.

Prayer

God, may we see in ourselves the things that bring brokenness with you. Amen.

Day 635 — Proverbs 7: The Company We Keep

> "While I was at the window of my house, looking through the curtain, I saw some naive young men, and one in particular who lacked common sense. He was crossing the street near the house of an immoral woman, strolling down the path by her house." Proverbs 7:6-8 (NLT)

Observation
Proverbs 7 is a little racy. It deals with the topic of an immoral, adulterous woman. It is the final lesson in Proverbs where the father addresses the son. Told in the form of a story, it offers the wisdom of not having any association with an adulterous woman. Solomon's warning to his son (sons) is to be carefully guarded. Solomon wants his son to practice wisdom with his external actions and his internal character. Solomon's story of the immoral woman spans verses 6-23. He assumes that his son is walking on the right "life" path, but wants to encourage him to remain on it, thus the story. From his window, Solomon sees a foolish young man who has dared to traveled too close to the corner where this woman lives. He seems aimless. She seems intentional. She wears provocative attire and uses alluring words. She tells him that her husband is away and won't return for many days. She invites him in and he is quickly caught in the current of her sinful deception. Solomon states that her bed is the "den of death." Solomon clearly wants his sons to know that danger is always present as soon as you let your thoughts start to wander.

Application
The main character of Solomon's tale is described as a "foolish young man." He is vulnerable. He is easily deceived. He is quickly compromised. And part of the reason for his demise is the company that he keeps. Our focus verse describes him in the company of naïve young men. He is clearly surrounded by those who are unable to practice discernment and offer moral positioning. In fact, rather than sounding the alarm of danger, they most likely prod him into his unwise choices. The young man also finds himself in the company of an immoral woman. Again, because he lacks wisdom and discernment, he is quickly beguiled and taken by her charms. Better friends could have made the difference. The peer pressure of godly men may have led his steps in a different direction.

Consider for a moment the company that you keep. Are they encouragers or detractors? Do they make you better or pull you down? Do they lead you to make good choices or encourage bad behavior? Let's admit that all of us are swayed by the company we keep. Attitudes, behavior, thought patterns, even the language we speak is partially manipulated by our closest associates. So be careful of those you let into your world. Their power is great and their leadership all but inescapable. Choose well.

Prayer
God, may we consider carefully, the company we keep. Surround us with the godly. Amen.

Day 636 — Proverbs 8: Wisdom-Produced Joy

> "Joyful are those who listen to me, watching for me daily at my gates, waiting for me outside my home!" Proverbs 8:34 (NLT)

Observation
Proverbs 8 depicts "lady wisdom" speaking directly to the reader. She will speak of the benefits that she brings to any situation and person who seeks her counsel. She speaks publicly with a loud and clear voice longing to be heard in the city gates and in the crossroads of the community. In a metaphorical way, she stands in the crossroads hoping that all will hear and will choose the right path for their lives. Her voice is accessible for all who will listen. She declares that all men and women need her words. Wisdom is to be treasured beyond silver, gold, or rubies. A careful distinction is made in her words between wisdom and cleverness (shrewdness). Unlike cleverness, wisdom contains no hint of evil or wrongdoing. The purposes of wisdom are always noble, godly, and pure. Wisdom declares that all kings and rulers desperately need her. She also declares that she is as old as creation itself. She has always been a part of that which creates a successful relationship with God.

Application
On the day this devotional thought was written, Apple was introducing its latest line of smartphones. I watched some of the keynote address as the new phones were rolled out and their features described. What struck me as odd was the audience response. With each new model or feature, the crowd erupted with applause and even shouts. Really? You get so excited about a new phone that you stand and cheer? Here's the problem… the joy that such a newly-released phone brings to the owner, is very short-lived. There will always be the "next greatest phone," and soon the ones we cheer about today we will long to trade-in tomorrow. Joy that is centered in our possessions will always fade. According to Proverbs, the joy that lasts, is the joy that is produced through our pursuit of wisdom. Whenever we seek the right choice to make, or the correct path to take, we would do well to "not lean on our own understanding," but to seek the counsel of Almighty God, who longs to impart wisdom to all who eagerly and humbly seek it. It is in finding and implementing God's ways that we discover and live the best life… the most fulfilling life. Consistency is needed in our pursuit of wise living. Each day… this day… everyday… we must crave the wisdom of God. Because we are human and driven by human nature, we have the tendency to become self-reliant, thinking that we are smart enough, educated enough, and experienced enough to confront the cares of each day. Wrong. Better look her way as you start this day.

Prayer
God, grant us wisdom today and every day in our pursuit of the life you outline for us. Amen.

Day 637 — Proverbs 9: A Lengthening of Days

"Wisdom will multiply your days and add years to your life."
Proverbs 9:11 (NLT)

Observation
Proverbs 9 offers a choice between the call of the woman named Wisdom (vv. 1-6) and the call of the woman named Folly (vv. 13-18). Both offer invitations to come to the banquets they have prepared. The house of Wisdom is well built, with seven strong pillars. It is a large, solid house where God is worshiped and honored. It is a grand mansion fit for the meticulously prepared feast she offers her guests. There is wine, spices, and carefully prepared meat. The guests will enjoy the feast that she has prepared. She extends her invitation far and wide. The food she provides will give life to those who consume it. After an interlude (vs 7-12) where the ways of wisdom and folly are contrasted, Folly extends her invitation. In personality and approach, she is much like the adulterous woman mentioned in chapter 7. She calls out to the gullible and naïve. She is vying for the attention of foolish men. Her appeal is base and tawdry. She claims that her food is sweet and pleasant, yet it is the "dinner of death." The chapter concludes with a clear choice to choose wisdom that leads to life, or folly, which leads to death.

Application
Years ago, while doing some research for a class I was teaching on "Healthy Habits in the Life of a Minister," I came across some material written by author and biologist Lewis Thomas. He wrote a book titled *Medusa and the Snail*, which contains a series of essays and observations. One essay, "On the Magic in Medicine," he described the research he had done on healthy lifestyle habits. He discovered seven habits from verifiable, statistical data that can add 11 years to someone's life. Here they are: Eat breakfast every morning, exercise regularly, maintain normal weight, don't smoke, don't drink excessively, sleep eight hours a day, and don't eat between meals. Does that list surprise you? It's not exactly rocket science, is it? In fact, it's mostly common sense. But sometimes we don't always pay attention to the simple words of advice and wisdom that swirl around our lives. We might, in fact, live longer if we did.

The advice offered to each of us from Proverbs 9 is both straightforward and simple. Wisdom gives life. Folly leads to death. It doesn't take a lot of intellect to make the right choice. But what it does take is a lot of self-discipline. The pursuit of wisdom is a choice. We need to intentionally crave a knowledge of the steps to take, and then make deliberate choices to act on what we have learned. Wisdom is the ability to take knowledge and apply it to our daily living. The discipline needed, is the discipline to turn from the alluring, easy path that leads to destruction in order to gain the wise path that leads to life.

Prayer
God, I pray that this day, we will choose a wise pursuit and a godly path. Amen.

Day 638 — Proverbs 10: Leaving a Lasting Impression

> "We have happy memories of the godly, but the name of a wicked person rots away." Proverbs 10:7 (NLT)

Observation
From chapters 10 to 22, many wise sayings or proverbs are offered by King Solomon. Many themes are discussed, but without discernable order in terms of subject matter. Solomon seems to offer advice in a "stream of consciousness." In terms of the study of Biblical numerology, where each letter of the Hebrew alphabet is assigned a numerical value, the name "Solomon" has a value of 375. In this section (chapters 10-22) there are exactly 375 proverbs, which suggests intentional organization on the part of King Solomon. The opening verse of the section provides a link to the material that has preceded it. The theme of a father giving wisdom to a son is once again raised. The remainder of the chapter offers a variety of themes, including a contrast between the way in which the wise and foolish use their money, the foolishness of being lazy, the wise of heart, how to choose the right path, and the length of days given to the wise versus those who are foolish.

Application
Over the course of 32 years of pastoral ministry, I've performed many funeral services. It is probably more correct to call them memorial services because of the attempt in those messages to call to memory the good qualities and life accomplishments of the deceased. Each life has a story to tell, and I always found it meaningful to tell about important moments in each of the lives I was memorializing. The memories were good, helpful, and in many ways healing. Telling someone's story brings them to life again for a few moments so that they are honored and their good lives remembered. But notice what Solomon says of the wicked. Their name, along with their stories, simply rot away over time. Those who share little, who extend no mercy, who offer no help in times of need, who speak ill of their neighbors… are soon forgotten, and perhaps, gladly so. Their existence is lost to the sands of time. Like walking through a cemetery of old headstones where the names, once etched in stone, are now unreadable, the lives of the wicked are soon forgotten. Most of us want to leave a lasting impression. We want it to have mattered that we once walked on the planet. We want to make a difference. We want to change things for the better. How do we do that? We must live lives of kindness, civility, and respect. We must care for others. The care we offer in life is reflected in the ways we will be remembered in death. My challenge for us is to work on that lasting impression.

Prayer
God, may our lives bring honor to you and in so doing to ourselves as well. Amen.

Day 639 — Proverbs 11: The Joys of Generosity

> "The generous will prosper; those who refresh others will themselves be refreshed." Proverbs 11:25 (NLT)

Observation

Chapter 11 continues the wise sayings and counsel of King Solomon. He offers practical guidelines for managing daily life. Like the previous chapter, Solomon addresses many topics. For example, the opening verse deals with business ethics and the use of dishonest scales. Solomon is clear in declaring that God detests dishonesty in business. Verse 4 contrasts the rich and the righteous. In this case, the rich are those who have defrauded people and have lined their purses with ill-gotten gain. Their wealth may buy them some level of security but it cannot help them to purchase their way out of God's wrath. Verses 10 and 11 describe the blessings that flow into the life of a city or community when righteous people prosper. Their benevolence encourages others and helps to alleviate need. Verse 14 offers some very practical advice for political leaders. Those who govern well have learned to surround themselves with wise counselors. The theme of physical beauty is touched upon in verse 22, in which Solomon compares a beautiful but impure woman to a pig with a gold ring in its nose. The idea being that physical beauty does not always equate to noble character or correct behavior.

Application

Our focus verse speaks of the prosperity of the generous. Think for a moment about the most generous person that you know. Consider the joy in thier life. The more they give to others, the more they seem to be blessed. Not only do they experience the joy of helping others in need, but their prosperity seems to continue to increase. It seems the more they give away, the more they have, both financially and emotionally.

Like many of you, I have prayed to be wealthy. "God just let me win the lottery and I will be the best rich person on the planet." God knows if that's an empty promise because God already knows the generosity of our hearts. If we have not shared out of the abundance that we already have, why would God expect us to suddenly share from full purses? Maybe a better prayer is not for God to make us rich, but for God to make us aware of the ways in which we can bless others, regardless of our bank statements. Generosity is a state of mind. Sharing with others is a result of seeing needs and recognizing our required involvement. Generosity requires us to acknowledge that all that we have is a result of God's blessings and that those blessings are intended to be surrendered from our hands at any moment God directs.

Prayer

God, teach us generosity that flows from a grateful spirit. Amen.

Day 640 — Proverbs 12: A Lesson on Leadership

"Work hard and become a leader; be lazy and become a slave."
Proverbs 12:24 (NLT)

Observation

Like the previous chapters, this chapter continues the wise sayings and counsel of King Solomon. He continues to address several topics. Verse 1 affirms that all people make mistakes, but that the wise person learns from them and receives both correction and discipline. Verse 4 contains a word for the bachelor seeking a wife. A good wife will be like a crown that adorns the head… a shameful wife will be like a cancer growing in his bones. Verse 9 gives wisdom concerning good, hard, honest work… even the work of a slave. Better to have food as a result of one's work, than to be self-important (too proud to work) and go hungry. Caring for the needs of animals is the theme of verse 10. Learning to handle anger is mentioned in verse 16. Verse 26 reminds the reader that the godly person gives good advice to his friends.

Application

Our focus verse offers a lesson in leadership. Good leaders, according to Solomon, have risen to their positions because of hard work. And although there are several qualities that make for a good leader, surely hard work and effort must be on everyone's list. Leaders have a vision for what they want to become and for the ways they want to lead. It then becomes a fidelity to that vision that brings the hard work, dedication, and effort to achieve something great. Notice the second part of the proverb: "be lazy and become a slave." This theme of slothfulness is woven into many of the proverbs. The refusal to work hard will only result in a poor reputation and a lack of advancement. Who elevates the lazy to a position of leadership? All of the key leaders that I know, have worked hard to achieve a level of success, and they continue to work hard at maintaining that success.

But allow me a word of caution in terms of Kingdom work. Sometimes great work and effort doesn't always show up in someone's metric for success. There are few scales that measure changed lives, or inspired thought, or life-saving renewal. In fact, most ministers I know plant a lot of seeds that only slowly grow to fruition. I know many very successful pastors who have labored hard for many years, with little quantitative results to show for their efforts. So understand… the Kingdom measures success in vastly different ways. The Kingdom counts qualities like faithfulness, dedication, generosity, and long-suffering in ways the world will never understand. Some faithful servants of God will only find reward and recognition in the life to come. But still it is important to heed the advice of Solomon. In whatever you are called to do, or to become, work hard. Give such a task the very best of your efforts.

Prayer

God, may we be faithful and dedicated to whatever calling you provide. Amen.

Day 641 — Proverbs 13: Walking with the Wise

> "Walk with the wise and become wise; associate with fools and get in trouble." Proverbs 13:20 (NLT)

Observation
And the beat goes on… Chapter 13 contains more wise sayings from Solomon. Verses 1-3 tell of the importance of listening and speaking wisely. The wise person is teachable and accepts correction. In verse 4, laziness is addressed again. It is only the result of hard work that a person prospers. Verses 7-8 contain an interesting word about wealth and poverty. It is not always readily apparent who is rich and who is not. Appearances can be deceiving. Conspicuous consumption is prideful and haughty. The wise person controls wealth carefully rather than being controlled by it. The value of patience is described in verse 11-12. The role of a reliable messenger is discussed in verse 17. In the ancient world messengers played a vital role in government, commerce, and personal relationships. Verse 24 is the old, "spare the rod, spoil the child" proverb. In fact, Solomon insists that those who neglect the discipline of their children actually display a hatred towards their children because of an unwillingness to train them properly.

Application
Our focus verse has a lot to say about the influence of others on our lives. We've all experienced that, haven't we? I notice when I travel back home for a few days that my Southern accent becomes more pronounced. It's like I get a booster shot of "Southern Culture" and suddenly words are pronounced differently. The same thing happens at a ballgame. When the crowd is excited and cheering loudly, I tend to get caught up in the moment as well. At other moments, I feel the influence of others in my clothing choices, my political opinions, and in my social media banter.

Solomon makes a valid point. He says that if we associate with wise people, we become like them. If we associate with fools, our behavior will soon take on foolish characteristics. It really does make a difference… this company we keep. We will feel the influence. We will feel the tug. We are always blown along in the wake of others' behavior. So, the question to ponder this morning is this, "Do my associations help me or hurt me? Do they make me better, wiser, happier, or healthier?" We can't control all the influences of our culture, but we can control where we invest our relational lives. There is enough negativity, anger, and disrespect to go around. Such qualities will flow over into our lives unless we guard our key associations carefully. Walk with the wise. Spend time with the godly. Live among those who pursue Christ.

Prayer
Father God, teach us to guard our lives from the negative influences around us. Amen.

Day 642   Proverbs 14: Be Angry and Sin Not

> "Short-tempered people do foolish things, and schemers are hated."
> Proverbs 14:17 (NLT)

Observation

Proverbs 14 contains more words of advice... more words of wisdom to share. As in the previous chapters, several themes are addressed. Verse 1 continues a theme of using wisdom when choosing a wife. A good wife will promote the well-being of her entire family, not just her husband. Verse 3 talks about the proud talk of a fool. It will become like a rod that will return to beat his own back. Ownership of oxen is discussed in verse 4. They take a great deal of care and feeding but ultimately are of such value to the farmer. Very little labor is done without the use of oxen. Verse 9 provides a little insight into the topic of guilt. Though most of us would long to avoid it, Solomon states that the wise person acknowledges it and seeks reconciliation because of it. Verse 13 talks about the temporary relief that laughter can provide in a time of grief. The theme of caring for a neighbor is found in verse 21. Solomon says that the man who helps the poor (neighbor) will be blessed by God.

Application

Our focus verse talks about the volatility of anger. Anger is an explosive emotion, seemingly just below the surface in our psyche, waiting to erupt at almost any moment. Surely, we have all felt that. Given the right moment or the right cause, and our fuse becomes very short. We lash out with words or strike out with our hands because for a moment, the anger we feel takes control of our better selves. Anger forces us to say things we will regret and do things that surprise even ourselves. We can't avoid anger, but we need to learn how to control it. It's the old rivalry between human nature and being Spirit controlled. Solomon is exactly right... whenever we are short-tempered, we do foolish things. On the other hand, Paul insists that part of the fruit of the Spirit is self-control. The key is to own our anger and focus the energy it gives off in productive ways, not in destructive behavior.

    I once read about a couple who had learned an effective strategy for dealing with anger in their marriage. They established Thursday as the official "fuss day." Any grievance, any spat, or any emotional anger had to be diverted until the following Thursday. They could not fight or fuss on any other day. What they discovered by practicing self-control was that by the time Thursday rolled around, the emotion had seeped away, and the anger had all but dissipated. It seemed to work for them. It may be a silly strategy, but the point is well made. If we act in anger without practicing the discipline of restraint, we will surely regret our actions.

Prayer

Father God, may we be quick to listen and slow to anger. Amen.

Day 643

Proverbs 15: Saints and Salads

> "A bowl of vegetables with someone you love is better than steak with someone you hate." Proverbs 15:17 (NLT)

Observation
Verses 1-2 remind the reader that wise speech is both restrained and edifying. In a moment of conflict, a wise person will answer with self-control. A gentle word in a heated moment will deflect anger. Verse 3 is a reminder that God sees all things. In verse 4, we are reminded that the right words can soothe. The sacrifices offered by the wicked are the topic of verse 8. Such sacrifices are "detestable" to God. God is not moved by the wicked person's attempt to gain favor. It is the heart of those offering the sacrifices that matter to God. Verse 13 reminds me of a childhood song… the proverb reads, "a glad heart makes a happy face." I want to sing, "If you're happy and you know it, then your face should surely show it." Verse 20 declares that a wise son brings joy to his father because of the honor that is conveyed. Verse 28 is a reminder that the godly person thinks carefully before speaking… the wicked let their mouths "overflow" with all kinds of foolish talk.

Application
I picked up a mantra from Norm on the old television series, *Cheers*. He used to say about choosing the best food to eat, "If it's green it's trouble, if it's fried, get double!" I affirm that statement. I must admit that I'm not much of a salad guy. I'd much rather enjoy a plate of meat and potatoes than a bowl of lettuce and bean sprouts. But I get it… we all need to think of balance when considering our diet. But notice what Solomon says… "Eating vegetables with someone you love is better than steak with someone you hate." Sometimes, the joy of a meal has nothing to do with the food you consume, but instead, with the company that you keep. The image underneath Solomon's choice of words has to do with poverty or wealth. Better to be poor and happy, than to dine at a rich man's table and be miserable.

Surely some of the best moments that we spend are those spent in the company of good friends while seated around a table of good food. What makes the moment great is not the careful preparation of the food, but the carefully crafted relationships. Sometimes, it doesn't matter what you are eating, as long as you are with the ones you love while you dine. I'd gladly eat a salad any day, as long as I could eat it in the company of good friends. May God bless you with good food and good people with which to enjoy it.

Prayer
Father God, today we thank you for our food and for those joining us at the table. Amen.

Day 644 — Proverbs 16: The Glory of the Gray

> "Gray hair is a crown of glory; it is gained by living a godly life."
> Proverbs 16:31 (NLT)

Observation

This chapter of Proverbs begins with a nine-verse section that deals with the sovereignty of God over human affairs. The reader is reminded that man can plan out his days, but nothing will come to pass apart from God's sovereign will. Solomon also states that God examines the motives of every heart. Also, the wise person commits all that he/she does to the Lord. Verse 4 teaches that everything, including evil, can be used of God for His purpose. Verse 7 offers a great word of insight about living a godly life. Those who live to please God will discover that they will have good favor with other human beings. The remainder of the chapter includes these and other themes: A good king speaks with divine wisdom (v. 10). As previously stated in 11:1, God insists that scales and weights be fair and accurate (v. 11). Verse 18 is the familiar "Pride goes before destruction, and haughtiness before a fall." Verse 26 speaks once again of hard work. A worker who has an appetite will urge himself on to working with diligence.

Application

When I was a kid, the hair style of the day was a slicked-back, greasy look. Brylcream commercials insisted that, "a little dab will do you," and that Brylcream would give men, "the look that ladies love." But then the dry look came into vogue and suddenly men started using hairdryers instead. My dad bought into the dry look and quit using the greasy stuff. His hair went from black to gray almost overnight. He's been completely gray for many years and, because we share his DNA, my brother and I are quickly seeing more of the gray stuff on the top of our heads!

King Solomon insists that gray hair is a crown of glory. (I'm going to stick with that mantra.) But read a little more deeply into his words. The reason that gray hair is a crown of glory is because it is the result of having lived a long life… a long, godly life. Make the connection. When a person pursues godly living, attempting to practice faith on a daily basis, offering kindness, grace, and civility towards others, that person tends to live a longer, healthier, safer life. And the result of a healthy life is a long life… which brings on the gray hair. The crown of glory is not simply a full head of gray hair, but the result of a long life, lived out in a pleasing way to God. Go back to the 10 Commandments. Do you remember the secret of a long life according to the fourth? "Honor your father and your mother, that your days may be prolonged in the land which the LORD your God gives you" (Exodus 20:12 NASB). Same thought, right? Living to God's standards helps to promote a long life. So, be grateful for the gray… it's a crown.

Prayer

Father God, may we pledge ourselves anew this day to living a God-pleasing life. Amen.

Day 645 — Proverbs 17: The Healing Balm of Forgiveness

> "Love prospers when a fault is forgiven, but dwelling on it separates close friends." Proverbs 17:9 (NLT)

Observation
Chapter 17 is filled with Solomon's advice and counsel. In verse 1, Solomon speaks of the value of living in a peaceful household: "Better to eat dry crust in peace than a house filled with feasting and conflict." Verse 3 describes God's refining work in testing each heart like a craftsman who refines silver and gold with fire. A strong word of rebuke is offered in verse 5 to those who mock the poor, for in doing so they mock God. Showing contempt for those who have been victimized by poverty or calamity is both wicked and foolish. Remember the phrase, "Trickle-down economics"? Solomon describes "trickle-down wisdom," suggesting that wise parents teach wisdom to their children, who in turn, teach wisdom to the next generation. Verse 10 is a reminder that you "can't beat wisdom into a fool." The closing verse is a reminder of the value of silence and how, at times, it is best to say nothing. Solomon writes, "Even fools are thought wise when they keep silent."

Application
I have a friend whom I once helped through a very difficult chapter in his life. He was a drug addict seeking help. I offered him compassion, advice, and even help with some of his over-due bills. What I didn't realize at the time was that he was lying to me and was still using drugs. When exposed, he confessed to me the error of his ways. It would have been easy to condemn him, to berate him, to forget him. But love won out and I chose to forgive him through the mercy of Christ, so abundantly received in my own life. (How could I not offer to him what Christ continues to give to all of us?) Because the fault was forgiven, we remain good friends. There is no awkward distance… no guilt-infused tension.

The Gospel makes a hard demand of us when it teaches us to forgive and forget. Such a notion cuts against the grain of human nature. Sometimes it's the last thing that we want to do, but it's how we long to be treated by God and by others. We don't want to be judged by our worst day or by a terrible season of poor choices. The burden of the past can be a terrible weight to bear. There is a healing balm called forgiveness that can soothe a lot of pain, and hopefully you have found renewal through Christ. Chances are there is someone in your life that needs to have their fault forgiven. There is a relational distance that can be bridged by your offer of grace. Why remain separated when you can reclaim a relationship that is broken?

Prayer
Father God, as we have received grace, so may we extend it towards others. Amen.

Day 646   Proverbs 18: Forging Friendships

> "There are 'friends' who destroy each other, but a real friend sticks closer than a brother." Proverbs 18:24 (NLT)

Observation

I had a friend whose father offered him this advice as he made his way off to college… "Read a proverb every day and try to apply the wisdom it provides." Good advice, right? And probably not a bad way to approach the book of Proverbs. There are so many proverbs, covering so many topics, that it is difficult to absorb all of the important lessons. This chapter is no exception. There are many important themes. The opening two verses speak a warning against headstrong, self-centered decision-making. Fools listen only to their own opinions and suffer as a result. Verse 3 teaches that the actions of the wicked will be exposed to the community, resulting in terrible shame. Verses 6-7 insist that fools will talk themselves into trouble. Their own mouths will lead them to ruin. Verse 8 describes gossip as a "dainty morsel." Fools enjoy it and greedily devour it. In verse 11 the rich are warned against thinking that their riches will provide them with a wall of protection.

Application

In our study of this particular focus verse, we would do well to look to the Hebrew language to provide us with a little insight. Twice in the verse, the word "friend" is used. But in the Hebrew text, the words are very different. The first use of the term "friend(s)" actually refers to someone who is a fellow or a companion… someone who may join us for some of the moments of our lives. The second use of the word is drawn from a Hebrew word that means "beloved." It refers to a depth of relationship. Such a friend is more than a simple, occasional companion… they are life-long supporters, encouragers, and confidants. We could almost substitute the word acquaintance in the first of the proverb… someone who lacks any emotional connection with us, who could quickly turn on us in a time of need or emergency. On the other hand, our friends are with us for the long-haul… through thick and thin.

I hope that most of us have a couple of real friends. We count on them. They stand with us. They show up in the critical moments of our lives and offer their prayers, their support, and their counsel. If you don't have someone like that in your life, it's not too late to develop such a friendship. Remember that relationships are two-way streets, and to develop a deep level of friendship with someone will surely take the best of your efforts. Think of it as an investment. You will receive the benefit of what you are willing to invest. It may mean taking the initiative. It may require patience. It may cost some time and a lot of effort. May God grant you the joy of having a few good friends.

Prayer

Father God, we thank you for those in our lives who stand closer than a brother. Amen.

Day 647 — Proverbs 19: The Rewards of Kindness

> "If you help the poor, you are lending to the Lord—and he will repay you!"
> Proverbs 19:17 (NLT)

Observation

Here are more words of wisdom from King Solomon, the man to whom God gave unparalleled insight. Verse 1 speaks of character, insisting that ethical qualities are more important than material possessions. Verse 2 speaks of the foolishness of undisciplined enthusiasm. Haste can lead to mistakes if actions are not infused with wisdom. Being angry with God is the subject of verse 3. Expressing one's anger toward God will surely lead to foolish behavior. Verse 5 speaks about those who perjure themselves in court and seemingly get by with their deceit. Solomon warns that such people will not escape God's day of justice. Verse 16 speaks of obedience to the commandments of God. Those who forsake God's laws will put themselves on a pathway to death. Verse 20 speaks of the life-long pursuit of wisdom. Gaining wisdom is a process… a journey. Solomon suggests getting all the wisdom that you can for as long as you can.

Application

There are a lot of ways to help the poor. You can always roll down the window and give a few bucks to the shivering guy standing on the corner with a cardboard sign in his hands. Or you can put some loose change in the jar next to the register at the gas station. Or you can donate a few unwanted clothing items at the local charity shop. Or you can click on the link and give some money to the local food bank through their website.

Or you could do more. Don't get me wrong, the things listed above are good things to do. They will help. But, in and of themselves, there are not the solution to poverty. Helping the poor must become a mindset. The poor should not be seen as individuals to pity, but as human beings who are loved by God and thus stand as our equal in terms of Kingdom worth and value. Perhaps a little, "there but by the grace of God go I" mentality would serve us well. Rich Christians in an age of poverty should automatically think, "as long as there is a need and I have the ability to help alleviate it, I must act." But beyond the dropping of coins in the offering plate, or the purchase of an extra biscuit to give to the lady on the corner, we must do more. We must consider what drives the economic disparity in our land. We must ask why some people remain marginalized with little access to good pay, good jobs, or to advancement within their companies. We must consider our wealth as a platform to speak of change and not as a privilege to look at others with pity and disdain while ignoring their plight.

Prayer

Father God, give us a generosity of both spirit and wallet. Amen.

Day 648 — Proverbs 20: Seeing Our Gifts

> "Ears to hear and eyes to see—both are gifts from the Lord."
> Proverbs 20:12 (NLT)

Observation

The offering of wise sayings and insight from King Solomon continues in this chapter. Verse 1 talks about the use and abuse of alcohol. The use of alcohol is not condemned in the Bible, but drunkenness is. Drinking in excess leads to a lack of self-control. The theme of being lazy and refusing to work hard is a common theme in the proverbs. In this chapter verses 4 and 13 both speak about the folly of the lazy. In one case, the lazy man refuses to plow at the right time to receive produce at the time of harvest. In the other case, the lazy who prefer to sleep rather than work will find only poverty. Verse 9 speaks of the depravity of humankind, insisting that no one possesses a clean heart before the Lord. Verses 10 and 23 echo a recurring theme of dishonest scales and evil merchants. Verse 22 speaks about the role of God when we desire to revenge a wrong in our lives. Solomon insists that we must wait for the intervention of God. Verse 25 speaks of the foolishness of making a rash vow before the Lord. (It reminds me of the story of Jepthah in Judges 11:29-40.)

Application

Ever ponder this philosophical question… "Which would you most hate to lose, your ability to see or your ability to hear?" Tough question, right? Either would be devastating. The answer might be impacted by one's talent or occupation. Ask the artist and she would give up sound before sight. As the musician and he would want to hear the melody more than observe those who play the notes. The world comes alive around us when we can see it and hear it. The ability to see and hear truly are gifts from God, as Solomon expresses in our focus verse. But beyond the appreciation we should have for the two important senses, I think Solomon is pointing to something even more important. Seeing and hearing give us the ability to perceive and understand. We gain wisdom as these senses connect us with the world around us. We can see God's creative acts. We can see God at work. We can see the power of God demonstrated in many ways. As we hear, we listen to what the Spirit is saying. We hear the words of God through a messenger. We hear and experience the beauty of God through a child's voice or through a well-played instrument. It's not just about seeing and hearing… it's about experiencing and knowing who God is. To be able to encounter, experience, and know God is truly a gift. Maybe this morning, your prayer needs to be that God will open your eyes and your ears in ways that let you truly perceive who God is and what God longs to do through your life this very day.

Prayer

Father God, thank you for eyes with which to see and ears with which to listen. Amen.

Day 649   Proverbs 21: What Goes Around, Comes Around

> "Those who shut their ears to the cries of the poor will be ignored in their own time of need." Proverbs 21:13 (NLT)

Observation
When I was young, my family had a little plastic container that looked like a loaf of bread. And in that little plastic loaf, there were memory verses printed on small cards. The idea was to take one each morning and read it to the family. I view the reading of the proverbs in much the same way. It is almost overwhelming to read too many in a single sitting. It's almost too much to take in. One or two a day can provide a lot to consider. Chapter 21 is filled with still more wise sayings of Solomon. Verses 5-7 speak of God's judgment on various types of wicked people... the worker who takes shortcuts in his work, the person with a lying tongue, and a person who commits violence. Verse 8 contrasts the ways of the guilty with the innocent. The guilty walks a crooked path in a zig-zag pattern while the innocent pursues a straight path attempting to follow God's instruction in all things. Verses 9 and 19 both deal with a contentious wife using two different metaphors. Solomon says it's better to live in the attic in a cramped uncomfortable space than to live in the house with a quarreling wife. He goes on to say that it is better to live in a desert than with a contentious wife. Verse 27 addresses the theme of worship. Solomon insists that the Lord is not impressed with religious practice without a heart dedicated to God.

Application
Our focus verse offers an important word of warning... a "what goes around, comes around" type of thought. Solomon insists that if we shut our ears to the plight of the poor, ignoring their needs, then we will find no aid in our own times of crisis. Or as Jesus echoes in the Beatitudes, "Blessed are the merciful for they shall receive mercy" (Matthew 5:7 NASB). There is a give and take in terms of meeting needs and finding comfort in one's own life. Those who take on the world with a spirit of compassion, healing, and benevolence, will find that such a spirit will boomerang back into their own lives. In other words, those who extend grace and mercy to those in need, will find it in their own lives during a time of need or crisis. Please don't misunderstand... if our only purpose for helping the poor is to safeguard our own lives, then we have missed the point. We help the poor because it is the right thing to do. We help the poor because we have been put into a position to help based on our resources. So, let us not see the poor and their needs as a nuisance, but as God-led moments to ease the burdens of another. It is when we show compassion, care, and interest in the lives of the less fortunate that we become very Christ-like. The poor will always be with us. Let's always be ready to help.

Prayer
Father God, give each of us a heart of kindness so that we reflect your heart. Amen.

Day 650 — Proverbs 22: A Fly in the Ointment

> "Throw out the mocker, and fighting goes, too. Quarrels and insults will disappear." Proverbs 22:10 (NLT)

Observation
Most of this chapter continues a recitation of the wise sayings of Solomon. The latter part of the chapter does indicate a slight shift in style. In verse 1, there is a warning about wealth. It is not to be valued above reputation. Money alone cannot secure a reputation. Verse 2 reminds the reader that there is a common denominator between the rich and the poor man… both are created in the image of God, and because of that, neither is superior to the other. There is prudence in planning for the storms of life, according to verse 3. The wise man plans carefully while the simpleton steps blindly into trouble and suffers because of it. Verse 6 is a well-known proverb and often quoted. It speaks of the responsibility and result of parenting that infuses wisdom into the life of a child. It reads, "Train up a child in the way they should go and when they are old, they will not depart from it."

A special section of scripture begins in verse 17 and continues until chapter 24:22. It is subtitled, "30 Sayings of the Wise." These words of wisdom are probably collected from various wise teachers from the nations of the world. It is thought that perhaps Solomon has heard them and has incorporated them into his counsel. Many of the themes are the same (the dangers of debt and the oppression of the poor, for example) as other portions of the book of Proverbs and yet are expressed with a slightly different style.

Application
You've probably heard the old expression, "There's a fly in the ointment." The expression, of course, means that it only takes a little impurity to ruin a pure substance. Or in the case of this proverb, it only takes a single negative or nasty person to ruin a community of folks. The expression, by the way, has its origin in scripture: "Dead flies make a perfumer's oil stink, so a little foolishness is weightier than wisdom and honor" (Ecclesiastes 10:1 NASB). Solomon was certainly aware of the negative effect of a "mocker or scoffer" within the context of the community. Troublemakers tend to spread the seeds of strife, contention, and even anger among what had been a relatively peaceful group. He advises that removing the troublemaker will end the conflict. He's right. Have you ever noticed how quickly the negativity of a single person can sour a moment or infect a group? Like a cancer spreading through a healthy body, a negative person can bring discord to an entire community. The key, according to Solomon, is to remove the mocker. For the sake of harmony and productivity, it is best to name the troublemaker for who they are and refuse to let them infect a group.

Prayer
Father God, may we have the courage to cast out negativity from our lives. Amen.

Day 651 Proverbs 23: That Which Brings Joy to a Mother's Heart

> "So give your father and mother joy! May she who gave you birth be happy." Proverbs 23:25 (NLT)

Observation
When reading this chapter, you will notice that 2-3 verses are devoted to a particular theme rather than a single verse conveying a word of wisdom as in the rest of the book. For example, verses 1-3 are written as a warning to someone dining in a ruler's home. The warning is to be careful of the food set before you… there may be strings attached or expectations that come by consuming a lavish meal. Verses 4-6 speak of the fleeting value of wealth. Though it may take years to obtain it, in a moment it can be taken. Verses 10-11 warn once again about moving the ancient boundary markers that define property. This proverb is a particular word of warning about land owned by defenseless orphans who have no one to advocate for them. They were often taken advantage of by unscrupulous men. Verses 13-14 contain an interesting word to parents who are afraid to discipline their children. A large section, verses 29-35, warn of the dangers of spending too much time in taverns abusing alcohol. Alcohol will bite like a "poisonous snake."

Application
You've heard the old expression, "Ain't nobody happy if momma ain't happy." Meaning that when momma isn't getting her way, she will make everyone miserable. To be honest, I've never really cared for that sentiment. I think it's a little demeaning and casts mothers in a poor light. The desire should be that of pleasing our mothers, not for sake of avoiding her anger and wrath, but for the sake of honoring them for the love, encouragement, and wisdom they provide. Solomon states that we are to bring joy to our mothers… make them happy that they brought us into the world. It begs a question… how can each of us bring joy to our mothers' hearts? What can we do that brings them honor and contentment? Be an honest person. Be respectable. Be kind. Be trustworthy. Be courteous. Be noble. Be fair. Be generous. Possess a good reputation. Treat people with civility, respect, and decency. When we are at our best, displaying our best selves, our mothers are most pleased. If we live well, it reflects on the upbringing they have provided. Could there be a greater joy found in the heart of a mother than that of knowing her child has turned out well? So, whenever Mother's Day rolls around again, instead of just taking her to lunch or buying a nice bouquet of flowers, why not present yourself as an honorable son or daughter?

Prayer
Father God, may we live in a way that brings joy to the heart of our mother. Amen.

Day 652 — Proverbs 24: Poor Prior Planning

> "Do your planning and prepare your fields before building your house."
> Proverbs 24:27 (NLT)

Observation

This chapter contains more "sayings of the wise." For those reading the entire chapter, you will notice a break at verse 23. The remaining verses are titled, "More Sayings of the Wise." These verses are an apparent addendum to the original collection with similar themes and writing style. The earlier verses of the chapter continue to address several topics. Verses 1-2 deal with those who would envy evil men. This is a dangerous practice. The evil have hearts that plot violence and their words stir up trouble. Verses 8-9 speak of the value of a person's reputation. Those who plot evil will be known as troublemakers. A clear command to rescue those who have been unjustly sentenced to die is contained in verses 11-12. Those who know of their plight cannot plead ignorance and fail to get involved. Verses 17-18 warn against gloating when enemies fall. God doesn't appreciate the "trash-talk" when people stumble.

Application

Our focus verse speaks to those living in an agrarian context. When building a house, it would be important to consider the amount of land surrounding the house… as to whether the land could support the needs of the household. The admonition is to plan carefully. As the old saying goes, "Poor prior planning, prevents proper performance." The wise farmer would plan his estate with plenty of surrounding fields to produce adequate food and allow livestock to graze.

I must admit that I tend to be one of those "fly-by-the-seat-of-your-pants" kind of people. I've always been a little impulsive… a little see-it and buy-it kind of person. And because of that, sometimes I don't always make the best decision. I might buy the latest tech on a whim. I might purchase a pair of pants without trying them on first. I might even buy a car just because I like the color. (Take for example the Hyundai Sonata that I once bought because it was painted crimson. Roll Tide, y'all.) But there are some decisions that we dare not rush. We need to think carefully before buying a home, or committing to a church, changing jobs, or starting a family. Such choices have a great impact on our lives. And so, we must seek the wisdom of the Lord in such moments. We pray. We carefully consider. We seek the wise counsel of others. As you begin to plot the course of this day, or the month ahead, or even the year that stretches out before you, let me encourage you to discipline yourself long enough to invite the Lord, who has wisdom to offer, into your planning. Just ask.

Prayer

Father God, grant us wisdom for the living of this day, and every day. Amen.

Day 653

Proverbs 25: Building the Wall

> "A person without self-control is like a city with broken-down walls."
> Proverbs 25:28 (NLT)

Observation

This chapters begins a unique section of proverbs within the greater collection. Chapters 25:1-29:27, represent a group of Solomon's proverbs collected much later in the history of Israel by a group of scholars and wise men who were commissioned to do so by King Hezekiah, who was the king of Judah (southern kingdom) from 715-687 B.C. The northern kingdom had already fallen to the Assyrians. Hezekiah was desperately trying to bring reform and revival to Judah and this collection of proverbs was an attempt to infuse Solomon's wisdom into the psyche of the nation. The first five or six proverbs in this collection are directly related to how a person might deal respectfully with the king. There was a sense in which the king had an intermediary role between God and the people. The king would gain wisdom and insight from God and then pass it on to his subjects. Verses 6-7 warn about taking the seats of honor at the king's table. Jesus reflected these words in Luke 14:7-11. I found verse 16 to be interesting. The Proverb warns against eating too much honey. Overdo it and you will get sick. Good advice to those who tend to overindulge in any aspect of their lives.

Application

Can we admit that most of us are not too good about practicing self-control, at least in certain areas of our lives? In fact, I was speaking to a friend recently about eating donuts. I found myself saying, "You know, I don't think that I have ever turned down a donut, no matter if I was hungry or not." Sometimes we over-indulge our television consumption. I mean… how many football games can you watch in a single day? (I recently watched four from start to finish!) The folks at Apple added a feature that's a little convicting. Once a week, your phone displays a brief message indicating how much "screen time" you have averaged each day.

So, why do we struggle with self-control? I think part of the answer is found in our human nature. We are drawn to that which catches the eye or satisfies some craving. To practice self-control, we have to willingly make choices against our nature. Paul reminds his readers that part of the fruit of the Spirit is self-control. Self-control, therefore, comes as we lean into the leadership of the Spirit and away from the pull of human nature. It takes willful, deliberate choices. It takes having a desire to live our "better selves," than be taken in by those things that seek to defeat us. We must build a strong wall around our wants, desires, and passions. With the power of the Spirit within us, we really can say no to the tempting voices.

Prayer

Father God, may we have the power to overcome self, even this day. Amen.

Day 654 — Proverbs 26: Stop Fueling the Fire

> "Fire goes out without wood, and quarrels disappear when gossip stops."
> Proverbs 26:20 (NLT)

Observation
The beginning of this chapter describes the actions of a fool... someone who fails to act wisely. The first three verses warn against giving honor to a fool. It is not fitting to do so and could cause real damage. A fool also can offer a curse without cause. His words will be meaningless. The proverbs also indicate that a fool only understands harsh force like a beating with a rod on his back. Words alone will do nothing to persuade a fool. Verses 13-16 all address the actions of the lazy person. According to verse 13, the lazy will look for any excuse not to go out and work. In this verse, the lazy stays at home with the excuse that a lion might be out on the road. Verses 17-28 speaks about those who cause trouble with their words. I like the colorful image of verse 17... "Interfering in someone else's argument is as foolish as yanking a dog's ears." A dangerous practice indeed!

Application
We own one of those portable little firepits that families sometimes gather around on a cool evening in the fall. We generally use our firepit only twice a year... once in the driveway each Halloween as we hand out candy, and once on the back deck when the family is in town over Thanksgiving. The problem is always finding some wood to burn in the fire. I don't keep a pile of firewood in the backyard. I just don't need it often enough. And so, to prepare for one of our "conversational fires," I run to the store to buy a pack or two of plastic-wrapped wood logs for the fire. And for some reason, I never seem to buy enough. The fire always seems to go out way too early because there is no more wood to fuel it.

Notice what Solomon says about a firestorm of gossip in our focus verse. Eliminate the fuel for the fire, and soon the flame is extinguished. He's right. A lot of our quarrels, disagreements, and angry exchanges can be eliminated if we remove idle and caustic chatter from our conversations. Some things just don't need to be said. Some complaints don't help. Sometimes the more you continue to bring up a silly discourse, the more the anger arises. Fire goes out without wood. Our quarrels will cease without edgy words to keep them alive. I'm not suggesting that difficult conversations need to be avoided. Sometimes such conversations are essential to moving forward and correcting behavior. But I am suggesting that words that only serve to enflame, agitate, or anger should be avoided. We are called to be peacemakers in our relationships and not fire-starters.

Prayer
Father God, give us words seasoned with grace, gentleness, and love. Amen.

Day 655 — Proverbs 27: The Need for Iron

> "As iron sharpens iron, so a friend sharpens a friend." Proverbs 27:17 (NLT)

Observation
Verse 1 describes the foolishness of boasting about one's activities for tomorrow. The wise man does not brag about that which he cannot control. Because of the uncertainty of each new day, why boast about things not yet unaccomplished? Verse 4 speaks of the power of jealousy. The writer suggests that its power is beyond that of anger and revenge. Jealousy causes a person to defy reason and moderation, leading to out-of-control behavior. Verse 8 speaks of the wanderer who strays from home, whose life is unsettled and isolated because that person has lost touch with the key anchor points that home and family provide. Verse 15 is a repeat of an earlier proverb. It speaks of a quarrelsome wife, comparing her, in this instance, to "a leaky roof in a rainstorm" (NIV). Take gender out of the proverb and certainly there is universal application to anyone who is contentious. The final five verses of the chapter compose a lesson on diligence and prudence using an extended agricultural metaphor.

Application
In the world of metallurgy, it is proven that iron can sharpen iron. In other words, a metallurgist can take an iron instrument, like a hammer with an anvil, and use it to shape and mold an iron instrument. The use of one iron instrument can make another iron instrument more effective. Solomon suggests that in the same way a hammer can shape a sword, a friend can sharpen another friend. I hope you have found that to be true.

We tend to fare poorly when we embrace the world as lone rangers. Somehow, we have talked ourselves into being self-reliant, believing that we can handle any situation, any temptation, and any problem all on our own. What a false notion. Whether we care to admit it or not, we need the help of a supporting cast. We need people in our lives who will speak truth into our hearts, gently correct our errant ways, and offer wise counsel when we struggle with having only our own opinions and thoughts to guide us. We need the iron of friendship to sharpen us, mold us, and make us better.

So, who is in your peer group… your cluster of friends… your circle of influence? Who is making you better, wiser, and more accountable? We need such "iron" in our lives. Without it, we will surely falter. We need fewer people who will enable our poor behavior and more people who will condemn it. And when called upon to do so, we need to provide a voice of reason and sanity, instead of a voice of accommodation in the life of another.

Prayer
Father God, surround us this day with the iron needed to sharpen our lives. Amen.

Day 656 — Proverbs 28: The Mystery of Generosity

> "Whoever gives to the poor will lack nothing, but those who close their eyes to poverty will be cursed." Proverbs 28:27 (NLT)

Observation

Verse 1 of this chapter describes the unsettled life of a wicked person as opposed to someone who is godly. The wicked has no rest, constantly running from real or imagined enemies because of his wayward actions. In contrast, the godly man lives in confidence and boldness. The theme of political and social chaos is addressed in verse 2. When there is "moral rot" within a nation, the government topples. Wise leaders, however, bring stability. Verse 6 repeats a common theme… integrity is of greater worth than wealth. Better to be poor and honest than rich and crooked. Verse 8 describes the righteous settling of finances. Those who exploit the poor with high interest rates will never enjoy their profit. Instead, those who treat the poor with kindness will be remembered. Are there prayers that God doesn't answer? According to verse 9 God detests prayers offered by the rebellious. And though God will hear the prayers of every sinner, God will respond differently to those who are faithful. Verse 15 reminds the reader that a wicked ruler is a danger to the poor… like a roaring lion or attacking bear. The poor must be defended and protected from social systems and leaders that exploit them.

Application

I can't fully explain what I am about to describe, but I know it to be true. Generosity brings blessings… greed robs both the pocket and the soul. It has been my discovery and experience, that God supplies the needs of the generous. The stingy person, however, lives in misery. It's really all about trust. The generous person has learned to trust in the provisions of God. The stingy person trusts only in their own resources and thus constantly feels the encroachment of poverty. In other words, those who consistently bless the lives of others through their generosity seem to enjoy abundance. Those who greedily hoard their wealth find little peace, contentment, or joy in their lives. I have never regretted an act of generosity. I have never looked back and said to myself, "I wish I hadn't helped that person. I wish I hadn't given to that cause." Instead, my regrets have come when I have failed to respond with generosity to the needs that have been revealed to me. The joy comes through giving. The sadness comes through the regret of not having done so. God blesses us with intentionality. God intends for us to be a blessing to others. Though some may find a sense of security in their wealth, those who share find a sense of joy. Where and how we invest our wealth indicates our trust in God to provide for our needs.

Prayer

Father God, may we possess a sense of generosity… abundant generosity. Amen.

Day 657   Proverbs 29: Razor Wire

> "There is more hope for a fool than for someone who speaks without thinking." Proverbs 29:20 (NLT)

Observation

Verse 1 repeats a very common theme in the collection… that of the ability of the wise to learn from experiences, even criticism, while the foolish person remains too stubborn to accept criticism and learn from it. Verse 2 describes the emotional stability of people living in two very different societies. When the godly are in control, the nation flourishes and the people experience joy. When the wicked rule, the people groan under oppressive and foolish policies. The contrast between flattery and encouragement is discussed in verse 5. Flattery is deceptive and destructive. Using flattery with a neighbor is like laying a net to entrap their steps. Verse 7 speaks of showing concern for the poor. The godly see the needs of the poor and respond appropriately. The wicked ignore their plight. Several verses speak about the problem of anger. Verse 11 speaks of the way in which anger is controlled by the wise but is loosed by the wicked. According to verse 22, the angry person starts a fight and with their hot temper commit all kinds of sins.

Application

A couple of years ago, I participated in a mission trip experience to a remote area of the Dominican Republic. One of the tasks for the week was to string razor-wire along the top of a brick wall, which surrounded the buildings of both a church and school. Knowing of the dangers of working with razor-wire, my working partner and I carefully strategized each step of the process. We knew to take things very slowly. We both put on thick gloves and long pants as protection against the extremely sharp wire. We were less than a minute into the process when a section of the wire touched my forearm, cutting a 2-inch gash. It's just that dangerous. It takes extreme caution and I hope you never have to deal with it.

Our words carry the same volatility. They are packed with power… power to destroy, hurt, and wound… or the power to heal, redeem, and encourage. The foolish man throws his words around with reckless arrogance with little regard for the potential of misuse. The wise man, in contrast, selects words carefully and cautiously, using them with great control and restraint. According to experts, women speak about 20,000 words a day. Men speak about 7,000. (I'm not even going to chase that rabbit…) But here's my point. If words are how we communicate, if they express the emotions of our heart and the thoughts of our minds, then isn't it important to choose all of them well. Be careful of your words… they are like razor-wire.

Prayer

Father God, may we be careful and cautious of the words we will use today. Amen.

Day 658 — Proverbs 30: I Can't Get No Satisfaction

> "There are three things that are never satisfied— no, four that never say, "Enough!": the grave, the barren womb, the thirsty desert, the blazing fire."
> Proverbs 30:15b-16 (NLT)

Observation

This chapter is attributed to "Agur, Son of Jakeh." The identity of this writer is unknown. Some suggest that it is a pseudonym for Solomon, while most modern scholars reject that idea, claiming that Agur is a relatively unknown Hebrew writer or perhaps even a Gentile proselyte. The second line of the opening verse is difficult to translate. The New Living Translation, the Holman Standard Christian Bible, and others state, "I am weary and worn out, O God," which seems to fit the verses that follow. However, many reliable translations, including the New American Standard Version, translate the Hebrew words quite differently, suggesting proper names like Ithiel and Ucal, as though Agur is addressing his sons or even his disciples. (The name Ucal, used only in this single place in scripture, was my paternal Grandmother's name. She had 13 brothers and sisters… surely all the other good names were taken, but props to her parents for knowing this reference.) The chapter is structured differently than those before it. The first half has groupings of verses while the last half uses more of the traditional one verse per proverb format. Verses 7-9 display the writer's plea for contentment with what he has, for in his words, he has "enough." He doesn't pray to become rich fearful that he would deny God. He doesn't pray to become poor, fearful that he might steal and thus dishonor God.

Application

Our focus verses deal with the ongoing desire to possess more, have more, own more. There is a weariness to the quest for satisfaction. Agur points to four things that are never satisfied… the grave that always craves the dead, the barren womb that always wants a child, the thirsty desert that longs for water, and the blazing fire that needs to consume in order to survive. I am fearful that we have not learned much in the past two or three millennia. Our cravings are seldom satisfied. If we have wealth, we want more. If we have possessions, we build bigger barns to store them so we can attain more. If we have power, we want more control. If we have clothes on our backs, we want the newer styles. Perhaps Augustine was right in suggesting that "Our hearts are restless until they find their rest in Thee." Created within us is a desire to know God, experience God, understand God, and please God. If our days are filled with the quest to satisfy our souls with anything but God, our efforts will be futile and exhausting.

Prayer

Father God, may we be content in you alone. Amen.

Day 659 — Proverbs 31: The Vital Role of a Mother

> "The sayings of King Lemuel contain this message, which his mother taught him." Proverbs 31:1 (NLT)

Observation
This final chapter of Proverbs is not attributed to Solomon but to an individual named King Lemuel. His name means "belonging to the Lord," yet there is no record of any Hebrew king with this name. The wise sayings he shares in this chapter are drawn from the things that his mother taught him. It is unusual not to include the instruction of the father. Had the father died? Was Lemuel's mother a widow? No one knows. Verses 2-9 are admonitions directed to the king from a mother's heart. She speaks of Lemuel as being the "son of her vows." (My interpretation of that phrase is that she has made many vows and offered many prayers on his behalf.) She admonishes him not to guzzle wine or crave alcohol, fearful that it might lead to poor behavior. She teaches him to stand up for the poor and marginalized and to offer justice to those who are oppressed. The final section, verses 10-31, are very familiar… among the most well-known of the entire book. They are filled with the virtues of a capable wife. The verses speak of hard work, diligence, beauty, and kindness. To find a woman of such reputation and nobility is rare. Such a woman, according to verse 29, surpasses the worth of all the other women on the earth.

Application
There is a special bond between mother and child. The depth of love is unmatched. The desire for success is unparalleled. The hope of a bright future is unsurpassed. Mothers give life to their children. They invest in their children. They dream for their children and love them with intensity and courage. How blessed are those who have known the love, kindness, and instruction of a mother.

We learn from our mothers not only by words of instruction, but also by observation as they role-model behavior, ethics, proper words, and healthy attitudes. Many of the life skills I possess, I learned from my mother. I learned patience, graciousness, forgiveness, inclusion, dedication, hard-work, and most of all joy. There was a lot of laughter in my house growing up. My mother, to this day, is quick-witted, insightful, and always intensely supportive of my brother and me. She hauled us around in the station wagon to every possible event. She sat on a lot of hard bleachers watching me play ball, wincing each time I got hit on the field. She cried the day I drove off to college. Every day that I live, I am assured of two things… her never-ending love, and her constant prayers on my behalf. I've lived like a king because I had the right mother. (My mother passed away a year or so after I wrote this devotion. I continue to be assured of her love and prayerful support.)

Prayer
Father God, thank you for the love, dedication, and instruction of every mom. Amen.

Day 660 — Ecclesiastes 1: Old Dogs... Old Tricks

> "History merely repeats itself. It has all been done before. Nothing under the sun is truly new. Sometimes people say, 'Here is something new!' But actually it is old; nothing is ever truly new." Ecclesiastes 1:9-10 (NLT)

Observation

According to verse 1, the Book of Ecclesiastes is written by "Qohelet," which translates, "Preacher or Teacher." Most agree that this wise teacher is King Solomon. Certainly, the wisdom, wealth, and power of Solomon was unparalleled and would have given him the perspective reflected. Given the tone of this book, Solomon could have written it late in life when he had begun to turn away from the Lord (1 Kings 11). Some argue that the writer was not Solomon but someone who wrote much later than Solomon's reign because some of the grammar and vocabulary reflect a much later form of the Hebrew language. The book is not written in a straight linear form, but is episodic, repetitive, and developmental. The key theme is expressed in verse 2, "Everything is meaningless," says the Teacher, "completely meaningless!" It is the discovery of the writer that human existence, life lived out under the sun, is utter vanity. The wise would look to life beyond this mortal existence. To illustrate the futility of life on earth, he writes about three of earth's wearying cycles... the sun that rises and sets only to rise again, the winds that blow that are stilled and then blow again, and the rivers that keep flowing into the sea but never are able to fill it.

Application

The writer of Ecclesiastes suggests that there is nothing new under the sun... that human habits, emotions, longings, and perversions continue with each new generation in a never-ending cycle. He may be right. Certain behaviors, lifestyles, and vices seem to become too engrained into the lives of families to see substantive changes. For example, there are many in the world who are born into extreme poverty. They lack a way up and out. They lack access, education, and opportunity and so the poverty cycle continues to grind its way forward into one generation and then into the next. Think in terms of human behavior. The same vices, temptations, and distractions live on through the centuries. Though each generation may be lured, intrigued, and trapped by something with a new name or face, the underlying temptations remain the same. Cycles of sin exist because of one fundamental choice that most refuse to make between the easy pull of human nature or the difficult obedience of a God-led life. Nothing about human nature has changed since day one. Humankind loves to play with the possibilities of disobedience. Our human nature seeks pleasure, power, and pain-free living. Obedience to God demands surrender to God's purpose.

Prayer

Holy Father, may we have a passion to follow you and nothing else. Amen.

Day 661 — Ecclesiastes 2: Joy in the Simple Things

> "So I decided there is nothing better than to enjoy food and drink and to find satisfaction in work. Then I realized that these pleasures are from the hand of God. For who can eat or enjoy anything apart from him?"
> Ecclesiastes 2:24-25 (NLT)

Observation
Chapter 2 begins with the search for meaning as the Teacher explores pleasure and the impact that the pursuit of pleasure has on human life. In verses 2-3, he explores the joy of laughter and wine and finds both to be meaningless and foolish. In verse 4-8, he discusses all his activities as a great king. He mentions his huge homes, vineyards, slaves, herds, great amounts of silver and gold, singers in his court, and the vast number of women in his harem that offer sexual pleasure. He concludes that it is all vanity and devoid of meaning. His pursuits are like "chasing after the wind." He does acknowledge that wisdom has some advantage over folly... but in the end both the wise and the foolish will die. His brutally honest and pessimistic outlook is briefly interrupted by the words of our focus verse in which he acknowledges that the only pleasures that bring any semblance of enjoyment are gifts from the hand of God.

Application
I once read the story of a young boy who used to sit on the riverbank near his small hometown, fishing away many lazy afternoons. Occasionally, a plane flew overhead. He looked to the sky and thought, "That's the life! One day, I want to be a pilot and fly planes across the country." Years later, he fulfilled his dream, became a pilot, and spent many days in the air... a career that somehow became tedious through the years. One day he was flying high above his former hometown. He looked down and saw the bend in the river, near the place he used to spend those lazy afternoons fishing. There was a longing in his mind to return to that simple life. He said to himself, "That's the life. I wish I could just sit on the bank and fish."

There is something to be said for contentment. Sometimes we fail to appreciate and enjoy the simple pleasures that life affords us. The simple things that contribute to our daily lives that make life better, are often overlooked. Today I took a warm shower and dressed in clean clothes. I ate a hot biscuit and drank an ice-cold coke. My car transported me safely to work. My office was clean, and the temperature was regulated. Simple things, right? But all of which are a part of God's grace in my life and in yours as well. Today, I hope that you find joy in the simple things. Rather than wistfully long for that which you do not possess, why not take a moment to be grateful for the things that you do possess. Learn to appreciate even the simple things. All things, both great and small, are gifts from above. Be mindful. Be grateful.

Prayer
Holy Father, forgive our lack of gratitude. Thank you, this day, for our blessings. Amen.

Day 662 — Ecclesiastes 3: A Discernment of Time

"A time to search and a time to quit searching." Ecclesiastes 3:6 (NLT)

Observation
The first portion of Chapter 3 (vv. 1-8) are by far the most memorable and repeated verses in the entire book. These words have been set to music and often quoted in various ways. They are a discussion of the various rhythms and seasons of life. Solomon suggests that every event under the sun (human life) has a proper time because all of it has been ordained by God. What may seem like endless futility from a human perspective, is in reality, a part of God's design for human life. Each of the verses in this section offers pairs of opposite life events such as, birth and death, planting and harvesting, killing and healing. Verse 5 is open to interpretation… "A time to scatter stones, a time to gather stones." This could refer to the sabotaging of a field during a time of warfare. To scatter stones would ruin the field, making it unusable for planting. To gather stones would clear the land to become once again productive. Another interpretation could be that of gathering stones to build a wall that separates or scattering the stones to tear down the walls of division. The tearing and mending of cloth in verse 7 probably refers to the experience of human grief. There is a time to rend one's clothing in remorse and eventually a time to repair and rediscover normal living once again. All these verses speak to the impermanence of life. Seasons come and go, but eternity is set in the human heart by God Who watches over all things.

Application
Years ago, I knew a couple who owned a gift store in Gatlinburg, Tennessee. Their store was filled with all kinds of nice trinkets, paperweights, mugs, and vases. (They were also the first to introduce Cabbage Patch dolls to the region and thus made a fortune!) Their home was a reflection of their shop. Every table, every nightstand, every inch of counter space was filled with beautiful keepsakes. To celebrate a special anniversary, the husband gave the wife a beautiful and expensive diamond ring. Once, when leaving the house for a few weeks of vacation, and not wanting to take along her precious ring, she hid it in one of the hundreds of keepsakes in her home, thinking that it would be hard to find if someone were to break-in while they were away. Here's the problem… when they returned, she could not remember where she had hidden it. She searched for weeks until finally concluding that it was lost for good. There are some things that are so precious that any search must be extended, while for others, that which is lost must be forgotten and the search abandoned. We are in the first category. We are so precious to God, that God will never stop searching for our hearts until they are claimed by grace.

Prayer
Father, thank you for your relentless search for each of us. Amen.

Day 663 — Ecclesiastes 4: Never Alone

> "A person standing alone can be attacked and defeated, but two can stand back-to-back and conquer. Three are even better, for a triple-braided cord is not easily broken." Ecclesiastes 4:12 (NLT)

Observation
This chapter continues a very pessimistic and dark viewpoint of life and its futilities. There are many injustices and difficult realities faced by all those who live "under the sun." In the opening verses, the Teacher speaks of the oppressive people and systems in place causing suffering, disruption, and misery for many. He insists that those "yet unborn" are the only fortunate ones because they have yet to be exposed to the harsh realities of life on earth. In verses 4-6 he discusses the futility of labor. So much of one's hard effort never leads to enjoyment. At least the dedicated worker has some sense of contentment in his labor as he enjoys the affordable, simple things. Verses 9-12 speak of the advantages of companionship in this desperate existence. Companions make life easier. They help in times of need. They comfort in times of difficulty. They give aid in harsh moments. The Teacher closes with a discussion of the futility of political power. All those who eventually rise to power will quickly be replaced. Power is never permanent.

Application
Recently, I journeyed to Tegucigalpa, Honduras, to lead a group of bi-vocational pastors in a week of study. It was a strange city, the native language unfamiliar, and the culture very different from my own. Unlike all the other international mission experiences I have had, this time I traveled alone. I boarded the flights, navigated customs, and worked my way through passport control solo. It was a bit intimidating… a bit scary, to be honest. All my fears and anxieties would have been greatly lessened by the presence of a companion… someone to make the journey with me.

There is great power in companionship. We are better, stronger, and wiser when we stand with others. It's hard to "do life" all alone. We need the support of friendship, the prayers of the faithful, and the comfort of family. Notice what Jesus said to his own disciples the moment he stepped away from the planet, knowing they faced the fear and anxiety of uncertainty. He said, "I am with you always…" (Matthew 28:20 NASB). He offered them, and us, the promise of continual presence. We are never alone. We have not been left to fend for ourselves. Isaiah 40:10 echoes the same refrain, "Do not fear, for I am with you; do not be afraid, for I am your God. I will strengthen you; I will help you; I will hold on to you with My righteous right hand" (CSB). You will not walk through this day alone… You have a companion.

Prayer
Father, thank you for your continual presence in our lives… even this day. Amen.

Day 664 — Ecclesiastes 5: Promises You Can't Keep

> "When you make a promise to God, don't delay in following through, for God takes no pleasure in fools. Keep all the promises you make to him. It is better to say nothing than to make a promise and not keep it."
> Ecclesiastes 5:4-5 (NLT)

Observation

This chapter has several distinct sections. Verses 1-7 deal with the futility of improper worship. There is advice about entering into the presence of God. First, be careful of offering meaningless sacrifices. The attitude of one's heart matters more than the sacrifice of animals. Second, be careful of praying with indifference. Hastily made prayers are meaningless and devoid of substance and real commitment. Third, when making a vow before the Lord, fulfill it. Breaking a vow reflects a lack of respect for God. Fourth, fear God in worship... meaning, approach God with reverence and awe. Verses 8-9 speak of the abuse of political power and influence. Solomon confesses that there is always too much bureaucracy that leads to corruption. Verses 8-20 speak of the futility of amassing wealth. Lusting and craving after wealth always create an insatiable appetite for more. The more wealth a person obtains, the more reckless his spending habits become. Wealth will slip through the fingers of the foolish. Wealth does not provide comfort beyond the grave. (The old "you can't take it with you" phrase comes from this passage.) As a final word, Solomon indicates that most of the rich never enjoy the money they have amassed.

Application

Sometimes we make promises in an attempt to get out of a "sticky" situation. For example, let's say that you forgot to fill up your wife's car as promised. You know you failed to honor that promise and so you make another promise or two to prove your reliability and trustworthiness. You might say something like, "I promise I will remember the next time. I will never let your car get below ¼ tank again." That's just a silly scenario, but you understand the mentality behind it. Whenever we make a promise, there is always the potential of breaking the promise, which gets us further and further into trouble. We do the same with God. Sometimes we make a foolish vow to God, promising some corrected behavior, some better conduct, some greater commitment. "If you just get me out of this tight spot... I will promise to do better." We make promises to God to secure blessing, favor, grace, and goodwill. We forget that God already longs to bring such things into our lives. We are already the objects of God's love and goodwill and yet, we make promises we can't keep or even worse, ones that we know we have no intention of keeping. Let's do better. Let's be honest when we talk to God. Let's don't make foolish promises in an attempt to secure blessings.

Prayer

Father, as the recipients of your grace, may we live honestly and obediently. Amen.

Day 665 — Ecclesiastes 6: The Joy of Contentment

> "Enjoy what you have rather than desiring what you don't have. Just dreaming about nice things is meaningless—like chasing the wind."
> Ecclesiastes 6:9 (NLT)

Observation
In this chapter, the "Teacher" gives a troubling example of wealth's inability to bring satisfaction or contentment. He describes the life of a person to whom God gives "wealth, honor, and everything they could possibly want," but no opportunity to enjoy his prosperity. In fact, when he dies, someone else, even a stranger, will enjoy his wealth. The Teacher calls this a sickening tragedy. In verses 3-6, the Teacher offers a deeper description of such a person and situation. He says that person could be richly blessed with 100 children and many years of life but still know no satisfaction. "What's the use?" he ponders. In verses 7-9, he compares the appetite for wealth like a hungry man craving food. Neither are ever satisfied with what they have. He ends his reflection on the futility of life on earth with verses 10-12. He states, with pessimism, that each life has already been determined by God and each person's destiny already set. The living of one's days are but a shadow. They are hollow and devoid of meaning.

Application
Consider the evolution of our obsession with television viewing. In the early days, a 20-inch black and white set was mesmerizing, stunning, and enjoyable. Then color sets came on the market. I remember our first one... a big cabinet model. We wondered how things could ever get any better... but they did. Better technology led to better televisions. Suddenly there was surround sound, flat screens, and larger pictures. We went from 720 dpi to 1040, and suddenly 4K "smart" TVs became the standard. Now, if there is a screen on your wall that is fewer than 70 inches, you must be living in the dark ages. That's just a simple example of the lack of contentment that most of us have with the things we possess. We want a bigger house, a sportier car, a greener lawn, a better phone. We long so much for what we have yet to obtain that we fail to find the contentment of enjoying what we already have. Don't get me wrong... when it comes to our growth and development as human beings, we need to continue to strive towards maturity, wisdom, and understanding. It's not enough to be content with old opinions, antiquated attitudes, and oppressive ideologies. We must push to become our best selves. But in terms of the things that we own, or should I say, the things that own us, we need to find the joy of contentment. Our "things" should be the tools that allow us to enjoy relationships, spend time together, and enjoy better health. They should add to our lives, not define them. So, if you find yourself chasing after the newest, the latest, or the greatest, just realize that meaningful life is never found in such things.

Prayer
Father, forgive us when we chase after the wind rather than meaningful life. Amen.

Day 666   Ecclesiastes 7: What Goes Around, Comes Around

> "Don't eavesdrop on others—you may hear your servant curse you. For you know how often you yourself have cursed others."
> Ecclesiastes 7:21-22 (NLT)

Observation

This chapter is reminiscent of the wise sayings of Solomon contained in the book of Proverbs. There are several key themes woven into the text. Verse 1 speaks of the importance of a good reputation. The Teacher suggests that it is valuable, like costly perfume. It is important in life and will become even more important in death. The wise person should strive to be well-remembered. Verses 2-4 speak of the value of pondering the reality and finality of death. With sober reflection, each person should consider the topic carefully. Verses 5-7 speak of the value of a wise man's correction. The praise of a fool is short-lived, but the counsel of a wise man will lead to lasting results in the hearer's life. Having patience and controlling one's anger is the topic of verses 8-9. Verses 11-14 suggest that wisdom and money both provide protection, but wisdom is of greater value because it will remain when wealth runs out. The final section, which actually extends to the first verse of chapter 8, offers a reflection on the connection between righteousness and wisdom.

Application

I've done a lot of public speaking in my life. Often, I am "wired-up" with a microphone on my lapel, or one of those that wraps around your head making you look like you are about to take orders at the drive-thru window. It's critically important to know when the microphone is on and when it is not. When turned on, every conversation can be heard. Even a whisper can be broadcast unintentionally to an audience. As a public speaker, you learn to guard your words very carefully.

In our focus verse, the Teacher cautions against eavesdropping on others. Just as it is important to guard our words when speaking, it is also important to guard our *listening*. The temptation to overhear others may backfire. We may hear words that we later wish we had not. We may discover that we are the objects of an unkind remark. Just as we are sometimes tempted to gossip about others, someone else may gossip about us. Gossip ruins a lot of friendships and reputations. It is a cancer in the life of any organization. The wise person learns to deal with gossip appropriately, choosing to disregard it, ignore it, and never pass it along. What good comes from the spreading of a rumor or the telling of a falsehood? Typically, those who are prone to spread gossip will soon become the ones victimized by it. So… if you can't say something good… think about not saying anything.

Prayer

Father, forgive us when we offer caustic and hurtful words. Amen.

Day 667 — Ecclesiastes 8: God Moves in a Mysterious Way

> "I realized that no one can discover everything God is doing under the sun. Not even the wisest people discover everything, no matter what they claim."
> Ecclesiastes 8:17 (NLT)

Observation
Chapter 8 of Ecclesiastes deals with life's frustrations. Specifically, the Teacher speaks of the dangers inherent while living in an ancient political system ruled by a monarchy who is able to rule unilaterally. Whenever the king has the authority and power over the life and death of his subjects, those who approach him must do so with great caution. He advises being careful not to get caught up in an evil and destructive plot against the king that could potentially backfire. Later in the chapter, the Teacher speaks more about the weakness of human wisdom and ability. Humans cannot control the wind, the day of their deaths, or the events that might impact a person's life. He also speaks about the paradox of earthly justice where the righteous sometimes get what the wicked deserve and vice versa. He concludes that humans are to leave ultimate justice in the hands of God.

Application
Sometimes, we can only see God's movement retrospectively. It is as we think back over the unfolding events of our lives that we begin to see how God carefully arranged people, place, and circumstance for God's purposes. Though we are constantly being woven into the fabric of that plan, we often fail to see how God is at work among us. We discover that God is very active and involved in our lives, though in the meantime, we don't always see God's hand, writing the script of our lives. The writer of Ecclesiastes is correct, "Who can discover all that God is doing under the sun?" We must live with the assurance that God is very much at work and moving us all towards the day when the Kingdom will come on earth as it is in heaven.

I took a class in college called Games and Recreation. It was part of a Youth Ministry track that I was studying. As a class requirement, each student had to keep an index card file of games to be played with youth groups. They had to be arranged by the level of activity, the number of people who could play, the appropriate age-level, etc. It was very time consuming. And at the time, I thought it was the dumbest thing I ever had to do. Three or four months later, I was called to serve as the Minister of Youth at a large church in Montgomery. Suddenly, I was planning retreats, after-church fellowships, and youth group outings. And every single week I found myself desperately flipping through that index card file to find just the right games to play. That was a long time ago, but the same story has been repeated in my life a hundred times over. God prepares us for our lives in mysterious ways.

Prayer
Father, we thank you this day for your careful investment in our lives. Amen.

Day 668 — Ecclesiastes 9: Death & Taxes

> "So go ahead. Eat your food with joy, and drink your wine with a happy heart, for God approves of this!" Ecclesiastes 9:7 (NLT)

Observation

Chapter 9 primarily deals with death. The Teacher sees death as the great leveler of all men. No one knows what awaits them in this life, but death is a certainty. Even wisdom is no guarantee of success. God's purposes are not manipulated by the acquiring of wisdom nor the lack of it. In the leveling of death, all are included… the wise and foolish, the rich and the poor, the godly and the wicked. It is better, the Teacher asserts, to be alive than dead. Those who are alive, live with the hope of being able to enjoy all that is good in this life. (He specifically mentions the joy of having a wife.) He further asserts that having a knowledge of the reality of death, should teach everyone to value the present. Therefore, because of the unpredictability of when death comes, all should live well in the present.

Application

We all know too well the expression, "the only two things that are certain in life, are death and taxes." For most of us, the coming of April 15 makes us wince a little. We understand "Tax Day" as a day of reckoning. We know that every year we must submit our tax return and pay any balance owed. And because we know that the day is coming, we plan accordingly… at least if we are wise. We ensure that our employer is taking out enough tax from our paycheck. If we are self-employed we make sure to put away enough each month to support the potential tax liability. We do not want to get caught with an "April surprise." We don't want to get caught having made no preparation.

We would do well to treat the coming day of death with the same precautions. Though we may not know the day of our death, we do know with certainty that it will eventually come. And so, we must make preparation. We must do the things necessary now to ensure success when that day comes. Many foolishly prepare the wrong way. Many try to earn salvation through good works, generous contributions, or noble endeavors. Certainly, such things should be the outflow of our faith, but never a substitution for it. The Bible is crystal clear on the topic of salvation and life after death. There is one, and only one, qualifying requirement, and that is a belief in Jesus Christ as Savior and Lord. To profess Christ is to prepare well. It is crucial. It is vital. We're reminded, "He who has the Son has the life; he who does not have the Son of God does not have the life" (1 John 5:12 NASB). Next April 15 your taxes will be due again. You better prepare now for that day. And sometime… the day will come when your life on earth will end. You better prepare for that day as well.

Prayer

Father, may we prepare well for that which will surely come. Amen.

Day 669 — Ecclesiastes 10: An Unused Skill

> "If a snake bites before you charm it, what's the use of being a snake charmer?" Ecclesiastes 10:11 (NLT)

Observation

Chapter 10 begins with a reminder of the power that wisdom provides, yet also adds a warning against the power of foolishness, which can be equally strong. A little foolishness... a little unwise action... a little perversity of thought can lead to great destruction. The Teacher also warns in verses 5-7 against the foolish practice of a ruler who puts people in positions of leadership who do not possess the wisdom to lead. It is equally foolish to take someone of great ability and put them in a very lowly position where their skills and intellect are wasted. Such foolish management leads to dire circumstances. Verses 8-11 remind the reader that not even wisdom can prevent every accident from occurring, but when wisdom is consistently applied to all facets of life, many accidents can be prevented. Knowing that the future is unpredictable, verse 14 suggests the use of wise action in all things. The final verses, verses 16-20, contrast the differences between wise and foolish leadership.

Application

Many of us develop some skill sets along the way. There are things that we learn to do that help us to accomplish a task or goal. For example, I have a passion for flying. Many years ago, I learned to fly. I took the tests and now carry a private-pilot license. But here's the problem... I don't use those skills very often. I haven't soloed in a plane in several years. When such a skill goes unused, it becomes wasted. Here's another example... for many years I coached little league baseball. In fact, I had a lot of success with the boys that I coached. I kept the same team together for 4-5 years and we won a lot of games and even a few city championships. But I don't coach anymore. I don't use those skills and so I've begun to forget a lot of my formula for success. Or... as many of you know, I spent 32 years as a preacher. I absolutely loved the process of preparing and presenting sermons. And because I don't want to lose those skills, I try to accept any and every opportunity to speak at churches on weekends.

Here's my point... if we have skills that are unused, they are wasted. The writer of Ecclesiastes suggests that if a snake charmer doesn't remember how to charm a snake, he's going to get bitten. All of us have been given amazing gifts, skills, and abilities by God, who intends for us to use them. Whenever we allow our gifts to atrophy, we are in danger of losing the ability to do great and mighty things for God. What is it that you do well? What are your strengths... talents... and gifts? Do not neglect the giftedness of God for your life. Find a place to serve, to volunteer, to exercise your gift.

Prayer

Father, may we be faithful in using the talents invested in our lives. Amen.

Day 670   Ecclesiastes 11: Just Do It

> "Farmers who wait for perfect weather never plant. If they watch every cloud, they never harvest." Ecclesiastes 11:4 (NLT)

Observation

Chapter 11 deals with the uncertainty and unpredictability of life. Though wisdom cannot remove either, it can help to prepare and cope with the unexpected. The Teacher offers counsel about two topics. The first, discussed in verses 1-2, is finance. He offers a wise maritime trading strategy that is risky, but potentially very rewarding. He suggests sending grain across the sea to various places, yet the wise trader should exercise care not to commit too great a percentage to any one location. The second topic is farming. The farmer is to act wisely despite the uncertainties of nature. Farming is always risky. Weather is unpredictable. But the uncertainty of the rain and sun cannot paralyze a farmer. He must keep planting, sowing, and harvesting with the knowledge that outcome is uncertain. The rest of the chapter offers advice to the young. The Teacher takes an upbeat posture suggesting that the young should enjoy life while they have the strength and health to do so. They are admonished not to worry and to keep their bodies healthy. Yet rather than a "sow your wild oats" mentality, youth are to conduct themselves under the scrutiny and authority of God.

Application

One of the greatest foes we face is fear. The fear of "what might happen" causes many of us to risk little, explore timidly, and live too cautiously. We let the fear of what might happen keep us from the thrill of living a life that opens new worlds, new relationships, and new experiences. Those who are afraid to fly will never cross the ocean. Those afraid to love will never know relationship. Those afraid to risk will never know the thrill of reward. Those afraid to show compassion will never know the joy of changing lives. In the case of our focus verse, the farmer who wrings his hands and watches the uncertain skies will never complete the planting and harvesting. It is not that the farmer should throw caution to the wind, but that he must be willing to step out in faith combined with hope so that the thrill of the harvest can be known. What fear is keeping you from experiencing the great adventure of life? Is it the fear of failure? The fear of embarrassment? The fear of risk? The fear of pain? The fear of rejection? When Christ calls us to an abundant life, we're called to rise above our fears, our worries, and our anxious thoughts. Be willing to risk so that you can find the rewards.

Prayer

Father, help us to conquer our fears so that we might know abundant life. Amen.

Day 671 — Ecclesiastes 12: Truth Hurts

> "The words of the wise are like cattle prods—painful but helpful. Their collected sayings are like a nail-studded stick with which a shepherd drives the sheep." Ecclesiastes 12:11 (NLT)

Observation
Considering the brevity of life and the certainty of death, this concluding chapter of Ecclesiastes offers an important word to the young. The Teacher admonishes the young to commit wholeheartedly to the Lord, carefully remembering God's authority and commandments. Trusting in God and obeying God's laws are the duties of each person (v. 14). The Teacher reminds the young to be faithful, knowing that the effects of age will soon come, when life's vitality and passions will dim. In fact, he gives a rather bleak look at aging. Included in his description of old age are these reminders… eyes will dim, days will be dark and cloudy, legs will weaken, shoulders will droop, teeth will fall out, hearing will diminish, energy will seep away, and there will be a loss of physical and sexual appetite. Not much to look forward to, right? So, in light of the relentless approach of death, honor God continually, before it becomes impossible to draw from the well of life. He concludes his remarks by saying that life is meaningless, vain, fleeting, and frustrating. Our only hope and joy are in honoring God and obeying God's commands.

Application
It may well be true that many of us can't handle the truth. Sometimes truth hurts. Let's face it, most of us enjoy living life by our own standards. We like setting the boundaries, making the rules, and self-judging our behavior. The truth, according to the way we define it, is easy, because it is our truth. The problem, however, is that our truth seldom aligns with real truth, ultimate truth, God's truth. God's truth states that we are all sinners in need of grace. God's truth states that Christ is the only hope of salvation. God's truth states that we are to love our enemies, pray for those who persecute us, welcome the stranger, feed the poor, and clothe the naked. God's truth says nothing about convenience, comfortable compassion, or many paths to salvation. Ultimate truth is not ours to legislate. Truth is not found in our opinions or prejudices. It is found only in God's ultimate purposes and plans. And sometimes that truth is painful.

When I was young, I longed to have the ability to dunk a basketball. But I possessed only average height and average jumping ability. And so, when I was unable to dunk on a 10-foot goal, I merely lowered the standard. I put up a shorter goal on which I could easily dunk. A lot of us do the same thing in terms of ultimate truth. When we don't like the ultimate truth of God, we simply lower the standard. We substitute our own version. We need a greater truth.

Prayer
Father, forgive us when we fail to set your truth as our standard. Amen.

Day 672 — Song of Solomon 1: Lipstick and Paint

> "How lovely are your cheeks; your earrings set them afire! How lovely is your neck, enhanced by a string of jewels." Song of Solomon 1:10 (NLT)

Observation

The book known as The Song of Solomon (literally, The Song of All Songs) is a series of songs describing the courtship between the king (Solomon) and a young woman who is identified later in the book as the Shulamite. The first section of the book describes the beginning of the courtship between the king and this woman. In verses 2-4, the Shulamite expresses her romantic desires for Solomon. She speaks of the attractive qualities he possesses like his kisses, his mouth, his love, his fragrance, and even his name. She longs to be brought into his chamber. Verse 4 also contains words spoken by "The Daughters of Jerusalem." This is a chorus of voices that will appear multiple times within the book. In verses 5-7, the Shulamite reveals a little insecurity about her appearance. Her skin has been darkened by the sun and her body has been shaped by hard work in the fields. And yet, the king is certainly drawn in by her charms. He praises her appearance with very flirtatious language as the chapter concludes. She too responds with beguiling words.

Application

As Solomon gazes at his love interest, he describes her physical beauty. In our focus verse, he speaks about her lovely cheeks and neck, both of which are enhanced by fine jewelry. He is obviously taken by her outward appearance... her physical beauty. It happens, right? Part of the initial attraction we feel towards others has to do with the physical appearance. Our eyes are drawn to their looks... the shape of their face, the color of their hair, the beauty of their smile. But sometimes the outward appearance belies the inner character and nature of a person. The wise person is the one who is willing to discover both inner and outer beauty. I once heard an old gentleman say, "Lipstick and paint make 'em look like they ain't!" He was referring to the sometimes deceitful claims of outward appearance. True love, true attraction, and true relationships must look well beyond the surface to the inner thoughts, the inner passions, and the inner joy of another's life. Real beauty is found in a graceful spirit and a loving heart.

Regrettably, our culture pushes us to think only in terms of the physical. Social media is filled with those who are most striking in appearance. We seem to undervalue those whose true beauty goes well beyond the surface. If we were to look at all others through the eyes of Christ, surely our perspective would change. We would see the beauty of loving hearts, kindred spirits, and sacred person. May God give us such vision.

Prayer

Father, may we see the true beauty in the life of all we encounter this day. Amen.

Day 673 — Song of Solomon 2: Love Demonstrated

> "He escorts me to the banquet hall; it's obvious how much he loves me."
> Song of Solomon 2:4 (NLT)

Observation
This chapter continues the flirtatious words of the Shulamite woman and Solomon as they express their longings for each other. She compares herself to a flower blooming in the plains of Sharon, which was a lush and fertile plain on the Mediterranean Coast. She compares her lover to an apple tree, full of fruit. He declares in response that she is indeed like a Lilly among the thorns... to be set above all others. She values the praises that he offers her. She takes delight in his company. She also revels in his public declaration of love for her. He brings her into the banquet hall and places a banner declaring his love. In verse 5-6 she expresses that she is indeed lovesick and finds strength and protection in Solomon's love. Verse 7 is a word of advice and warning offered to the virgin girls of Jerusalem, telling them not to enter into love foolishly or casually. The remainder of the chapter describes the anticipation each has to be together. There is the hint of desire and fulfillment as he calls her to a hidden country rendezvous.

Application
The Shulamite woman declares "it's obvious how much he (Solomon) loves me." Solomon has demonstrated his love in very public and meaningful ways. I am reminded that we make obvious the things we love most. The things we love most claim the priority of our attention, our time, and even our wealth. I know people whose love for their car is obvious. They care for it in a meticulous way, devoting both time and energy towards it. There are some who love their yards. The extent to which they are willing to go to maintain their lawn indicates that the yard is important to them. Others love the clothes they wear. They go to great lengths to insure they have the newest style and the most expensive designer on their bodies. Jesus once declared that there were only two things that we are called to love most... God and people. Remember Mark 12:30-31, "And you must love the Lord your God with all your heart, all your soul, all your mind, and all your strength. The second is equally important: Love your neighbor as yourself. No other commandment is greater than these" (NLT). The question becomes, "Is it obvious that we love these things?" How is our love demonstrated in the day-to-day moments of our lives? Do we live with devotion? Do we prioritize the moments we spend in the presence of the Almighty? Do we pray? Do we read the Bible? Do we reflect on God's interaction with us? And what of the people we encounter each day? Do we forgive abundantly? Do we share willingly? Do we heal compassionately?

Prayer
Father, may it be obvious to all, the things we love the most. Amen.

Day 674 — Song of Solomon 3: The Best of Days

> "Come out to see King Solomon, young women of Jerusalem. He wears the crown his mother gave him on his wedding day, his most joyous day."
> Song of Solomon 3:11 (NLT)

Observation

As this chapter opens, the Shulamite expresses her fear of losing Solomon, the love of her life. After a time of courtship (see chapter 2), Solomon has returned to Jerusalem. She is so in love that the time of separation is all but unbearable. She recounts searching for him in the dead of night. It seems that she is recalling a recurring dream or nightmare. She goes throughout the city at night, desperately searching for him everywhere. The power of romantic love is illustrated by her willingness to risk safety and societal status by undertaking such a desperate and dangerous search. When she finds him, she takes him into her mother's house and into her mother's bed and refuses to let go of him. Perhaps this is a nod to the idea that only in the context of covenant marriage is the place where romantic desire and intimacy are to be found. Marriage arrangements were established by the mother of the bride in the ancient world. This reference to the mother's bed is certainly a reference to the impending wedding. The final six verses of the chapter speak of the wedding procession as Solomon arrives in the city, making his way to the mother's house to claim his bride. It is an elaborate procession complete with a lot of detail concerning his horse-drawn carriage and security detail.

Application

In our focus verse, Solomon's wedding day is described as "his most joyous day." That's probably true for most of us. The day of our wedding arrives with such hope and promise and love. The celebration is joyful and happy. (It is unfortunate, of course, that for many, the euphoria of the day diminishes over time and many couples are unable to experience a long-lasting relationship.) There are no perfect marriages because there are no perfect people. But what if things could be different? What if the joy of marriage was unending, life-changing, and always exciting? The New Testament describes the Church as the bride of Christ. Many passages speak of Christ's coming to claim the church and all those who follow him into a perfect, forever, union. Imagine being chosen by Christ. Imagine being loved by him forever with perfect devotion and celebration. Imagine every fear being erased and every disappointment being destroyed. Imagine being loved, accepted, and cherished for all of time. Here's some good news… you don't have to imagine such a life, because you can claim it. Christ already welcomes you into his heart and life and celebrates the uniqueness of who you are each day. May knowing him always be your most joyous day.

Prayer

Father, we thank you for the loving, forever embrace of Jesus. Amen.

Day 675   Song of Solomon 4: What Captures Your Heart?

> "You have captured my heart, my treasure, my bride. You hold it hostage with one glance of your eyes, with a single jewel of your necklace."
> Song of Solomon 4:9 (NLT)

Observation
For those thinking that the imagery of the Bible can get a little steamy… this chapter doesn't disappoint. It opens with Solomon's description of the Shulamite woman's beauty. He praises seven beautiful features of her body. He describes her eyes, hair, teeth, lips, temples, neck, and breasts. He poetically compares the parts of her body to elements found in nature. In verse 4, he compares her neck to David's tower. (Although this may be a great comparison, there is no other mention of this tower in scripture. This tower is sometimes called the citadel of Jerusalem and remains to this day as the tallest structure in the ancient city.) Solomon sums up his description by saying in verse 7 that she is "altogether beautiful" and without blemish. Verse 8 records Solomon's request for her to come and be his bride. It is an invitation to share the wedding night. As he continues to praise her beauty, he states that she has "captured his heart." In verses 12-15, he praises her beauty. The chapter ends with the Shulamite inviting him to explore her body in sexual intimacy.

Application
What captures your heart? What is your treasure? What holds you hostage? For Solomon, it was the beauty of his bride. He was completely taken by everything about her. As we read his description of her, we almost blush with embarrassment. What a joy to be so truly in love and so taken with the beauty of physical form.

But let's take a moment to move away from the imagery of physical love described in these words. Let's consider the other things that often capture our hearts. We are captivated by ideas, by possessions, by pursuits, and by our passions. There are moments in which we are so taken by such things that we can think of nothing else. We can't rest until we write the last paragraph, or make the last donation, or watch the final episode, or possess the latest version of some electronic device. It's great to be passionate… to be overtaken… to be completely consumed by something. Let's just make sure that our hearts are captured by things that really matter. At the end of the day, it is not our passion for a sports team, a political candidate, nor a degree on the wall that will change the world. It will be our passion for the hurting, the marginalized, the suffering, or the lost which will define our legacy. Take a moment to consider what holds you in its spell this day. Seek that which is noble, pure, and of lasting worth.

Prayer
Father, may we be passionate for the things that capture your heart. Amen.

Day 676

Song of Solomon 5: The Need for Praise

> "Why is your lover better than all others, O woman of rare beauty? What makes your lover so special that we must promise this?"
> Song of Solomon 5:9 (NLT)

Observation

Because Solomon uses the past tense form of each verb in verse 1, it indicates the completion and satisfaction of his sexual desires. He and his bride have consummated their union. He declares that his bride is his to exclusively enjoy. Six times in the verse he used the word "my" as an indication that she now belongs to him as his beloved wife. His words are written with a sense of joy, contentment, and fulfillment. As the narrative continues there are insights about the maturing of the relationship. There is even a hint of an interpersonal problem to be overcome. Apparently, a moment comes when the Shulamite had offered excuses and hesitated to give herself to Solomon, which resulted in resentment. Apparently in another dream sequence, she relates how she refused to answer the door when he came for her. He leaves. Distraught, she ventures out into the dark night to search for him. The watchmen of the city mistake her for a prostitute and beat her. She calls out to the Daughters of Jerusalem (chorus) to help her. She then awakens to the reality of how much she loves and desires her husband. As he had done previously, she now offers a list of all his desirable characteristics… his head, his hair, eyes, cheeks, lips, hands, abdomen, and legs.

Application

If you were to ask me why I enjoy driving the car that I presently own, I would offer these types of words in response. I like the handling characteristics. I like the looks of the exterior. I like the feel of the leather seats. I like the performance when I hit the accelerator. I could list a lot of reasons. I could praise my little car in a lot of ways.

But what about offering praise for the people we love most? If I were to ask, "What makes your spouse so special? Why is your spouse better than all others? What do you prize about their qualities? What attracts you to your spouse?" Could you make a list? Could you offer words of praise about his/her special characteristics? It's been my discovery through many years of pastoral ministry, that many people are better at talking about their spouse to others, than they are at offering words of praise and thankfulness to them directly. Sometimes, as marriages mature, we lose the ability to offer words of praise, words of passion, and words of gratitude. We just "assume" that our spouses know how deeply we care for them and appreciate all that they do to make our lives full and complete. But just maybe, they need to hear such words directly. Everyone needs a little praise. Everyone needs to feel valued, wanted, and needed. Why not take a moment this very day to tell your spouse about your love?

Prayer

Father, thank you for the people we love most. Help us to express our thoughts. Amen.

Day 677 — Song of Solomon 6: The Perfect Smile

> "Your teeth are as white as sheep that are freshly washed. Your smile is flawless, each tooth matched with its twin." Song of Solomon 6:6 (NLT)

Observation

Back in Chapter 5, the narrative speaks about a separation of the two lovers (Solomon and the Shulamite) caused by the Shulamite's indifference to Solomon's sexual desires. The chapter contained a dream sequence in which she misses him and desperately goes searching for him. In this chapter, awakened from her dream, she seeks him, and they once again share in a continuation of their sexual intimacy. She uses garden imagery and language to describe their sexual activity. Verse 3 affirms the Biblical concept of the one flesh concept of marriage. "I am his and he is mine…" Verses 4-10 record Solomon's description of the beauty he sees in his lover. She is without peer. Her beauty is above "countless women" (v. 8). The chapter winds down with the Shulamite expressing her overwhelmingly strong desire for her husband. Just as the coming of Spring has awakened the world of nature, her love has been rekindled once again.

Application

In describing the beauty of his wife, Solomon mentions her smile. She apparently has perfect teeth in a time and culture where dental hygiene could not have been all that great. Certainly, in our culture, a lot of importance is placed on having a beautiful smile. We know that a beautiful face can be diminished by bad teeth. And so, we go to great lengths to create a nice smile. If we are willing to go to the expense and effort to do so, we can certainly change the way our teeth look. We can have them whitened, straightened, capped, or even replaced. But sometimes, a beautiful smile can be a little deceptive. The outward appearance may not reveal the inward turmoil, pain, or anguish of a person's life. Having a better smile doesn't necessarily mean that we will have a better life.

Don't get me wrong… oral health is vitally important. You really should see your dentist regularly and take good care of your teeth. But emotional and spiritual health are also important. There are activities in which we must engage daily if we are going to maintain our strength, our hope, and our character. We must invest in scripture and learn how to apply its truth to daily life. We must spend time in dialogue with God each day, affirming our dependency with each prayer that we make. We need to find a sense of community and shared support that only corporate worship and church attendance can provide. We need to make sure that the joy and beauty on the inside is every bit as bright as the smile on the outside. Take care of your teeth… and more importantly, take care of your inner self.

Prayer

Father, we thank you for bright smiles and meaningful lives. Amen.

Day 678 — Song of Solomon 7: In Praise of Feet

> "How beautiful are your sandaled feet, O queenly maiden."
> Song of Solomon 7:1a (NLT)

Observation

As chapter 7 opens, Solomon offers praises for the sensuous beauty of his lover's body. Unlike previous descriptions in the book, he starts at her feet and moves all the way up to her hair. Perhaps his attention has been drawn to her feet because, as the scene opens, she is dancing before him. With very descriptive language he describes her feet, hips, navel, torso, breasts, neck, eyes, nose, head, and hair. And then, at the end of his description, he circles back to a description of her breasts and using the imagery of a palm tree, he speaks of his desire to "climb the tree and take hold of her fruit." It is a very vivid description of his desire for her. She responds in verses 9-10 using the imagery of wine. Like wine flowing through the lips and teeth, she desires his "sweet" kisses. In further response to his desires of intimacy, she welcomes him to claim her once again as his own.

Application

If we were tasked with describing someone's beauty, we probably wouldn't talk first about their feet! Feet are often forgotten, neglected, and taken for granted until they give us some form of trouble. In fact, we often hide our feet by covering them with shoes. And though many enjoy the purchase and wearing of fancy shoes... still the feet themselves elicit little notice.

The Prophet Isaiah took notice of feet as he offers this description... "How beautiful on the mountains are the feet of the messenger who brings good news, the good news of peace and salvation, the news that the God of Israel reigns!" (Isaiah 52:7 NLT). The feet are made beautiful because of their purpose. They carry the messenger of God who proclaims the good news of peace and salvation. Feet are like a lot of things... seldom noticed, but extremely vital. Without our feet, our bodies could not walk, stand, or run. They propel us, move us, and transport us and yet without fanfare or complaint.

I am reminded that there are many servants of God who daily help to build the Kingdom in quiet and unassuming ways. They work in the background, never announcing their service or promoting their importance. And yet, their contribution is vital to the success of God's movement here on earth. They serve. They love. They heal. They pray. They encourage. You may be one of those persons. So, take courage if you are a humble servant today, far removed from the limelight of notoriety. Does it matter if your name doesn't appear in the bulletin or your presence is never required on the stage? The only one who really matters is watching every step you take and will reward you for your consistent and faithful work.

Prayer

Father, we thank you for the beautiful feet of your servants. Amen.

Day 679 — Song of Solomon 8: That's the Power of Love

> "For love is as strong as death, its jealousy as enduring as the grave. Love flashes like fire, the brightest kind of flame. Many waters cannot quench love, nor can rivers drown it." Song of Solomon 8:6b-7a (NLT)

Observation
As this concluding chapter opens, the Shunammite is expressing her desire for even greater intimacy with her husband, Solomon. In the culture of the day, husbands and wives were forbidden from public displays of affection. Only immediate family members could share an embrace or kiss in public. She states that she wishes Solomon was her brother and therefore they would be free to demonstrate their affections for each other without being shamed by others. In verse 4, she counsels the young women of Jerusalem not to "awaken love" until the time is right… which is in the context of a marriage relationship. Verses 5-14 offer a conclusion to the book that emphasizes the strength and power of love. She compares love to a seal made by a signet ring. It binds a heart to the heart of another. She also compares the strength of love to the strength of death meaning that it is powerful and inescapable. Even a flood of mighty waters cannot wash it away. The final verses trace the history of the relationship between the two. She was protected by her brothers when she was young, met Solomon in a vineyard, and finally discovered the joy of marital love.

A lot of time and energy has been spent explaining the presence of this steamy love story in the Old Testament. Why has it been included? Why has it been carefully preserved? Some suggest that it displays God's design for marriage… that love is to be exclusive, passionate, and sacrificial. Others argue that it is intended as a metaphor used to explain the extravagant, overwhelming, and unending love of God for all of God's children.

Application
The power of love really is an amazing thing. Love emboldens. Love sacrifices. Love gives. Love protects. Whenever a person is caught up in a loving relationship there is no hardship too great to endure, no distance too great to span, no brokenness too great to heal. If you have ever been in love, you know its power, its ability to captivate and dominate every waking thought. You know how it makes your heart sing and your spirit rejoice. And remember this… the brightness of human love dims in comparison to the love God has for each of us. We are loved beyond measure, beyond our comprehension, and yes, even beyond our sinfulness. We are caught up in the powerful, never-ending, redemptive embrace of God.

Prayer
Father, we thank you for the love you lavishly offer to each of us. Amen.